THE
HIGH-PERFORMANCE
TWO-STROKE ENGINE

THE
HIGH-PERFORMANCE
TWO-STROKE ENGINE

Dr JOHN C. DIXON

Senior Lecturer in Engineering Mechanics
The Open University, Great Britain

Haynes Publishing

First published in April 2005

A catalogue record for this book is available from the British Library

ISBN 1 84425 045 8

Library of Congress catalog card no. 2004100810

Published by Haynes Publishing, Sparkford,
Yeovil, Somerset, BA22 7JJ, UK
Tel: 01963 442030 Fax: 01963 440001
Int. tel: +44 1963 442030 Int. fax: +44 1963 440001
E-mail: sales@haynes.co.uk
Website: www.haynes.co.uk

Haynes North America, Inc.,
861 Lawrence Drive, Newbury Park,
California 91320, USA

Printed and bound in England by J. H. Haynes & Co. Ltd, Sparkford

Contents

Preface

The spark ignition two-stroke engine is widely used for competitions in both motorcycle and kart racing. The mechanical simplicity of the engine gives it a tremendous appeal. This apparent simplicity certainly makes it a tempting target for tuning. The information presented here is intended to help would-be engine improvers to better understand the engine and the processes within it, and so obtain better results. It cannot be described as light reading throughout, and is not intended to be read once and discarded. Repeated reading will be required for a full appreciation of the science behind these fascinating engines, and will give the reader who has made the effort of coming to terms with the technicalities a distinct advantage over anyone who has ignored them.

As in my previous work, I have tried to present the basic core of theory and practice, so that the book will be of lasting value. I would, of course, be delighted to hear from readers who wish to suggest any improvements to presentation or coverage.

John C. Dixon, The Open University,
Milton Keynes, England.

CHAPTER 1:

Introduction

1.1 Introduction

The crankcase-scavenged two-stroke is a device of deceptive simplicity. With no valves in the head it is economical to manufacture and light in weight. It is easy to take apart and service, and tempting to modify. However, improving engine performance is always a challenge. Take a little too much metal off a port and performance may be worse, not better.

The key to successful development and modification of any engine, not to mention design, is understanding its operating principles. The two-stroke engine may seem simple, but it has all the subtle complexity of any engine. This book explains its operation in a way that will enable the reader to solve many of the problems of tuning and design.

Engine tuning is often a matter of trial and error. Modifications are put repeatedly to test. However, with the right knowledge the reader can move assuredly in the right direction. As well as providing that knowledge, this book presents a source of ideas to investigate. Some of these might even save you wasting time by repeating old mistakes.

This book has been written with the engine tuner in mind, but also provides a sound technical basis for the engine designer. Although computer simulations can help predict the effect of design changes, the basic analysis presented here gives an insight into what is happening within the engine. At times this can be even more useful.

The term 'engine cycle' belongs to the jargon of thermodynamics, for example Otto cycles and Diesel cycles. To the engine designer or tuner, working with flow resistances, gas dynamics, mechanical design, lubrication and reliability theoretical cycles hark back to student days. They don't belong here.

There are two distinct categories of two-stroke. They range from the remarkably simple engines of motorcycles, karts, boats, and model aircraft, to the very large diesel two-stroke engines used for ship propulsion. With their exhaust scavenging and separate compressors, these are occasionally mentioned just for comparison.

The defining characteristic of nearly all the engines considered here is that they are crankcase-scavenged, in which the mixture of fuel and air is drawn into the crankcase before being transfered into the cylinder. The resulting simplicity and low parts-count explains their appeal and low capital cost. This simplicity stems from Joseph M. Day's 1891 invention of the classic 'three-port' two-stroke. In Day's original engine, the inlet to the crankcase was controlled by the lower edge of the piston skirt, as in Figure 1.1.1. This is probably the simplest layout for a working engine. In his first engines the mixture was transfered from the crankcase to the cylinder by a flap-valve in the piston itself. The idea of a transfer port, with its bypass passage, actually came from his colleague Frederick Cock, in 1892. With the troublesome piston flap-valve eliminated the ultimate cheap, simple engine was born.

Today's high-power competition two-stroke therefore owes its origin to Day. In it:

1. Air/fuel mixture is drawn into the crankcase

2. The mixture is passed to the cylinder via transfer ports

3. A tuned exhaust system draws the burnt gases from the cylinder

When competition demands power first and foremost, as it often does, this layout can give tremendous specific power. This type of engine is the main subject of this book.

However, competition doesn't always demand raw power. Other characteristics, such as high torque at lower speed, low fuel consumption, very light weight or good controllability can dominate. These factors call for variations in design, and are included for their own merit and to place the modern racing two-stroke engine in a broader context. Their influence on design may include other configurations of transfer ports, and other types of exhaust system.

Contrast the early design of Figure 1.1.1 with Figure 1.1.2, which shows a modern road-going sports engine. Note the essentially flat piston crown, the large transfer passages, the main shaft supported in ball bearings, and the rotary disc mounted on the right hand end of the shaft for control of the inlet. Note too the large cooling fins.

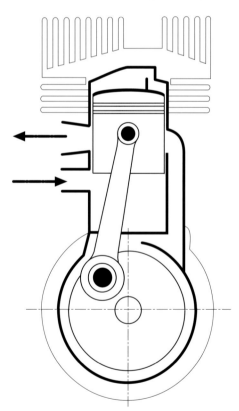

Figure 1.1.1. Inlet control using lower edge of piston was a feature of Day's original two-stroke, patented 1891.

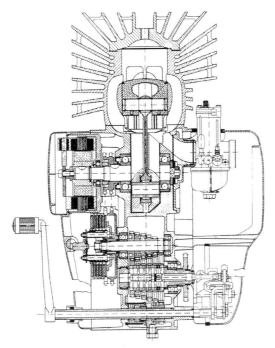

Figure 1.1.2. The Maico MD 250 – a modern sports engine in cross-section.

1.2 Early History.

Day's simple two-stroke invention called for a considerable background of knowledge. The first engines of any kind had been very large stationary ones used for pumping water out of mines. The earliest small-engines in the nineteenth century were for propelling the first motorcars. Early road vehicles required compact engines of modest output with good reliability and efficiency. As early as 1838, Barnett, in England, had described how to use separate air pumps to scavenge a cylinder in a two-stroke engine. Fundamental theoretical work by Beau de Rochas resulted in a French patent of 1862, which laid down the principles of four-cycles of engine operation – the four-stroke. His list of desirable features included:

1. Small internal surface area of the combustion chamber in relation to volume

2. Quick combustion followed by fast expansion

3. Large expansion ratio

4. High operating pressure

The first two give reduced cooling of the burned gas, improving the efficiency and giving more energy for a given fuel consumption. The third also improves thermal efficiency. The last two improve power. For conventional engines, expansion ratio and compression ratio are effectively the same thing, but nowadays we tend to use the latter term. Unfortunately, de Rochas failed to produce a practical design.

The first marketable small engine came from Frenchman Jean Lenoir (1822–1900). This had a thermal efficiency of about 5%, and was in fact a two-stroke, firing every revolution. Five thousand were made between 1860 and 1865. The low efficiency meant low power and high fuel consumption.

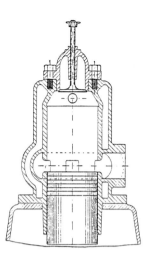

Figure 1.2.1. Port arrangement of Clerk's original axially-scavenged engine, showing poppet inlet valve. His very first engine had a sliding inlet valve.

Low efficiency was a handicap that others sought to overcome. German engineer Nikolaus Otto (1832–1891) raised efficiency to about 10% in 1867. Otto preferred the four-stroke cycle (firing on alternate revolutions), which he considered more compact and lighter than the two-stroke designs of that time. It also allowed higher compression ratio, which gave better efficiency. His engine first ran in 1876, and sold 50,000 units between 1877 and 1890.

Engines of those days ran at a stately few hundred revolutions per minute – fast compared with their large stationary engines, but very slow by modern standards.

In 1878, Scottish engineer Sir Dugald Clerk (1854–1913) produced the first two-stroke using axial scavenging, in which the fresh gas passed down the cylinder, through a poppet inlet valve in the head and out by exhaust ports around the cylinder wall (Figure 1.2.1). There was a separate scavenge pump. This was the precursor of today's large marine two-stroke. In recognition of this, the two-stroke cycle is sometimes called the Clerk cycle.

In 1884, German engineer Karl Benz marketed a two-stroke engine with 'crankcase pre-compression' including a valve in the cylinder head.

In 1885, Gottlieb Daimler (1834–1900), who had once worked for Otto, patented an improved, lightweight, high speed (800 rev/min *was* high speed in 1885) four-stroke which was effectively the ancestor of today's motor car engines. He also made the world's first one-off motorcycle in 1885.

In England in 1887, Edward Butler commercially produced a two-stroke tricycle.

Trained as an engineer in Bath, England, Joseph Day (1855–1946) set up his own company making air compressors. In 1884 he patented a flap valve for fluid in pipes. Turning his talents to the growing demand for small engines, he patented in 1891 a two-stroke with crankcase induction and a flap-valve in the piston crown through which the mixture passed from crankcase to cylinder. In 1892, Frederick Cock, working for Day, proposed a transfer passage and port (the bypass system), thus giving us the modern small 'three-port' engine, with crankcase scavenging and no valves, as in Figure 1.1.1. Inlet to the crankcase was by a piston-controlled port or through a sprung poppet valve, and the transfer and exhaust ports were both at the lower end of the cylinder, providing loop scavenging rather than axial scavenging. The head, upper cylinder and piston, freed of valves, gave the special mechanical simplicity that has become the essence of the small two-stroke engine. The Day-Cock three-port engine was granted US patent protection in August 1895.

With Cock, Day formed a company to manufacture their engine. Simplicity of manufacture should have ensured success, but they lacked business acumen and became embroiled in court cases. Nevertheless, Day successfully licensed the design in the USA, where it became popular for powering small motor boats. By 1912 the Palmer Brothers had made 60,000 units. The royalties enabled Day to establish the Day Motor Company in London. Unfortunately, Day wrote little about his work, but one of his early machines is in London's Science Museum, and another in the Deutsches Museum, Munich.

In 1892, English engineer J. D. Roots produced a two-stroke engine of the Day-Cock type for use in a tricycle. This was the year when Rudolf Diesel (1858–1913), working in Germany, invented his principle of injecting liquid fuel at high-pressure direct into the cylinder. Used for both two-stroke and four-stroke engines, Diesel thereby eliminated the then unreliable electrical spark ignition, though five years passed before the first practical diesel engine appeared in 1897.

James Robson should also be mentioned for his early (pre 1900) two-stroke.

Thus, the nineteenth century ended with the fundamental three-port or Day-type two-stroke established and in commercial production. Low cost, reliability and reasonable thermal efficiency were the early targets of development. Power outputs in terms of mass or swept volume were very modest by modern standards.

1.3 The Early Twentieth Century
An early twentieth century development was the introduction of the rotary disc valve. Gerard patented one of these in France as early as 1906, (Figure 1.3.1). Mounted directly on the crankshaft and pressed against the inside face of the crankcase, this was in effect an internal rotary disc valve.

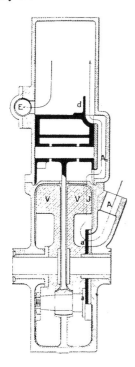

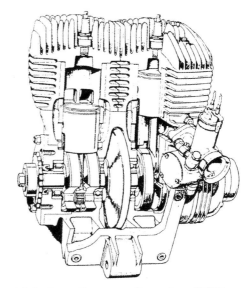

Left: Figure 1.3.1. Gerard's rotary-disc valve of 1906.

Above: Figure 1.3.2. Scott's twin-cylinder motorcycle engine of 1920.

As interest in motor transport grew, car and motorcycle racing soon became a public attraction. English engineer Alfred Scott (1876–1924) made his name with two-stroke racing motorcycles. His engines, developed between 1900 and 1925, were noted for quality and aesthetic appeal. In the first decade of the twentieth century, he developed an original and compact mechanical configuration of three-port two-stroke with twin cylinders and a single flywheel between the two single-throw cranks in independent small-volume crankcases. Scott's layout remained in production engines into the 1950s.

In the 1920s, E. Schnürle in Germany invented his now ubiquitous transfer port configuration, though this had little impact on competition engines at the time. However, the innovative motorcycle German manufacturer, DKW, founded by Jörgen Rasmussen (1878–1964), did produce a sports bike using Schnürle's porting in 1929. The name Schnürle is often misspelled. The two dots on the ü (*umlaut* in German) are sometimes rendered in English by adding letter e after the u, but <u>not</u> before it. Also, in German, a final letter e is not silent. Hence, the name is correctly pronounced *sh-noorl-uh*, which probably explains why they are sometimes called 'snarl ports'!

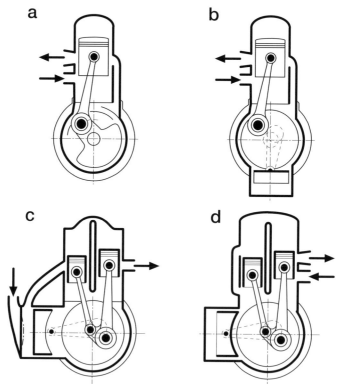

Figure 1.3.3. DKW racing developments 1932–1937:
(a) Standard three-port engine used up to 1932, with piston-controlled induction. (b) Supercharging pump added opposite the main piston in 1932, acting in phase with the piston. (c) The URe 250 had the Garelli-type 'split-single' cylinders. The supercharging piston, left, draws air in through a large reed valve. (d) The 1935 UL 250 with piston-controlled induction was developing 22 bhp at 4,800 rpm by 1937.
(H.W. Boensch, Der Schnellaufende Zweitaktmotor, *Motorbuch Verlag Stuttgart, 1993, and* S. Rauch, DKW – Die Geschichte Einer Weltmarke, *Motorbuch Verlag Stuttgart, 1988*)

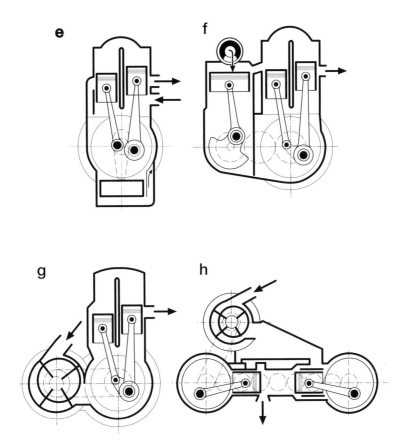

Figure 1.3.4. DKW racers 1935–1939.
(e) The four-cylinder 350 production racer (two cylinders shown) gave 32 bhp at 5,500 rpm. The supercharging piston is double acting for the four-cylinder, its lower surface coupled to the crankcase of the other pair of cylinders. (f) In the ULd 250 of 1938, the supercharging piston ran on a separate crankshaft geared to the main shaft. Inlet to the charger, originally via a reed valve at the top of the cylinder, was superseded by a rotary valve, as shown. (g) Under development in 1939 was a similar split-single with a vane compressor. (h) Again with vane compressor, this unit has true axial scavenging with opposed pistons and all three shafts geared together.
(H.W. Boensch, Der Schnellaufende Zweitaktmotor, *Motorbuch Verlag Stuttgart, 1993, and S. Rauch, DKW* – Die Geschichte Einer Weltmarke, *Motorbuch Verlag Stuttgart, 1988)*

During the 1930s the centre of development shifted to Germany, the most successful racing two-strokes being the supercharged DKWs. The balance between two-strokes and four-strokes in the competition world has always been a fine one, often decided by the whims of rule-makers.

The supercharged U-piston configuration or 'split-single' two-stroke (Figures 1.3.3 to 1.3.6), dominated the Thirties. This type of engine scavenging was introduced by the Italian Garelli concern in 1923. One cylinder has the transfer ports (cylinder inlet) and the other has the exhaust ports, the ports being low in each cylinder. The gases pass axially up the first cylinder, and then back down the second, driven by the scavenge pump. This is rather like an

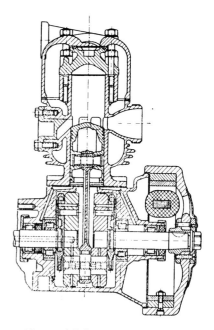

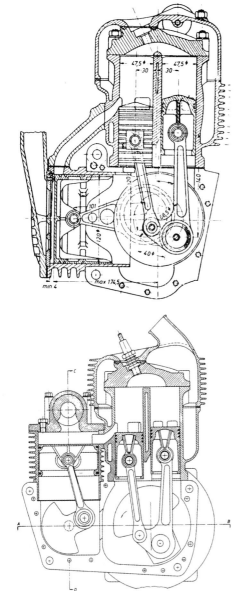

Above: Figure 1.3.5. DKW URe 250, circa 1935, showing the large bore supercharging piston. Note the small bore/stroke ratio and the long pistons with three rings each. The exhaust ports are to the rear of the right-hand cylinder. (S. Rauch, DKW, Motorbuch Verlag Stuttgart, 1988.)

Left: Figure 1.3.6. Cross-section of the DKW ULd 250 of 1938, showing the rotary valve at the top left, supercharging piston, and auxiliary connecting rod for the second combustion piston. Note the change of combustion chamber from the URe engine. (S. Rauch, DKW, Motorbuch Verlag Stuttgart, 1988)

opposed-piston engine folded over in the centre of the cylinder. If the two crankshafts are geared, at a 1:1 ratio of course, but with a suitable displaced angle, or if a Y-shaped conrod is used, the piston motion may be phased by 10 to 15 degrees. The exhaust then opens before the transfer opens and closes before the transfer closes. This is an ideal set-up for supercharging as the charger can pressurise the cylinders after the exhaust closes. Otherwise, a supercharger could only speed up the scavenging without significantly raising the cylinder charge pressure. It would be little more than a scavenge pump. However, the required phasing also causes a period of nearly constant combustion volume during which heat is lost from the gas. This is something engine designers try to avoid.

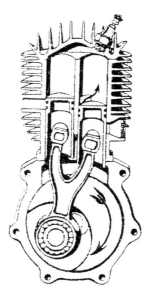

Figure 1.3.7. Puch split-single construction with a forked connecting rod. (The Motor Cycle).

Garelli's original did not have this asymmetrical timing. It was left to DKW to develop the system progressively up to almost 40 bhp (30 kW) from 250 cm^3 in 1939. A 250 cm^3 engine prepared for motorcycle speed records achieved 49 bhp on methanol fuel. There was also a 48 bhp 350 cm^3 racer. These are modest figures now but were tremendous at the time.

When superchargers were eventually banned, many variants of the 'folded' cylinder remained in use. The original Garelli system had the two pistons cantilevered out from a central connecting rod on a long gudgeon pin (wrist pin), which is poor structurally. DKW favoured a secondary connecting rod pivoted on the main rod. Puch used a forked Y-shaped rod to obtain favourable port timing, but this called for a complex little end with the gudgeon pin sliding in the rod, (Figure 1.3.7). TWN used a more conventional twin-throw crankshaft with the big end journals in better angular relationship. One other arrangement was tried by DKW and others, with two crankshafts geared together at the appropriate phasing, with the cylinders angled in towards each other to meet at the common combustion chamber.

For the normal unsupercharged three-port two-stroke, the power was significantly boosted in the 1930s by the development of the resonant inlet pipe, which works well with a piston-controlled inlet. This involves careful choice of inlet diameter and length, researched by Ing. Dr. Ulrich Schmidt, who showed how the theory of the Helmholtz resonator could be applied. He published his findings in 1938.

DWK also tried reed valves in their racing engines, but found them unreliable. In the 1930s, rotary disc valves within the crankcase had become popular for two-stroke outboard motors for boats. Other transfer configurations were under development. The standard Day type engine with transfer and exhaust ports diametrically opposite each other required a piston baffle, like a wall across the piston to deflect the transfer flow upwards. This baffle cools the combusted gas and reduces the thermal efficiency but can help to vaporise the fuel droplets that strike it. However, it generally makes the piston hotter, causing thermal distortion and complicating the head design, resulting in thermal losses, so designers were keen to discard it for competition work and use a flat-topped piston. Initially, this was done by having a pair of diametrically opposed exhaust ports, with one pair or two pairs of opposed transfer ports between them, these being angled steeply up to prevent charge loss. An engine of this type was marketed by Villiers in this period. Barnes & Reinecke also used peripheral 'ring-of-drilled-holes' porting.

Eventually, better results were found with a single exhaust port and a pair of transfers set near the exhaust but directed away from it and at a low angle to the piston crown. This was the work that Schnürle patented in 1925.

1.4 The Late Twentieth Century

After World War 2, manufacture under the name DKW moved to West Germany, whilst the original DKW factory, in East Germany, became MZ (Motorräderwerke Zschopau). Racing continued in Germany, mostly with pre-war equipment, and it was on the German racing circuits that many of the new developments took place, especially of inlet and exhaust systems. For example, in the late 1940s, MZ tried, and abandoned, cross-flow rotary inlet valves, having failed to minimise flow resistance.

Considering the 'other end' of the engine, it was well known that the length of the exhaust pipe, still a plain constant diameter in those days, was important in boosting power at a particular engine speed. However, the effect was limited by a rule that the exhaust pipe had to end behind the rear axle, too long for any real power benefit by the methods then known.

By 1948, Karl Döring was using a megaphone exhaust on a supercharged DKW 125. A year later, Ernst Ansorg adapted the rotary disc valve for motorcycles, building a modified DKW with the innovation of placing the disc in a separate chamber, with improved passage shape. In 1950, MZ returned to racing (entering as IFA), and had a single-piston 125 cm^3 supercharged engine in use with a long megaphone. Then, in 1951, superchargers were banned. Even with the shorter exhausts permitted, the two-stroke could no longer compete with the four-stroke, so two-stroke designers had to seek new ways to enhance power.

That same year came a further development of the rotary inlet valve in a remote chamber, the work of tuner Daniel Zimmerman, working on MZ engines. MZ took out some rotary disc valve patents in 1951. Walter Kaaden (1919–1996) went on to develop the disc valve independently, using a modified circular saw blade! Shortly after that, he joined MZ officially, becoming head of their racing department. The disc now used a thin flexible rotor with axial float on the shaft. This rotor was light, so imbalance from the inlet cut-out was much reduced, as was rotor friction. In 1954, the MZ inlet still had a rather short period of 165°, but by 1958 it was up to a modern 210°.

More important, though, were the exhaust system developments. In 1952, DKW raced with an exhaust system using a header pipe followed by a divergent cone, followed by a convergent cone and a tailpipe – the divergent-convergent or 'di-con' exhaust. This was of great significance for the future of the racing two-stroke. Adler soon had an additional tailpipe restrictor. MZ tried such systems but found no improvement, so they returned to plain megaphones through to 1955. By 1956, MZ again had full divergent-convergent systems having discovered the need for an earlier exhaust opening to create a strong exhaust pulse to enhance the supercharging effect.

Hence, by the mid-1950s the racing two-stroke had its modern configuration, despite detailed improvement to come. By then the leading engine designers knew, and by the late 1950s it was widely known, that the exhaust system is a dominant factor, and that the engine must be designed with the exhaust system in mind. It is not a bolt-on extra.

Walter Kaaden added the boost port in 1959. This was a bridged double port, directly opposite the exhaust, facilitated by the use of disc induction rather than piston-controlled induction, the former type of inlet making space available at this part of the cylinder. This raised power and the peaking speed by 5% or so.

In 1961, MZ rider Ernst Degner defected to Suzuki, taking Kaaden's know-how to Japan. Suzuki, previously struggling, promptly produced the competitive RT62 125 cm^3 single. The transferred know-how included a better exhaust-system profile and long exhaust timing. Thus the centre of two-stroke development shifted to the Japanese, who were willing to spend heavily, using racing to promote world-wide marketing of low and high technology road-going motorcycles and production racers.

Since then there have been considerable power increases, due to piston and liner metallurgy, plus many detailed improvements to exhausts and porting, but the basic German format remains the same, despite the introduction of four-cylinder engines in various arrangements.

The resonant divergent-convergent exhaust, as introduced on racing motorcycles, is effectively a supercharger with no moving parts. It left untouched the two-stroke's mechanical simplicity. Indeed, by doing away with the mechanical supercharger, it actually made it simpler. Even the early engineers knew that the two-stroke was a subtle device. Despite its fewer parts it is just as complex in its operation, its thermodynamics, its fluid mechanics, and its materials, as any engine.

1.5 Performance Levels

Table 1.5.1 shows the performance levels of significant racing motorcycle two-strokes since the 1920s, showing the general upward trend. For better comparison of the peak power and peaking speed, the equivalent performance at a 125 cm^3 cylinder size is included, and calculated as explained in Chapter 2. This allows for the variation of thermal efficiency with cylinder size. The apparent competitive power level varies because the engines listed are not all GP engines.

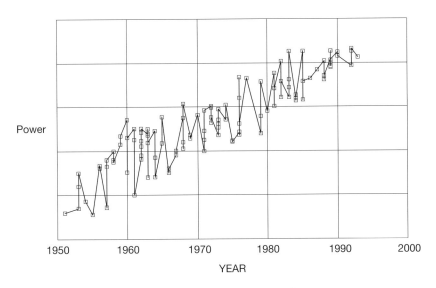

Figure 1.5.1. Racing motorcycle power outputs (125 cm^3 equivalent cylinder) from 1950 to 2000.

Table 1.5.1. Racing Motorcycle Two-Stroke Engine Power Output History

Year	Make	Model	Swept Volume	No of cyls	Power max	Speed Pmax	Cylinder vol	Power max 125 cm³	Speed Pmax 125 cm³	Torque Pmax 125 cm³
			(cm^3)	(-)	(BHP)	(krpm)	(cm^3)	(BHP)	(krpm)	(Nm)
1923	Garelli	350 SS	350	2	16.0	4.0	175.0	6.2	4.5	9.9
1931	Puch	250	250	2	18.0	4.5	125.0	9.0	4.5	14.3
1932	DKW	250	250	1	17.0	5.0	250.0	10.0	6.3	11.3
1935	DKW	URe	250	2	26.0	4.7	125.0	13.0	4.7	19.7
1936	DKW	URe	250	2	30.0	5.0	125.0	15.0	5.0	21.4
1938	DKW	ULd	250	2	35.0	7.0	125.0	17.5	7.0	17.8
1951	Puch	250TF	250	2	12.0	4.5	125.0	6.0	4.5	9.5
1953	Puch	250SG	250	2	14.0	5.8	125.0	7.0	5.8	8.6
1953	MZ	125/3	125	1	12.0	8.0	125.0	12.0	8.0	10.7
1954	Puch	250SGS	250	2	17.2	6.0	125.0	8.6	6.0	10.2
1955	Yamaha	YA1	125	1	5.6	5.5	125.0	5.6	5.5	7.3
1956	DKW	350	349	3	45.0	9.7	116.3	15.8	9.5	11.9
1956	MZ	125	125	1	17.0	10.0	125.0	17.0	10.0	12.1
1957	Yamaha	YD1	250	2	14.5	6.0	125.0	7.2	6.0	8.6
1957	MZ	125	125	1	18.0	9.2	125.0	18.0	9.2	14.0
1958	MZ	125	125	1	20.0	10.7	125.0	20.0	10.7	13.3
1959	EMC	125	125	1	23.5	10.0	125.0	23.5	10.0	16.8
1960	EMC	125	125	1	27.0	11.0	125.0	27.0	11.0	17.5
1960	Kreidler	50R	50	1	7.5	10.0	50.0	15.1	7.4	14.7
1961	MZ	125	125	1	25.0	10.8	125.0	25.0	10.8	16.5
1961	MZ	250	250	2	45.0	10.0	125.0	22.5	10.0	16.0
1961	Yamaha	RA41	250	2	20.0	10.0	125.0	10.0	10.0	7.1
1962	Yamaha	RD48	250	2	42.0	10.0	125.0	21.0	10.0	15.0
1962	Suzuki	RT62	125	1	24.0	11.0	125.0	24.0	11.0	15.6
1962	Kreidler	50R	50	1	11.0	11.5	50.0	22.2	8.5	18.7
1962	Everett	250	250	1	31.0	7.4	250.0	18.2	9.3	13.9
1962	MZ	125	125	1	25.0	10.8	125.0	25.0	10.8	16.5
1963	Yamaha	RD56	250	2	50.0	11.0	125.0	25.0	11.0	16.2
1963	Yamaha	RA97	125	2	28.0	13.0	62.5	23.8	10.3	16.5
1963	Bultaco	TSS	125	1	24.0	10.0	125.0	24.0	10.0	17.1
1963	MZ	250	250	2	48.0	10.8	125.0	24.0	10.8	15.9
1963	Suzuki	125	125	2	26.0	12.5	62.5	22.1	9.9	15.9
1963	Villiers	Inch.	250	1	37.0	8.5	250.0	21.7	10.7	14.5
1964	MZ	250	250	2	49.0	10.5	125.0	24.5	10.5	16.6
1964	Yamaha	RD48	250	2	37.0	9.5	125.0	18.5	9.5	13.9
1965	R-Enfield	250	250	1	37.0	8.2	250.0	21.7	10.3	15.0
1965	Yamaha	RD56	250	2	55.0	11.5	125.0	27.5	11.5	17.1
1965	Yamaha	RD05	250	4	65.0	14.4	62.5	27.7	11.4	17.3
1966	Yamaha	TD1B	250	2	30.0	10.0	125.0	15.0	10.0	10.7
1967	Yamaha	TD1C	250	2	38.0	10.0	125.0	19.0	10.0	13.6
1968	Q.U.B.	250	250	2	55.0	11.0	125.0	27.5	11.0	17.8
1968	Yamaha	TD2	250	2	44.0	11.0	125.0	22.0	11.0	14.3
1968	Yamaha	250	250	4	72.0	15.3	62.5	30.6	12.1	18.0

Table 1.5.1. Racing Motorcycle Two-Stroke Engine Power Output History (cont)

Year	Make	Model	Swept Volume (cm³)	No of cyls (-)	Power max (BHP)	Speed Pmax (krpm)	Cylinder vol (cm³)	Power max 125 cm³ (BHP)	Speed Pmax 125 cm³ (krpm)	Torque Pmax 125 cm³ (Nm)
1969	Yamaha	TD2	250	2	47.0	11.0	125.0	23.5	11.0	15.2
1969	Jawa	350	350	4	70.0	13.0	87.5	23.0	11.5	14.2
1970	Alpha	Centuri	125	1	28.0	12.0	125.0	28.0	12.0	16.6
1971	BSA	Bantam	125	1	20.0	11.0	125.0	20.0	11.0	13.0
1973	Yamaha	TD3	250	2	52.0	10.8	125.0	26.0	10.8	17.2
1973	Kreidler	50R	50	1	14.5	14.2	50.0	29.3	10.5	20.0
1974	Yamaha	TZ250	250	2	54.0	11.0	125.0	27.0	11.0	17.5
1976	Kawasaki	KR750	747	3	120.0	9.5	249.0	23.6	12.0	14.1
1976	Rotax	454	437	2	98.0	9.5	218.5	31.9	11.4	19.9
1976	Honda	MT-125	125	1	26.0	10.5	125.0	26.0	10.5	17.7
1977	Bultaco	50	50	1	18.0	15.5	50.0	36.3	11.4	22.7
1979	Yamaha	TZ350F	350	2	72.0	11.0	175.0	27.8	12.3	16.1
1979	Kawasaki	T2	250	2	71.0	12.0	125.0	35.5	12.0	21.1
1981	Honda	RS-RW	125	1	30.0	11.3	125.0	30.0	11.3	18.9
1981	Honda	RSRWT	125	2	40.0	14.0	62.5	34.0	11.1	21.8
1982	Garelli	125	124	2	47.0	14.6	62.0	40.2	11.6	24.8
1982	Yamaha	R2	250	2	71.0	12.0	125.0	35.5	12.0	21.1
1983	Honda	RS500	500	3	128.0	11.5	166.7	34.2	12.7	19.3
1983	Rotax	250	250	2	72.0	13.2	125.0	36.0	13.2	19.5
1984	Honda	RS250	250	2	66.0	11.5	125.0	33.0	11.5	20.5
1985	Kreidler	50R	50	1	21.0	16.2	50.0	42.4	11.9	25.3
1985	Suzuki	RG500	496	4	125.0	10.8	124.0	31.4	10.8	20.8
1985	Honda	NS500	499	3	133.0	11.5	166.3	35.6	12.6	20.1
1986	Exactweld	250	250	2	72.5	12.2	125.0	36.2	12.2	21.2
1988	Honda	NSR250	250	2	80.0	12.0	125.0	40.0	12.0	23.8
1988	Honda	RS125	125	1	36.0	12.0	125.0	36.0	12.0	21.4
1988	Yamaha	W4	500	4	147.0	12.0	125.0	36.7	12.0	21.8
1989	Honda	NSR500	500	4	170.0	12.5	125.0	42.5	12.5	24.3
1989	Aprilia	AFIV	250	2	78.0	12.5	125.0	39.0	12.5	22.3
1990	Honda	NSR500	500	4	169.0	12.5	125.0	42.2	12.5	24.1
1992	Honda	NSR250	250	2	85.0	12.8	125.0	42.5	12.8	23.7
1992	Rotax	125	125	1	43.0	12.5	125.0	43.0	12.5	24.5

All outputs are claimed, not independently verified.

Varied sources sometimes give conflicting data.

Fast-developing engine powers vary even during one season.

Imperial horsepower = 1.015 PS European.

Sources include:

H. W. Boensch, *Der Schnellaufende Zweitaktmotor*, Motorbuch Verlag Stuttgart, 1993.

H. Huetten, *Schnelle Motoren*, Motorbuch Verlag Stuttgart, 1994.

C. MacKellar, *Yamaha Racing Two-Strokes*, Crowood Press, 1995.

M. Walker, *MZ*, Transport Source Books, 1996.

M. Walker and R. Carrick, *British Performance Two-Strokes*, 1998.

C. MacKellar, *Honda GP Racers*, Crowood Press, 1998.

Figure 1.5.2 shows the variation over the years of peaking speed for the 125 cm^3 equivalent cylinder. This reached 10,000 quite early on, and has since increased to 12,500, possibly slightly more. It appears that the trend will settle at 12,500 to 13,000 unless there is a significant technical advance.

Maximum torque figures are not widely available. However, Figure 1.5.3 shows the progression of torque at peak power, which is easily calculated from the previous data. This shows a steady advance as scavenging has improved with better inlet, transfer and exhaust systems.

The above indicates that a 125 cm^3 cylinder can be persuaded to deliver around 42 bhp at 12,500 rpm (31.4 kW at 208 revs/sec). Subsequent chapters explain how. This performance level corresponds to a torque of 24 Nm at peak power (17.7lb.ft). The engine energy delivery is 150.8 J/rev. This requires a brake mean effective pressure of 1.21 MPa (175 psi) for the entire cylinder, or about 350 psi for the working upper half of the cylinder. Such figures would be even greater at the peak-torque speed.

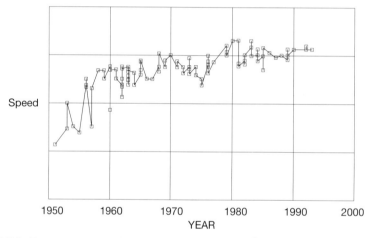

Figure 1.5.2. Racing motorcycle peaking speed (125 cm^3 equivalent cylinder) from 1950 to 2000.

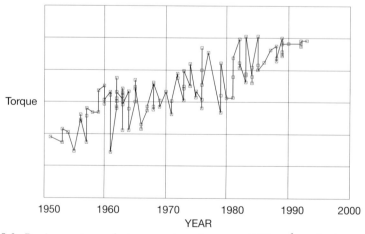

Figure 1.5.3. Racing motorcycle torque at peak power (125 cm^3 equivalent cylinder) from 1950 to 2000.

CHAPTER 2:

The Engine and its Components

2.1 Introduction

This chapter explains the practical operating principles of the engine, with a brief but necessary reference to the theoretical thermodynamic cycle. It reviews the layout and methods of construction, introducing bore, stroke, swept volume, port timing and terms such as 'efficiency'. Finally, the chapter looks at temperature distribution and related problems of thermal expansion and thermal distortion.

2.2 Principle of Operation

There are various ways of classifying engines:

1. Two-stroke or four-stroke cycle? What is called a complete 'cycle' of operation may be achieved in two strokes of the piston (one up, one down) or four. A single-cylinder two-stoke engine fires on every revolution. A single-cylinder four-stroke fires on every other revolution.

2. External combustion or internal combustion? In an external combustion engine the fuel is burned with air outside the cylinder. In internal combustion, the fuel is burned with the air actually inside the cylinder. Nearly all-modern engines are internal combustion.

3. Open cycle or closed cycle? In an open cycle, the working gas is replaced on completion of each cycle. The closed cycle retains and reuses the same working gas. Open cycles are usually internal combustion and closed cycles are generally external combustion.

The crankcase-scavenged two-stroke engine is therefore an open cycle internal combustion engine.

Most theory books are based on closed cycles, which do not relate well to the open-cycle engines of the real world. Figure 2.2.1 shows the famous Otto cycle – the theoretical basis of spark-ignition engines.

This 'idealised' Otto cycle relates reasonably well to slow closed cycle engines with external combustion, but not to modern high-speed open-cycle engines.

For instance, instead of ending the cycle with a cooling process, the practical IC engine ejects the used air and burnt gases from the cylinder (the exhaust process) and takes in fresh cool air, which substitutes for cooling in the theoretical closed cycle. This is called induction and transfer.

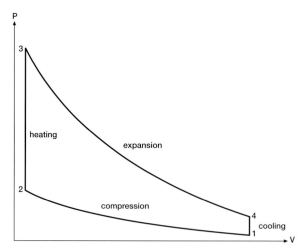

Figure 2.2.1. The ideal closed Otto cycle, basis of the spark-ignition engine.

The 'ideal' cycle also fails to represent the actual engine because the four theoretical gas processes are not in reality separated. Combustion does not occur instantaneously at top dead centre. For such reasons, the theoretical Otto cycle considerably overestimates the energy a real engine can yield. In fact, basic theory is of limited practical help to engine designers or tuners, but it is historically important because it revealed the significance of compression and expansion ratio.

Rather than thinking of the four idealised thermodynamic processes (compression, heating, expansion, cooling), it is better to think in terms of the physical actions that make an internal combustion engine operate. For a crankcase-scavenged two-stroke engine these actions are:

1. Induction
2. Transfer
3. Compression
4. Combustion
5. Expansion
6. Exhaust

Induction, transfer and exhaust are not strictly thermodynamic processes, but together (in the order exhaust, induction, transfer) they provide the cooling process of the ideal cycle. Hence, six physical processes correspond to theory's four 'ideal' thermodynamic processes.

Unfortunately the terms 'two-stroke cycle' and 'four-stroke cycle' are sometimes shortened to 'two-cycle' and 'four-cycle', and hence the term 'two-stroke engine' is sometimes rendered as 'two-cycle engine', with complete loss of meaning. One *cycle* of operation of the two-stroke engine consists of *two strokes.*

In crankcase-scavenged two-strokes, a mixture of air and fuel is drawn first into the crankcase. It is then transferred to the cylinder. The term inlet (or induction) means the process of drawing the mixture into the crankcase, and the term transfer (or bypass) describes the flow of gas from the crankcase to the cylinder.

Figure 1.1.2 of Chapter 1 shows the porting through which the fuel-air mixture is transferred from the crankcase to cylinder, and the exhaust through which the burnt gas is ejected from the lower part of the cylinder above the piston at bottom dead centre. The actual portions of the cylinder in which compression and combustion take place are individually far less than the total 'swept' volume. They may even be less than half for an engine with a long exhaust period as used with a tuned exhaust system. However, half is a useful approximation. The two-stroke engine may then be considered as using one half of the cycle for exhaust and transfer, and the other half for compression, combustion and expansion. In contrast, the four-stroke engine uses almost the whole stroke, but only on alternate revolutions. The more frequent firing of the two-stroke is therefore offset by a considerable reduction of the effective swept volume. It is far from obvious in advance how the performance of the two types of engine will compare for a given swept volume.

Two-strokes tend to run with a hotter piston, cylinder and head, because combustion takes place on every cycle. This is their Achilles' heel. Higher power brings more heat into the top end, with thermal distortion and loss of reliability. Piston and cylinder metallurgy become more important.

2.3 Construction

Figures 2.3.1 onwards show an assortment of engines. Constructional methods vary according to type, the period of manufacture, the event for which the engine was intended, cost limitations, and design philosophy.

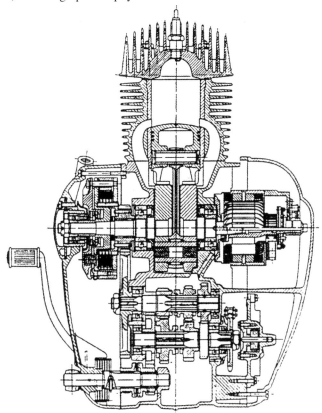

Figure 2.3.1. The MZ ES-250 road-going engine from the 1960s and '70s. 16 bhp at 5,200 rpm (1962) on a 28.5 mm carburettor. The last version gave 80 bhp/litre. The version shown is from 1962. The Schnürle transfers are conspicuous, with entry through cut-outs in the piston skirt below the wrist pin. Three piston rings. Squish-band combustion chamber.

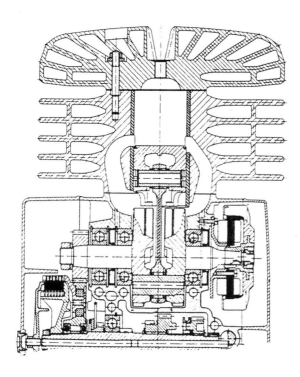

Figure 2.3.2. Sachs Sports 175, another road-going example: 26 bhp at 8,500 rpm (148 bhp/litre). Flat-top piston, again with squish band. Six transfer passages were used, of which the main and secondary are shown in section (not the ones furthest from the exhaust). The shaft is supported in three ball bearings with a cantilevered drive to the clutch on a lay shaft. Piston-controlled induction (not shown). Exhaust port not shown. Crank web diameter 1.80 S, rod length 1.70 S, main shaft diameter 0.40 S, little end pin 0.30 S, big end pin 0.36 S (see Section 2.4 for explanation of dimensions).

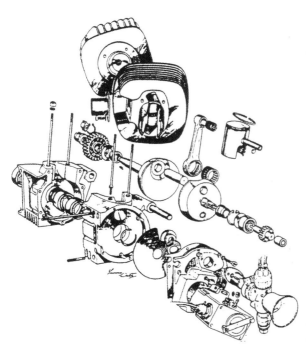

Figure 2.3.3. MZ 125 air-cooled racing single of 1961, the first to achieve 200 bhp/litre, producing 25 bhp at 10,800 rpm – the classic structure for a racing single. Note the pressed-together crankshaft and compact big-end, the rod having roller bearings at both ends. The two-part light alloy main crankcase is assembled around the crankshaft. The finned cylinder barrel is held to the lower alloy case by four studs that also hold the head. Induction control by rotary Zimmermann disc valve mounted directly on the crankshaft, operating in a remote chamber. Piston skirt cut-outs below the gudgeon pin allow gas entry to the bottom of the transfer passages, visible in the cylinder barrel. This was the engine being used by Degner when he defected to the Japanese.

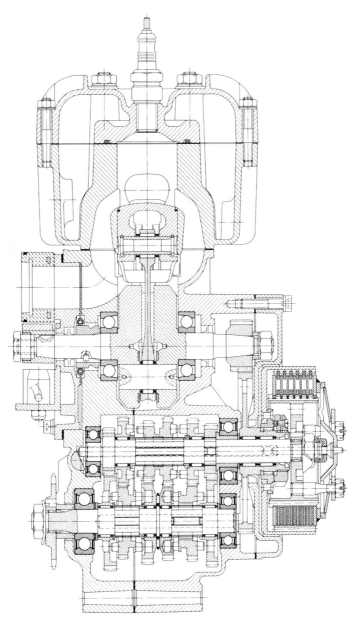

Figure 2.3.4. Water-cooled Kreidler 50 of 1983. 21 bhp at 16,200 rpm. 420 bhp/litre. Shaft supported on two ball bearings. Power take-off on the right to clutch on lay shaft. Very large rotary disc intake on the left. Large Schnürle transfer passages. Single piston ring. The domed piston is deceptive – piston crown radius is about 60 mm (1.5 B), which makes the exhaust port look lower than it really is. Port height should be measured from the piston timing edge. As drawn, the exhaust is in fact 54% of the stroke and the transfers are 30.5% of the stroke. Crank web diameter 2.0 S, rod length 2.13 S, main bearings 0.43 S, little end pin 0.30 S, big end pin 0.40 S, carburettor and intake hole diameter 28 mm, which is 0.70 S. Zimmermann intake disc diameter 2.75 S. The piston is particularly robust (see Section 2.4 for explanation of dimensions).

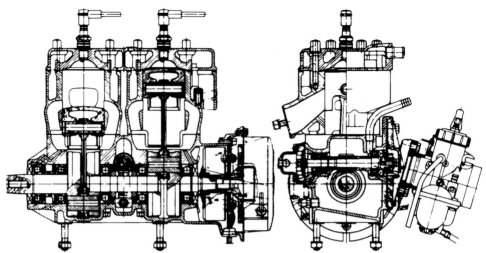

Figure 2.3.5. Rotax '454' of 1976. 437 cm³ giving 98 bhp at 9,500 rpm. 36 kg without gearbox. Bore x stroke 67.5 mm x 61 mm. Because twins pose an intake problem, piston inlets or reed valves are often used. With standard Zimmermann discs there must be one on each end of the engine, so power take off must be from between the cylinders. Rotax opted instead for a right-angled drive to an intake disc located on the side of the engine. The single timing cutout in the disc can serve the two cylinders alternately from twin carburettors. Note the severely downdrafted exhaust passage. Rod length 2.00 S, crank web diameter 1.67 S, inlet disc diameter 136 mm, 2.33 S.

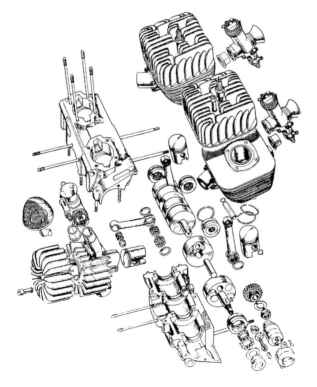

Figure 2.3.6. DKW three-cylinder 350 of 1956. 48 bhp at 9,500 rpm. One cylinder faces forwards, using longitudinal finning, while the other two, at 75 degrees to the first, are almost vertical, giving better cooling than three cylinders in line, where the centre cylinder has cooling difficulties. Also, the engine is narrower overall than an inline three. Piston-controlled induction. Four main bearings separating the three crank chambers. This layout was copied by Honda 28 years later, with water-cooling, and then won a World Championship. (Motor Cycle)

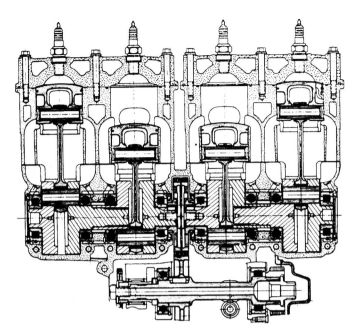

Figure 2.3.7. Yamaha 700 straight 4 (also in 500 and 750 sizes), circa 1990. Stroke 54 mm, bore 54, 64 and 66.5 mm – a combination of two twins, with central power take off . Layout not ideal for disc intake valves. Piston intake or reed valves, as used here, fit conveniently and make an impressive row of carburettors. The complex crankshaft is carried in four roller and four ball bearings. Rod length 2.00 S, crank web diameter 1.76 S, main shaft journal diameter 0.59 S at the ball bearings, 0.46 S at the roller bearings. Firing order 1&4, then 2&3, in diagonal pairs. Despite good balance, extreme width is a disadvantage (see Section 2.4 for explanation of dimensions).

Figure 2.3.8. The König flat four 500. Power output 113 bhp at 10,800 rpm, using a single inlet rotor with right-angle belt drive. A Zimmermann disc feeds two crank chambers from two carburettors. Similar in concept to the Rotax, but each chamber now serves two opposed cylinders. Obviously, this is only possible if the two cylinders sharing one inlet have pistons moving outwards simultaneously or there will be no crankcase depression to draw in the air. The rotor drive is shown at 1:1 crankshaft speed, thus the rotor must have one cut-out. The rear pair of cylinders fires at 180° from the front pair.

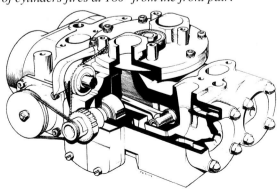

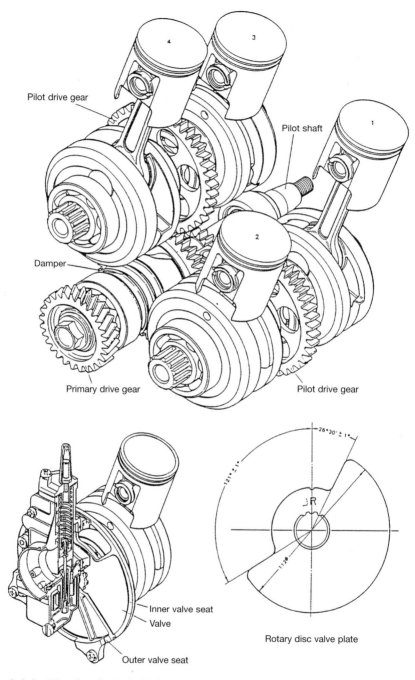

Figure 2.3.9. The Suzuki RG 500, circa 1990. Given an existing twin 250 with a Zimmermann inlet disc at each end and a power take off in the centre, it is not difficult to make a square four with two such twins geared to a common pilot shaft. Firing order 1&4, then 2&3, giving excellent balance. The overall layout is more compact than a straight four. Water or forced-air cooling is necessary.

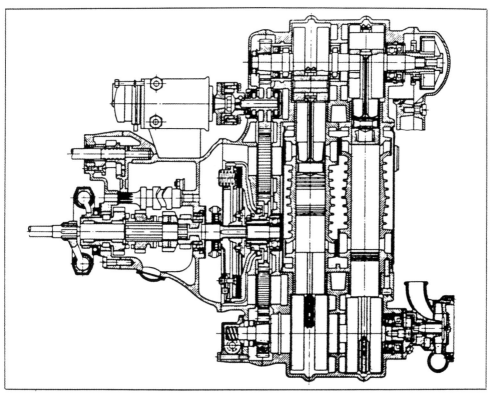

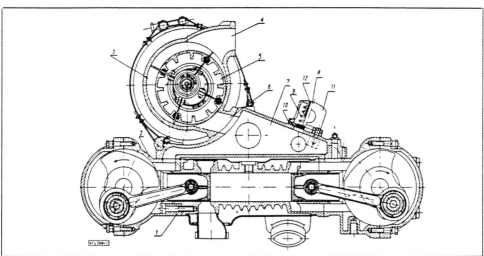

Figure 2.3.10. An ambitious and successful last fling by DKW was the four-cylinder opposed-piston GS 250, producing 47 bhp at 7,000 rpm – (a 350 gave 56 bhp). The crankshafts are geared together. Opposed pistons eliminate cylinder heads, compensating for the added weight elsewhere. Heat losses to the heads are eliminated, giving better thermal efficiency, with more power and better fuel economy. The engine layout is wide but low – more suited to cars than motorcycles. (S. Rauch, DKW, *Motorbuch Verlag Stuttgart, 1988.)*

Although not always the largest or heaviest individual part, the crankcase is considered to be the main component. It is usually made from aluminium alloy, cast in sand for small quantities, or in a steel die or by lost-wax investment casting for larger quantities. Magnesium alloys are sometimes used for lightness. Even for single-cylinder engines, crankcase design varies considerably. It may be a relatively large integral casting containing the crankshaft and a drop-in cylinder sleeve. At the other extreme it may be a fairly small part enclosing the crank web only, with separate shaft housings and a separate cylinder unit bolted on. Sometimes the cylinder barrel is removable, with a joint below the ports, giving access to the transfer passages for manufacture or modification. The cylinder barrel may be of cast iron, or machined from steel, or possibly of aluminium with a chrome-plated bore.

The fins may be integral with the cylinder, or they may form a separate fin barrel. If the crankcase also incorporates the cylinder fins (sometimes called monolithic), then the wearing surface of the cylinder may be chromed, or a thin iron or brass cylinder liner (sleeve) may be inserted. Where the liner and fin-barrel or crankcase are separate components, the fit of the liner in the fins may be free or shrunk to give what is called an interference fit'. Such details as the precise materials used, their coefficients of thermal expansion and the interference fit or otherwise may have a considerable effect on the performance and usability of the engine.

The crankshaft may be made in one piece, requiring a separable connecting rod big end for assembly. Alternatively, and normally for single-cylinder engines, the crankshaft may be in two main parts plus the crankpin, all pressed together. By using an assembled crankshaft, the connecting rod big end need not be split for assembly. This lightens the big end considerably, and reduces its size, which allows reduced crankcase volume and a much more compact crankcase.

The crankshaft is supported in the crankcase or shaft housing by plain journal bearings, ball bearings or roller bearings. The shaft may also have to accept significant axial loads, as from helical gears, as well as the piston/conrod loads from the crankpin. Most crankshafts are made from high strength steel. Titanium is an expensive low weight alternative.

Crankshaft features include the crankpin, the crank web and the bearing journals. The crank web is usually machined to provide balance. A full disc is sometimes called a crank disc. Larger engines usually have a Woodruff key for output torque transmission, with a threaded shaft end or stud for retention of the output gear. Where plain main bearings are used for economy or light weight, the shaft may run in aluminium bearings but bronze or cast iron bush inserts give longer life. Ball bearings or roller bearings are normally used as the main shaft bearings.

The connecting rod, or 'conrod', is usually made of steel or aluminium alloy. Titanium is sometimes used for specials. Only in low speed engines is the rod big end split for assembly. In the modern high-speed engines the rod big end is in one piece, usually with a roller bearing. Sometimes, both ends may have bronze bushes. These thin sleeves of bronze provide a better wearing surface than the main material of the rod. They are fixed by thermal shrinking or pressing.

The small-end or little end of the rod connects to the piston by the gudgeon pin, or wrist pin. This is usually of hollow steel. The piston, in larger sizes, is invariably of aluminium alloy. Piston alloys often have a high silicon content to reduce thermal expansion and improve hot strength. Silicon alloys are hard wearing but harder to machine. The gudgeon pin holes may be reinforced by brass or bronze bushes.

The gas pressure in the cylinder is generally retained by one or two piston rings, usually of iron. The thermal expansion coefficients of the piston and the liner/fin assembly must be compatible. Good results have been obtained with aluminium alloy pistons in chromium plated aluminium cylinders, with aluminium alloy pistons in iron liners, possibly chromed, with aluminium pistons in chromed brass liners, and with iron pistons in iron liners, with one of the two chromed. Iron pistons tend to be heavy, unless designed very carefully, but can have a very low wear rate. Iron is still a good choice of material for a low speed engine.

The cylinder head is normally separate, in which case it usually bolts onto the case or fin barrel, although a few engines have been made with integral heads. The head has its own head fins, distinct from those on the case barrel. Then there is the spark plug, but, of course, no valves. Water-cooled engines generally have no fins, and look totally different.

Inlet of fresh mixture to the crankcase may be controlled in various ways:

1. Piston control, using the lower edge of the piston skirt
2. Reed valves
3. Rotary valves.

For maximum power, the inlet pipe and carburettor must be of large flow area to give least resistance. This gives poor fuel suction, which can be problematic under hard acceleration, upsetting the fuel feed pressure (in the absence of a well-positioned float chamber). In some engines the fuel supply is pressurised. Fuel pumps, such as diaphragm pumps, are found mainly on engines that need to operate in unusual attitudes, such as chain-saw engines.

2.4 Dimensions

The length of stroke is, of course, twice the crank *throw*, which is measured from the shaft rotational axis to the centreline of the crankpin. The *swept volume* is the volume swept by the piston during one stroke. In other words, it is the volume between the piston crown at *bdc* (bottom dead centre) and at *tdc* (top dead centre). The swept volume is simply the area of the bore multiplied by the stroke. It does not depend on the shape of the piston crown or on the length of the connecting rod. The *combustion volume* is the volume above the piston at tdc. This may involve a volume in the head, in the plug, and in the cylinder, also allowing for piston crown shape, head gaskets, etc. The *crevice volume* is the total volume of small clearances, e.g. around the piston above the top ring.

The engine *capacity* is the swept volume plus the combustion volume. Competition regulations are usually based on swept volume rather than capacity. However, the term capacity is frequently used incorrectly for swept volume. Of late, the term *swept capacity* has been seen, meaning swept volume. This only adds to the confusion.

Given the two prime dimensions

1. Bore B
2. Stroke S

then the bore cross-sectional area is

$$A_B = \frac{\pi}{4} B^2$$

and the swept volume is

$$V_S = A_B S = \frac{\pi}{4} B^2 S$$

For comparing engines of different sizes, it is helpful to non-dimensionalise lengths, areas and volumes. This can be done by dividing lengths by the bore B or by the stroke S as appropriate. Areas can be divided by the bore area A_B, and volumes by the swept volume V_S.

This is called *normalisation*. However, *specific areas*, often used in discussing port sizes, are the area divided by the swept volume, expressed as cm²/litre or in²/in³. Specific areas are not non-dimensional.

For normalising lengths, whether it is preferable to normalise against B or against S depends on the actual dimension. The connecting rod length is logically related to the stroke rather than the bore. Port heights are often expressed as a percentage of the stroke. However, it is usually better to normalise head dimensions or port widths against the bore B.

The *reference area* is the cross-sectional area of the bore. An area such as a port area is then non-dimensionalised to give a normalised area

$$A_N = \frac{A}{A_B}$$

Normalisation of an area is particularly useful for expressing port areas or passage cross-sectional areas in non-dimensional form, and for comparing engines on this basis.

A volume is normalised by dividing by the swept volume,

$$V_N = \frac{V}{V_S}$$

This may be used to relate volumes such as the combustion volume, the crankcase volume, or the transfer passage volume to the engine swept volume.

As mentioned, it is also common practice to express port areas as specific areas rather than normalised areas, by dividing the area by the swept volume:

$$A_S = \frac{A}{V_S}$$

Specific areas are often expressed as cm²/litre or in²/in³. This has significant disadvantages compared with normalised areas, because it is not non-dimensional. If an engine design is scaled in exact proportion throughout, the *normalised* port area (port area / bore area) remains the same, but *specific* port area (port area / swept volume) reduces with increasing size.

In summary, *normalisation* involves dividing a length by a reference length, an area by a reference area, or a volume by a reference volume, and produces a non-dimensional result. However, *specific* areas are areas divided by the swept volume.

During the sequence of actions (the six processes) of the two-stroke cycle there is, of course, considerable overlap. This can be seen in the graphic angular 'timing' diagram of Figure 2.4.1, which shows the *port open period* in relation to shaft angular position. The example is for a high-speed racing engine. The shaft angle over which a port is open is called its *angular duration*, or just *duration*. The term 'dwell' is often used incorrectly and should correctly refer only to the sustained open condition of a poppet valve. For the example given, the port durations are:

$$\text{Inlet}: \quad \theta_I = 140 + 60 = 200°$$

$$\text{Exhaust}: \quad \theta_E = 184°$$

$$\text{Transfer}: \quad \theta_T = 130°$$

The time duration of a port depends upon the angular duration and the shaft speed. The duration of combustion is not known unless a pressure sensor is used in the cylinder head, and even then is not well defined because of the gradual start and end of the process.

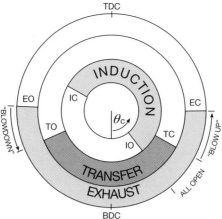

Figure 2.4.1   Angular timing diagram.

The time or crank angle between the exhaust opening and transfer opening is called the *blowdown period*. This is the time from when the exhaust has just opened and the cylinder pressure is falling, until the transfer opens. Hence, for conventional engines,

$$\theta_B = \frac{1}{2}(\theta_E - \theta_T)$$

This is 27 degrees in the example given.

The position of the top edges of the ports, and hence the port timing, can be very critical, even to one degree or less. For consistent good results the timing must be controlled very accurately.

For comparing different engines, the combustion volume can be expressed as a fraction of the swept volume, i.e. as a normalised volume. However, it is more usual to work in terms of the *compression ratio*, which is the capacity divided by the combustion volume. However, the racing two-stroke also has a *crankcase compression ratio*, or *primary compression ratio*, so the ordinary compression ratio is sometimes called the *secondary compression ratio* to avoid confusion.

Because of the presence of the exhaust port in the lower part of the cylinder, the *trapped compression ratio* is sometimes used. This is based on the trapped part of the swept volume, i.e. the volume above the top edge of the exhaust port.

Engines are sometime described as *efficient*, but there are many types of efficiency. The main ones are:

1. *Volumetric efficiency*. This is the quantity of new air drawn into the cylinder and retained there, divided by the swept volume.

2. *Indicated thermal efficiency*. This relates the indicated energy output (calculated from cylinder pressures measured by an 'indicator') to the energy of combustion of the fuel used.

3. *Brake thermal efficiency*. This relates the shaft energy output to the energy of combustion of the fuel used. It is so called because the power output was traditionally measured by means of a brake.

4. *Mechanical efficiency*. This relates the actual output at the shaft to the indicated output. Its shortfall from 100% is a measure of losses from pumping and friction.

As a matter of interest, the term *volumetric efficiency* is often used, incorrectly, as the air consumed by the engine per revolution divided by the swept volume. The correct term for this is the *delivery ratio*. The ratio of volumetric efficiency to delivery ratio is the *trapping efficiency*, indicating the fraction of air consumed that is successfully retained in the cylinder, rather than being lost directly from the exhaust port. Hence, the volumetric efficiency is somewhat less than the delivery ratio. The process of replacement of the old gas in the cylinder with new mixture is called *scavenging*.

2.5 Thermal Expansion

Because the two-stroke engine fires on every revolution, unlike the four-stroke which fires on alternate revolutions, the two-stroke tends to run hotter in the upper cylinder and head. In contrast, the bottom end may be well cooled by the fuel/air mixture passing through the crankcase. Larger cylinders lead to greater head and cylinder top-end temperatures, so scaling up an engine can give disappointing results. Although larger cylinders tend to be more thermally efficient, with proportionally lower thermal losses from the burned gases, they generally need better cooling. This is partly because of the longer metal conduction paths, especially from the centre of the piston crown. For a cylinder of a given size, the heat input to the piston, cylinder and head is directly related to the internal gas temperature and gas density. This is why a high output engine tends to run hotter, needing bigger fins, or water cooling. As temperature increases at sustained high output, power may be lost. Seizure of the piston or ring may even occur. In severe cases the piston crown may collapse. Such problems make two-stroke metallurgy particularly critical. High speed is not really the problem, though this may increase the frictional heating, of the rings for example. The greater problem is the high gas temperature and density that occurs when the engine has high torque for its size (high specific torque), or high brake mean engine pressure.

Because of the charge density and high combustion energy, the piston crown temperature of high performance engines can exceed the softening point of some aluminium alloys, causing failure. High piston temperature also causes extreme expansion. Aluminium-silicon alloys have proved to be the solution. These have better hot strength and lower thermal expansion. Table 2.5.1 shows the thermal expansion coefficient for some selected pure elements. Table 2.5.2 shows the typical effect of silicon in Al-Si alloy. Each one per cent of silicon reduces the thermal expansion coefficient by about 0.8 per cent of the original value, though the exact value depends on other alloying constituents. For example, 'Lo-Ex' alloy, which has a particularly low expansion coefficient, contains 1%Cu, 1%Mg, 1%Ni and 12%Si. Table 2.5.3 gives coefficients for other possible engine materials.

Although these coefficients, e.g. aluminium at 24 parts per million per degree C, may seem very small, in precision competition engines the expansion is significant. The actual expansion distance x is given by

$$x = \alpha(T - T_0)L$$

Internal engine temperatures can exceed 300°C above ambient. For pure aluminium, the product of the expansion coefficient and the temperature rise is then 0.0072. That is 7 mm/m, or 7 thou/inch. For a piston diameter of 50 mm (almost 2 inches), the increase in diameter is 0.36 mm (14 thou). With clearances between the cold piston and cylinder of much less than this, unless the piston and liner materials are carefully matched, seizure can easily occur because the piston simply becomes larger than the cylinder.

When an aluminium alloy piston is used in an iron cylinder, a suitable cold clearance of around 0.1 mm must be provided, depending on the operating conditions and on the materials involved. Increasing cold piston clearance may sometimes be a temporary fix for piston seizures, but use of a high-silicon lower-expansion piston is better, or use of a higher expansion cylinder. Most modern high-performance two-strokes use a chromed aluminium alloy cylinder.

Ring end-gap of the cold piston ring is necessary to prevent seizure in the liner. The ring gap depends on the materials of the ring and cylinder and on the severity of service. The ring itself gets hotter than the liner because it is heated by the hot piston and by its own friction against the liner. The optimum value of cold end gap depends on the type of iron used for the ring, the ring temperature, and the liner temperature and material. For most materials, a minimum value is 0.4% of the bore, although much greater values are sometimes needed. An end gap of 0.4% of the bore is 0.2 mm on a 50 mm bore, or 8 thou on 2 inches. Too large a gap will allow gas leakage, with performance loss and possible blow-by heating problems. Too small a gap is worse, causing severe problems when the ring expands. Once the gap has closed up, the ring will become tight in the bore, expanding hard against the cylinder, increasing friction and raising the temperature of the ring even more. This can result in a catastrophic runaway seizure of the ring. Bearing in mind that the ring gap allows for circumferential expansion, the fact that a ring needs about 0.4% bore clearance implies a clearance of 0.13% of the circumference. This suggests that the ring runs about 100°C hotter than the liner assuming the same thermal expansion coefficient for ring and cylinder.

Engines often have an iron cylinder shrunk into an aluminium cooling barrel. As they heat up, the barrel will expand more than the liner. If the liner becomes loose less heat will be transferred to the fins, so the liner gets even hotter. So long as there is an interference fit between an iron cylinder and aluminium fins, they will expand by the same amount despite the difference in thermal expansion coefficient. When the liner becomes free in the cooling barrel the loss of the interference fit will increase the thermal resistance of the joint, so the liner tends to heat up to follow the aluminium barrel size.

With a main shaft supported in one or two ball bearings, the outer race of the steel bearing is installed in the (usually) aluminium crankcase. The cold interference fit is about 0.08% of the ball race diameter, which is 0.4 mm on 50 mm diameter. The interference fit is necessary to hold the ball race firmly in place to withstand the combustion force and reciprocating forces. Friction causes the race and housing to heat up, which tends to loosen the fit. If friction were then to cause it to turn this would cause creep and wear of the housing.

Fitting the race in a tight housing inevitably reduces its internal clearance. Ball races are available with various free internal clearances so that the installed clearance can be controlled to the value required. Taking the thermal expansion coefficient of steel as 12 ppm/°C and that of the aluminium case as 24 ppm/°C, the uniform temperature increase required to free the ball race completely in the case is found from:

$$T = \frac{x}{(\alpha_1 - \alpha_2)D} = \frac{0.04}{(24 - 12) \times 10^{-6} \times 50} = 67°$$

This temperature increase is above the 'cold' temperature, in this case a room temperature of 15°C, so the actual free-up temperature is 82°C.

Pressing the ball race into and out of the cold case with this interference fit will quickly wear the case and loosen the fit. However, heating the case to 100°C will allow the race to drop in easily. Heating the case to 50°C above the temperature of the race would normally be enough during installation, but any delay will cause the race to heat up to case temperature. Another option sometimes used in difficult cases (severely tight fit) is to cool the race as much as possible, for example in a fridge or freezer. This can give an extra 20 degrees or 0.006 mm (0.24 thou). In extreme cases, even liquid nitrogen has been used. At −196°C, this will reduce a 60 mm ball race diameter by a tremendous 0.1 mm (4 thou). This will certainly allow free fitting, but handling can be a problem.

At uniform temperature, a component of uniform isotropic material will expand equally in all directions and retain its original shape at the new size. However, in engines the temperatures are not uniform, so the thermal expansion causes small changes, not just of size but also of shape. This is called *thermal distortion*. The term 'distortion' indicates an undesirable change of shape. Some distortions are unimportant and some are easily dealt with. Others are very problematic.

Piston and Cylinder

The cylinder may run at about 250°C at the top but possibly only 100°C at the bottom because the inner crankcase is well cooled by the incoming fuel/air mixture. Figure 2.5.1 shows temperature profiles in a cylinder for a 50 cm³ engine of moderate output. This illustrates the temperature variation along the cylinder, and shows the significant differences between exhaust and transfer sides. The temperatures will be higher for a higher performance engine. For a bore of diameter 50 mm, the diametral expansion for an iron liner is then about 0.09 mm (3.6 thou) more at the top than at the bottom. For a 19% silicon-aluminium alloy, it is about 0.15 mm (6 thou). Considering a piston of the same material as the cylinder, this will usually have an expansion slightly greater than the hot top end of the liner because the piston crown is somewhat hotter than the upper cylinder. The cylinder is often given a taper, with its diameter larger at the bottom. Then, when running temperature is reached, the bore is of more-or-less constant diameter, allowing the hot piston and ring to fit uniformly throughout the stroke. An aluminium cylinder will need extreme taper unless very high in silicon. If there is insufficient taper the engine will tighten when hot, with the piston scraping the bottom end of the liner.

Because of the scavenging pattern of most porting systems, the cool mixture of fuel and air goes up one side of the cylinder first, so the cylinder runs cooler on that side, and hotter on the exhaust side, as seen in Figure 2.5.1. This temperature difference increases because

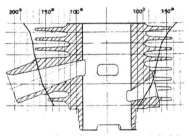

Figure 2.5.1. Axial temperature distribution in a 4.2 bhp 50 cm³ engine, measured by Kreidler, using thermocouple elements installed 1 mm beneath the inner surface of the chromed aluminium cylinder. A modern racing 50 would deliver four or more times this power, increasing the temperatures. Temperature difference from top to near to the bottom of the cylinder is about 60 °C and the exhaust side 30 °C hotter than the inlet side, causing differential expansion and thermal distortion. With air cooling, air is best directed onto the exhaust side first. Fin size should relate to the local heat flux, being larger at the top of the cylinder and head.

the exhaust gas heats the exhaust outlet. There is also a hot exhaust system attached to that side.

The lack of symmetry in the temperature of the piston and cylinder causes them to expand into a non-circular shape. These shape discrepancies, along with mechanical stress distortion, are generally dealt with by providing some clearance, and by careful running in of the engine until any tight areas are worn away to the optimum fit. Individually tailored shape adjustments to the piston and cylinder are also a possibility. Use of aluminium instead of iron may make the distortion problems worse, because, although the improved thermal conductivity reduces the temperature variations, the expansion coefficient is higher.

The usual way to accommodate piston and liner distortions is to use a free-fitting piston and to achieve the seal with a compliant piston ring that will adapt to the liner profile. The top land of a ringed piston (above the top ring) gets hotter than the rest, and needs to be reduced correspondingly in diameter to avoid seizure. In fact, the whole length of the piston may be carefully profiled. The ring is forced against the cylinder wall primarily by the cylinder gas pressure that acts behind it so the total ring friction is related to the number of rings.

The temperature difference between the exhaust and opposite sides causes the cylinder to expand into a curve, as shown in Figure 2.5.2. The initial length L expands slightly on both sides. For the expansion, with average temperature difference between the two sides of T,

$$L_1 - L_2 = \alpha T L$$

From the geometry of Figure 2.5.2, with the angle θ in radians,

$$L = R\theta$$

$$L_1 - L_2 = D\theta = \frac{DL}{R}$$

Considering some example numbers, for cylinder bore 50 mm and length 100 mm, with temperature difference a severe 100 °C, and thermal expansion coefficient 20 ppm/°C, the length difference is 0.20 mm. The angular bend is 0.004 radians and the radius of bend is 25 m. To obtain angular degrees from radians, multiply by 57.3, giving 0.23 degrees.

For a truly cylindrical piston to pass freely along a bent cylinder, the piston must be of reduced diameter. This diametral reduction d is given by the expression

$$d = \frac{L_P^2}{4R}$$

For the example numbers, with a piston length of 50 mm, this required diametral

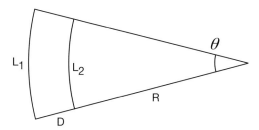

Figure 2.5.2. The cylinder, initially of length L and diameter D, subject to differential expansion, becomes longer on the exhaust side. The cylinder acquires a bending radius of curvature R and a total angular bend θ.

reduction is 0.025 mm (1.0 thou), which is certainly significant. This situation can be alleviated by deliberately shaping the piston to suit the thermally distorted cylinder.

Most engines have the exhaust port perpendicular to the axis of the crankshaft. In some cases the exhaust port has to be located over the crankshaft. To ease this problem, some manufacturers machine the cylinder axis on such engines about 0.1 degrees out of perpendicular to the shaft to partially compensate for the thermal distortion.

So far, this section has considered straightforward thermal expansion, in which the original size is recovered on cooling. However, this doesn't always happen. If metal is maintained at high temperature, as with the piston and cylinder of an engine, small, non-reversible dimensional changes occur. These are usually enlargements. To distinguish them from reversible expansion they are called 'metal growth'. This growth occurs for two reasons:

1. Thermal stress relief
2. Metallurgical changes

During manufacture, the metal acquires internal stresses that fight each other. High temperature relaxes these stresses, which sometimes results in dimensional changes. These small changes in size are called *creep*. Because the initial stresses are non-uniform, high temperature can also cause distortion.

Also, iron is sometimes quenched from high temperature to harden it. This captures the crystal metallurgical structure of the high temperature. If the metal is held at an intermediate temperature, as when an engine is operating, there is a gradual change to the low temperature equilibrium state, which will be dimensionally slightly different. This is why an iron piston or cylinder will grow, very slightly and slowly, with running time.

Another factor in piston-liner fit is worth mentioning because it is sometimes confused with thermal effects on metal and its growth. When castor oil is used as a lubricant, a thin layer of lacquer is deposited on the liner, and particularly on the piston. The rate of deposition increases rapidly above normal running temperatures. Some lacquer may be very helpful, keeping the metal parts apart and preventing metal wear. In an ideal situation, if the piston metal is not growing then the rate of lacquer deposition equals the rate at which it wears off and no piston metal is worn away at all. The higher temperatures of lean running will cause extra lacquer to be formed. This may help to protect the engine, but too much lacquer on the piston can reduce piston cooling to the liner. Lacquering does not occur with synthetic or mineral oils.

2.6 Example Engine

To give numerical values for analysis and discussion in this book, we will use an imaginary example engine – a high-performance single-cylinder with tuned exhaust. Its specification is given in Table 2.6.1. It is not really a motorcycle engine or a kart engine because the former would be 125 cm^3, and the latter, although using 100 cm^3, would have lower peak output because it needs a wider power band. A full-race motorcycle engine would use a longer exhaust timing (probably at least 194°, possibly as much as 202°) which would give a higher peak power potential but a very high peaking speed and a narrow power band. Also the inlet would probably close later, at 70° atdc or even as late as 80° atdc. The 184° exhaust timing would lose us about 20% power reduction, with a peaking speed possibly 10% lower. The 100 cm^3 swept volume will produce 16% less power than the 125 cm^3 cylinder, with a peaking speed 8% higher. The peak power is 21 kW, or 28.1 bhp.

Table 2.6.1. The example engine (100 cm³ swept volume)

Bore	B	50 mm
Stroke	S	50 mm
Bore area	A_B	19.635 cm²
Crank length (S/2)	L_C	25 mm
Swept volume	V_S	98.175 cm³
Rod length	L_R	90 mm (between centres)
Crank/rod length ratio L_C/L_R	λ	0.27778
Rod G position	L_{RL}	54 mm (from little end centre)
Shaft speed (peak power)	N_M	12,000 rev/min
Torque (at peak power)	Q	16.71 Nm
Shaft power	P_S	21.0 kW
Fuel	-	Gasoline (UK petrol)
Fuel energy of combustion	e_C	45 MJ/kg
Combustion volume	V_C	10.91 cm³
Compression ratio (geometric)	R_C	10.0
Mechanical efficiency	η_M	85%
Main shaft diameter	D_S	25 mm
Crankpin diameter	D_C	20 mm
Gudgeon pin diameter	D_G	15 mm
Inlet diameter	D_I	25 mm
Inlet length	L_I	160 mm
Transfer passage area	A_T	6 cm²
Transfer passage length	L_T	70 mm
Crankcase volume	V_{CT}	200 cm³
Timing:		
Inlet	θ_I	= 140 + 60 = 200°
Exhaust	θ_E	184°
Transfer	θ_T	130°
Blowdown	θ_B	27°
Exhaust port height abdc	H_E	22.31 mm
Transfer port height abdc	H_T	11.54 mm
Swept trapped volume	V_{ST}	54.37 cm³
Trapped comp. Ratio	R_{TC}	5.98
Piston mass	m_P	80 g
Ring mass	m_R	2.5 g each of two
Gudgeon pin mass	m_G	35 g
Conrod mass	m_C	60 g (36g + 24 g)

CHAPTER 3

Engine Geometry

3.1 Introduction

Engine geometry consists of shapes, lengths, areas, volumes and angles. Some aspects of the internal geometry are of special importance. Most obviously, cylinder size affects power output. The shapes of the ports and when they open and close (their timing) determine engine characteristics. The size and timing of the ports controls how their opened area changes with crankshaft position. This is usually studied by graphs of the port area against crank angle. Their shape, direction and cross-sectional area influence scavenging. Small areas (narrow passages) work well at low rpm but restrict top-end power. Larger areas give more power at high speed but are poor at low speed.

The crankcase volume also affects inlet and transfer behaviour. The cylinder head shape and volume influence ignition and combustion characteristics.

3.2 Scale Effects

Although the engine tuner can rarely change fundamentals such as the number of cylinders, swept volume or the bore/stroke ratio, these are vital parameters for the engine designer. They are decided early in an engine's development, and are a commitment that is difficult to change. On the other hand, the tuner can choose which engine to develop.

Compare a single-cylinder 500 cm^3 engine with a 50 cm^3 single. The 500 may have a lower peaking speed and a lower specific power, but a better specific fuel consumption. It may be tempting to assume that the larger engine is in a lower state of tune, the lower specific power and speed returning a better specific consumption. However, such a conclusion could be totally wrong. To compare engines of different sizes one must know the effect of cylinder size. We need to standardise performance parameters.

1. If the engine is uniformly scaled up to a new swept volume, how will this affect the maximum torque, power, peaking speed and fuel consumption?

2. For a given total swept volume, how does the number of cylinders affect the torque, power, peaking speed and fuel consumption?

These questions highlight the importance of scale effects.

Top racing engines are usually multi-cylinder ones, unless the rules dictate otherwise. The following is a logical basis for comparing engines of different cylinder sizes. The results of the analysis are in good agreement with the real engines of Table 1.5.1 in Chapter 1. Figure 3.2.1 shows how the power output of an engine of given total swept volume depends on the number of cylinders. The upper curve follows a simple analysis. The lower one includes the

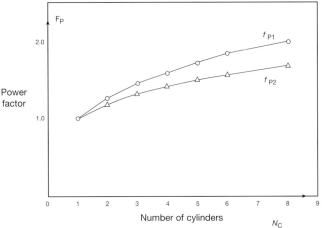

Figure 3.2.1. *The basic effect of number of cylinders (Nc) on power output for a given total swept volume.*

effect of variation of thermal efficiency with cylinder size. More cylinders give greater output.

Why is this so? What are its implications?

Start by assuming that each cylinder of a multi-cylinder engine has the performance of a single cylinder engine of the same bore and stroke. This is reasonable provided that the packaging of inlets and exhausts does not compromise the behaviour. Then multiply all linear dimensions by a scaling factor K_L on a single cylinder. Areas are therefore increased by the area scaling factor

$$K_A = K_L^2$$

Volumes, including the swept volume, increase by the volume factor

$$K_V = K_L^3$$

For example, a factor of 2.0 multiplies areas by 4.0 and volumes by 8.0. Dimensionless ratios, such as compression ratio, don't change. Component volumes, and therefore their weights, increase in proportion to K_L^3, as does the swept volume V_S. The engine mass per unit of swept volume is therefore constant.

Normalised areas (A/A_B) are non-dimensional and remain constant with scaling. Specific areas (cm²/litre) reduce with size, as $1/K_L$, because they are area per unit volume, L^2/L^3.

There is some scale effect due to air viscosity, though, as the gas flow in almost any engine will be turbulent, the effect of scale on the air flow is small enough to be ignored.

Also the primary (crankcase) compression ratio is independent of scale. This means that the pressure variations in the crankcase that drive the inlet and transfer flows, are independent of engine size. The pressure scaling factor is simply

$$K_P = 1.0$$

Therefore the air velocities in the engine inlet and transfer passages are independent of size too, so the gas-velocity scaling factor is also

$$K_{GV} = 1.0$$

The distance that air has to travel to scavenge the cylinder is directly proportional to K_L. But in a larger engine the gas must travel further. As the gas velocity is unchanged, the time taken for complete scavenging is therefore proportional to $1/K_L$. So a larger engine takes longer to scavenge, and the peaking speed (the engine speed for peak power) is lower. The crankshaft angular velocity scaling factor is

$$K_{AV} = \frac{K_{GV}}{K_L} = \frac{1}{K_L}$$

Slower scavenging means that peak power occurs at a shaft speed that decreases with the scale ratio, as $1/K_L$. For example, twice the linear scale will give eight times the swept volume, and half the engine speed for peak power.

The shaft speed (rev/min) scaling factor is the same as the angular velocity scaling factor:

$$K_{RPM} \equiv K_{AV} = \frac{1}{K_L}$$

This means that the peaking speed is inversely proportional to the cube root of the swept volume:

$$N_{M,P} \propto V_S^{-1/3}$$

This effect is seen in Table 3.2.2 by comparing engines of different cylinder sizes in the same state of development. The mean piston speed is proportional to the stroke times the shaft speed, and is therefore independent of scale, likewise the gas velocity.

The brake mean effective pressure is the energy yield in one revolution divided by the swept volume. Since scale has little effect on the gas pressures, the scaled engine will deliver an unchanged brake mean engine pressure, so

$$K_{BMEP} = 1$$

The torque of one cylinder will be directly proportional to the cylinder swept volume, being proportional to V_S or to K_L^3, so the torque scaling factor is

$$K_Q = K_L^3$$

However, the larger engine cylinder must operate at only $1/K_L$ of the speed of a smaller one, so delivering a power proportional to $K_L^3 \times 1/K_L$, i.e. the peak power output grows only with K_L^2. Therefore the power scaling factor is

$$K_{power} = K_Q K_{RPM}$$

$$= K_L^2$$

This result has major consequences for racing engine design. The power is proportional to K_L^2 and so to $V_S^{2/3}$ and so the specific power (bhp/litre) falls as size increases, in fact as $1/K_L$. Therefore, unlike the torque, the power is less than proportional to the swept volume. In fact with $P \propto V_S^{2/3}$ doubling the cylinder volume only increases the cylinder power by 59%.

For competition regulations specifying maximum total swept volume V_{SE}, increasing the number of cylinders N_C reduces the scale of individual cylinders. The individual cylinder swept volume is

$$V_S = \frac{V_{SE}}{N_C}$$

The result is a power output proportional to the cube root of the number of cylinders

$$P \propto N_C^{1/3}$$

Table 3.2.1   Effect of number of cylinders for a given total swept volume

Number of cylinders N_C	Cylinder swept volume V_S	Linear scale factor K_L	Relative power f_{P1}	f_{P2}
1	1.000	1.000	1.000	1.000
2	0.500	0.794	1.260	1.189
3	0.333	0.693	1.442	1.316
4	0.250	0.630	1.587	1.414
5	0.200	0.585	1.710	1.495
6	0.167	0.550	1.817	1.565
8	0.125	0.500	2.000	1.682

At constant engine total swept volume V_{SE}, increasing the number of cylinders N_C therefore improves the specific and actual engine power outputs, as in the power factor f_{P1} of Table 3.2.1 and Figure 3.2.1.

Thus going from 1 to 2 cylinders gives a 26% power increase. Going from 2 to 3 gives a further 14%, from 3 to 4 gives 10%, and so on. These increases can be decisive in power-based competitions.

The above scaling argument applies equally to two-stroke and four-stroke engines. It explains why large numbers of cylinders are used when permitted, for example V-8, V-10 and V-12 four-strokes in Indy and Formula 1 racing cars.

Why then have even more cylinders not been used when allowed, especially for two-stroke Grand Prix motorcycle and other sophisticated racing classes? For one thing, engines with a large number of cylinders are much more expensive to manufacture. However, there are also technical reasons. First, the packaging will be a problem for two-strokes beyond a modest number of cylinders. It is difficult to arrange the inlet and exhaust systems without the power output falling short of expectations. Also, good air-cooling is difficult to achieve so that water-cooling may be the only answer. Also, for a smaller number of cylinders the engine will tend to be lighter.

However, there is another scaling factor that applies even to an isolated single cylinder. As we have seen, when a single cylinder is scaled in the ratio K_L, the volume goes with K_L^3 but the area with K_L^2, so the specific area within the combustion chamber reduces, as $1/K_L$. The larger cylinder therefore provides proportionally less cooling of the combusted gases. Also, as heat conduction distances are longer, being proportional to K_L, the internal surface temperatures, as of the piston crown, tend to be higher for larger engines, whereas small cylinders give better cooling of the combusted gas. Therefore smaller cylinders fall short of the simply-scaled performance prediction, with a lower thermal efficiency and worse specific fuel consumption. An engine with many cylinders for a given total swept volume therefore has a markedly higher fuel consumption. Part of this goes in improving the output, but part is wasted in thermal inefficiency. The latter effect increases the cooling requirements, which may add weight and drag. Similarly, the increased specific area of a smaller cylinder means that the exhaust port and passage extract proportionally more heat from the exhaust, reducing the effectiveness of the resonant exhaust.

The influence of scale on thermal efficiency is difficult to calculate from first principles but is indicated by the known thermal efficiency of various sizes of engines. Very large two strokes, such as those used for marine propulsion, with a swept volume of 2 m^3 per cylinder, have a thermal efficiency of around 50%. At the other extreme, small 2.5 cm^3 model engines have a thermal efficiency of only around 12%. In between, racing two-stroke motorcycle engines have thermal efficiencies of around 20%. These figures suggest thermal efficiencies proportional to the swept volume to the power of 0.10. Hence the thermal efficiency η_T varies as

$$\eta_T \propto V_S^a$$

with the thermal efficiency scaling index $a = 0.10$.

The single-cylinder engine torque Q is then proportional to swept volume times this efficiency variation, giving

$$Q \propto V_S^{1.1}$$

Therefore, including allowance for the efficiency factor, torque increases faster than the swept volume, and specific torque (Nm/litre) and brake mean effective pressure improve with cylinder size.

Previously the power was proportional to the 2/3 (= 0.667) power of the cylinder size, but including the efficiency variation

$$P \propto V_S^{0.767}$$

Note, $0.767 = 0.667 + 0.1$, the latter figure being the effect of efficiency.
The specific power output is

$$\frac{P}{V_S} \propto V_S^{-0.233}$$

On this basis, the sensitivity of engine power to the number of cylinders N_C, like the specific power, reduces from the exponent 1/3 to 0.233, or approximately $\frac{1}{4}$, because the small cylinders have a lower thermal efficiency.

The predicted effect of number of cylinders on power output, including the effect of thermal efficiency, is shown in Table 3.2.1 and Figure 3.2.1 as curve f_{P2}, where the substantial loss of efficiency for a large number of cylinders is seen.

Actual racing engines show that such scaling effect analysis is realistic. V-12 racing four-strokes have more power than V-8 engines of the same swept volume and bore/stroke ratio but worse fuel consumption and greater cooling requirements, both of which add significantly to the weight of the vehicle. Figure 3.2.2 shows the predicted trend of thermal efficiency against cylinder size.

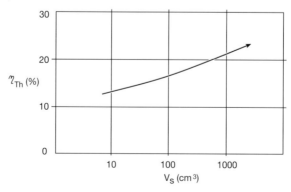

Figure 3.2.2. Variation of thermal efficiency with cylinder size (theoretical).

A few manufacturers have produced ranges of scaled sizes of different swept volume. Their comparative performance confirms the trends predicted. It also confirms the variation of peak-power speed with size, predicted to be inversely proportional to linear scale, or to the inverse cube root of cylinder swept volume.

Table 3.2.2   Predicted scale effect on the characteristics of a single cylinder two-stroke engine (efficiency scaling index a = 0.1)

Swept Vol (cm^3)	Power max (bhp)	Peaking speed (rev/min)	Torque (at Pmax) (Nm)	Thermal efficiency (%)	Brake MEP (MPa)	Specific power (bhp/litre)
25.0	6.22	17,461	2.54	17.4	0.64	248.6
50.0	10.58	13,859	5.44	18.7	0.68	211.5
100.0	18.00	11,000	11.67	20.0	0.73	180.0
125.0	21.36	10,211	14.92	20.5	0.75	170.9
250.0	36.35	8,105	31.99	21.9	0.80	145.4
500.0	61.86	6,433	68.59	23.5	0.86	123.7
1000.0	105.26	5,106	147.06	25.2	0.92	105.3

Figure 3.2.3 and Table 3.2.2 show the predicted peak-power rpm for a wide range of sizes. This table is based on the predicted scaling rule, assuming a peaking speed of 11,000 rev/min and power of 18 bhp for a 100 cm^3 cylinder, with 20% thermal efficiency. Obviously the peaking speed and power for a given size depend very much upon the state of tune, which in turn depends upon how narrow a power band is acceptable. For 100 cm^3, an 11,000 rev/min peak corresponds to a fairly high output engine with a resonant exhaust, though the peak could reach about 13,500, depending on the exhaust timing. Without a full resonant exhaust, but using a simple expansion box silencer, the peaking speed would be about 20% lower. This still assumes a well-ported engine designed for power. Restrictive porting, chosen for good low-speed behaviour, can easily halve the peaking speed. The thermal efficiency values may seem pessimistic, but the trend is apparent.

Fuel consumption figures at peak power are rarely published, but some data are available for the QUB500 (Blair, SAE 780745) as follows: 500 cm^3, peak power 64.5 bhp at 7,600 rev/min, specific fuel consumption 0.589 lb/bhp.hr, air/fuel ratio 12.63, delivery ratio 0.788. The following figures are for a gasoline of density 0.73 g/cm^3 and combustion energy 45 MJ/kg:

1. Volume of air per rev 394 cm^3
2. Mass of air per rev 0.473 g
3. Mass of fuel per rev 0.03743 g
4. Fuel energy of combustion per rev 1685 J
5. Power output 48.2 kW
6. Speed 126.7 rev/s (= 7,600 rev/min)
7. Energy output per rev 380.4 J
8. Thermal efficiency = 380.4/1685 = 0.226 = 22.6%
9. Fuel consumption 4.742 g/s, 6.5 cm^3/s

The thermal efficiency of this engine is therefore in fair agreement with the values above.

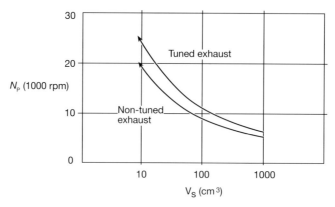

Figure 3.2.3. Variation of peaking speed with cylinder swept volume (with constant state of tune).

The downward peaking speed trend seen in Table 3.2.3 as cylinders increase from 50 cm³ to 500 cm³ is certainly observed on motorcycle engines. This doesn't imply that any engine will conform accurately to these tables and graphs. They merely indicate the trends and allow comparisons of different cylinder sizes.

The foregoing analysis shows that direct comparison of parameters like specific power, specific torque, thermal efficiency and so on, is not a good way of comparing the merits of different sizes of engine. Even a volume factor of one half (changing a single cylinder to a twin) gives a factor of 0.93 on thermal efficiency, 1.26 on peaking speed and 1.17 on specific power output. However, relating engine characteristics to a particular swept volume, say 125 cm³, according to the scaling rules offered, the design and performance may be fairly compared with other engines.

To compare different cylinder sizes, calculate the quality of their performance as follows. Choose a standard cylinder reference swept volume, e.g.

$$V_{St} = 125 \text{ cm}^3$$

The standardised peaking speed N_{PSt} is found for the measured peaking speed N_P by

$$N_{PSt} = N_P \left(\frac{V_S}{V_{St}} \right)^{1/3}$$

The standardised thermal efficiency, where the efficiency index a is 0.100, is

$$\eta_{TSt} = \eta_T \left(\frac{V_S}{V_{St}} \right)^{-a}$$

The standardised torque value is

$$Q_{St} = Q \left(\frac{V_S}{V_{St}} \right)^{-1-a}$$

This adjustment also applies to bmep (brake mean effective pressure). The standardised power is

$$P_{St} = P \left(\frac{V_S}{V_{St}} \right)^{-2/3-a}$$

The standardised specific power (bhp/litre) is

$$P_{S,St} = P_S \left(\frac{V_S}{V_{St}} \right)^{1/3-a}$$

Take the 1985 Kreidler 50 (single cylinder) as an example. From Table 1.5.1 this produces 21 bhp (15.69 kW) at 16,200 rev/min. Assume a thermal efficiency of 18%. The specific power output is 420 bhp/litre. At peak power the speed is 270 rev/s, the energy output is 58.11 J, and the torque is 9.25 Nm (see Chapter 12 for performance analysis calculations). Using the above equations to standardise to 125 cm^3 gives 42.4 bhp (31.68 kW) at 11,900 rev/min, 339.3 bhp/litre and 19.73% thermal efficiency. The exceptional speed (16,200 rev/min) and specific output (420 bhp/litre) are therefore seen to result mainly from the small cylinder size. These figures are reduced when standardised, but are still very good, though the designers would not be to blame for a low thermal efficiency.

Thus, in a racing event where multi-cylinder engines dominate, one is unlikely to be seriously competitive with a single cylinder, or with a twin against four cylinders, unless rules favour fuel efficiency or light weight rather than outright power. They might, for example, explicitly limit the amount of fuel consumed or carried.

3.3 Bore/Stroke Ratio

The other basic geometry problem is of proportion rather than size. In other words, the effect of the bore/stroke ratio with the cylinder swept volume kept constant. Four-stroke racing engines of limited swept volume are best when considerably over-square, i.e. having a high bore/stroke ratio. Should two-stroke engines be like this? If not, why not?

For a given cylinder swept volume, the ratio of bore to stroke is

$$r_{BS} = \frac{B}{S}$$

The bore area is

$$A_B = \frac{\pi}{4} B^2$$

Figure 3.3.1 illustrates the swept volume for a flat-topped piston for bore/stroke ratios of 2.0, 1.0 and 0.5 respectively. These may seem extreme values, but they are actually found in practice. Racing four-stroke engines may have a ratio of 2.0, and opposed-piston engines may have a ratio of 0.5. Table 3.3.1 gives area values. It is not surprising from this figure and table that a higher bore/stroke ratio gives a much larger bore area, with a larger head area at the top of the bore, of benefit to four-stroke engines with valves in the cylinder head. The performance of racing four-strokes depends on the breathing provided by such valves, so the extra bore is an advantage, even as high as 2.0:1.

Table 3.3.1 Effect of bore/stroke ratio on areas, for a 100 cm³ cylinder

B/S	2.0	1.0	0.5
B (mm)	63.4	50.3	39.9
S (mm)	31.7	50.3	79.9
B/B_1	1.260	1.00	0.794
S/S_1	0.630	1.00	1.587
A_B (cm^2)	31.57	19.87	12.50
A_W (cm^2)	63.14	79.49	100.15

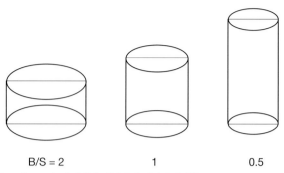

B/S = 2   1   0.5

Figure 3.3.1. Bore/stroke ratio (a) 2.0, (b) 1.0, (c) 0.5. These are extreme values.

If the bore diameter and bore area of a four-stroke engine is limited by its valves, doubling the stroke will not improve the rate of air flow through the valves, so it will take much longer to fill the cylinder. Theoretically, the long-stroke engine will deliver peak power at half the previous speed, giving twice the torque but only the same power. The power of a four-stroke depends on the bore area rather than on the swept volume. Actually, the longer stroke engine will have a larger combustion volume for a given compression ratio, with lower thermal losses, and perhaps slightly better breathing. Also, the lower speed of operation will require a different length exhaust system. The result is that the stroke increase actually gives only a small power increase.

The foregoing applies to four-stroke engines limited by the breathing of valves in the head. However, the racing two-stroke has its ports in the cylinder walls, not in the head, with the timing determined by the fraction of the wall area the ports occupy. Therefore the size of the ports of the two-stroke depends on the cylinder wall area, not on the bore area. Table 3.3.1 includes comparative wall area values for a 100 cm³ cylinder. The bore area is proportional to the bore/stroke ratio to the exponent 2/3, whereas the wall area changes with the exponent –1/3, and is larger for a smaller bore/stroke ratio.

Therefore, the very high bore/stroke ratios favoured for racing four-strokes limited by swept volume regulations are not appropriate for two-stroke engines. Also, the expression of power/bore area used for four-strokes is irrelevant.

Figure 3.3.2 shows the variation of the bore area and cylinder wall area as the bore/stroke ratio varies between the extreme values. The bore area increases, as $r_{BS}^{2/3}$,

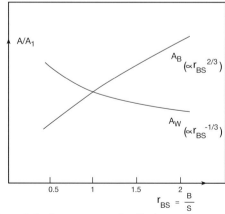

Figure 3.3.2. Variation of the bore area and cylinder wall area with bore/stroke ratio.

whereas the wall area reduces, as $r_{BS}^{-1/3}$. However, the greater wall area does not lead to very long stroke racing two-stroke engines. There are possibly two main reasons for this. For a long-stroke engine the scavenging gas has further to travel, up the cylinder and back down again, so scavenging will be slow and peaking speed slow, giving less power. Perhaps even more important, efficient scavenging of the cylinder is difficult to achieve with an extreme shape. Experience indicates that a bore/stroke ratio around 1.0 is best for crankcase-scavenged engines.

3.4 Cylinder Geometry

The main measurements of engine geometry include:

1. The bore, measured by vernier calipers in the cylinder.

2. The tdc and bdc piston depths in the cylinder, measured by depth gauge or caliper end.

3. The stroke, which can be measured on the shaft, or better by the difference of the above two measurements.

4. The port timing may be measured using a degree wheel fixed on the shaft, with a wire pointer fixed to the top of the case. Alternatively, the position of the top of the ports can be measured using a depth gauge or vernier calipers. When related to the bdc position of the piston, this gives the port height abdc.

5. The port shapes, i.e. widths, and bottom edge positions.

6. Corresponding measurements for the intake, possibly by piston control or as appropriate for rotary valves.

The cylinder measurements are represented on a diagram showing an internal development of the cylinder, as in Figure 3.4.1. Typically this will contain a bridged exhaust port, a pair of bridged transfers, and a single or bridged boost port. There may also be a piston-controlled inlet port lower in the liner, and feed holes to give extra flow into the transfer passages.

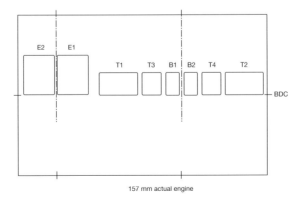

157 mm actual engine

Figure 3.4.1. Development of cylinder wall showing porting. Exhaust port E1+E2 is bridged. Main transfers are T1 & T2. Supplementary transfers are T3 & T4. The boost ports are B1 & B2. Port widths are circumferential values, not the straight line from one side of the port to the other. There is no piston-controlled inlet.

The gas flow capability of a port can be assessed in various ways:

1. Port maximum area
2. Port angular duration
3. Port time duration
4. Product of maximum area and angular duration
5. Product of maximum area and time duration
6. Integrated angle-area
7. Integrated time-area

Note that (6) and (7) are different from (4) and (5). The latter two are the integrated values. These are more difficult to evaluate but are the correct ones to use (see Section 3.7).

The transfer or exhaust port maximum area occurs with the piston in its extreme bottom position. The actual area may be defined as that on the developed inner surface of the cylinder, as was shown in Figure 3.4.1.

Since the flow of gas is not perpendicular to the wall, the port has a smaller effective area of discharge than the area on the developed cylinder. An alternative is to measure the port width as a linear direct measure from one side of the port to its other side, instead of around the circular bore. A discrepancy in effective flow area also arises from the actual direction at which the gas leaves the port.

Another option is to measure the effective port area transverse to the expected flow direction (Figure 3.4.2). However, the actual direction of gas flow is difficult to ascertain, and may require careful experiments. This is why a discharge coefficient is often used in computer engine simulations (Chapter 6). However, for similar types of engines the port areas make a useful comparison.

When quoting or using a port area or an effective port area, one must know how the area is defined. An advantage of the simpler methods is that they are true geometric properties of the engine. Estimates of flow direction are not always reliable, and are only attempts to represent what is happening in the engine.

Port areas are measured notionally in m^2, or practically as cm^2, or of course in square inches. For comparison of engines of different sizes, direct comparison of the port areas is meaningless. Therefore the port areas are adjusted to specific area or normalised area as described earlier.

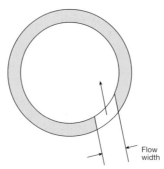

Figure 3.4.2. Effective flow width of a port, distinct from the edge-to-edge width and the circumferential width.

3.5 Port Timing

The complete port timing or angular duration, i.e. the port angular open period in crankshaft degrees, may be represented graphically by a timing diagram, as shown in Chapter 2, Figure 2.4.1. These diagrams are little more than a basic statement of the timing figures in degrees. They just illustrate the timing.

The effect of the ports depends on more than their timing. Obviously the port widths are also significant. Nevertheless, modern Schnürle porting is fairly uniform in its layout, so there are well-established ranges of values for port timing. In conventional engines, the transfer and exhaust are symmetrical about bottom dead centre. Piston inlet is symmetrical about top dead centre. Rotary valves have asymmetrical timing.

1. Exhaust

For a simple expansion chamber exhaust, and definitely not a tuned pipe of any kind, the exhaust port angular duration θ_E may be classified:

Exhaust Timing (Plain exhaust):	
125°	Very short
135°	Short
145°	Medium
155°	Long
165°	Very long

Values of below 130° would be used only for low revving engines (in relation to the swept volume, i.e. low normalised speed). Above 160° is definitely 'wild timing', likely to give little additional power. Peaking speed will be higher and the exhaust harder to silence. A short-timed engine has a longer expansion stroke. This tends to be more fuel efficient because of the larger trapped expansion ratio, and has less danger of wasting fresh mixture directly out of the exhaust port. Short exhaust timing also has the advantage of being quieter because the pressure is lower when the port opens.

For an engine with a tuned exhaust system, the exhaust port timing will normally be longer. This is because an early exhaust opening gives a strong exhaust pulse that makes a lot of noise, but is actually useful. The exhaust duration in this case could be classified as:

Exhaust Timing (Tuned Exhaust):	
125°	Very short
145°	Short
165°	Medium
185°	Long
205°	Very long

The highest timings are used for maximum power where a narrow power band is tolerable, whereas low timings are used where fuel efficiency or wide power band are of more interest than maximum power. Short timing allows a shorter tuned exhaust length, with help to boost the torque at a low rev/min and to give a wide power band with a weaker exhaust influence. The peak power for short-timed engines is much less than with long-timed exhausts.

2. *Transfer timing*

Transfer angular duration θ_T cannot be considered in isolation from the exhaust timing. However, the following classification might be applied:

Transfer Timing
100°	Very short
110°	Short
120°	Medium
130°	Long
140°	Very long

The longer timings generally apply to higher rev/min operation, i.e. high normalised speed.

There is no need for the transfer and boost ports to open simultaneously, or even to have level upper edges. There have been various fashions for unequal timing. The ports further from the exhaust may have a slightly longer duration or a slightly shorter duration. The transfer duration spread θ_{TS} is defined here as positive for a longer main transfer timing than boost timing. It could be classified as:

Transfer Spread:
± 2°	Very small
± 4°	Small
± 6°	Medium
± 8°	High
± 10°	Very high

This does not imply that any transfer duration spread is necessary or even desirable. Whether positive or negative spread is helpful depends upon the porting configuration, with positive spread perhaps working well with a level transfer stream, and a negative spread for streams inclined significantly upwards. Scavenging is inevitably influenced, with some effect on the peak power and power band.

3. *Exhaust lead (blowdown)*

The angle through which the crankshaft turns from the opening of the exhaust port to the opening of the transfer port is called the *exhaust lead angle* or *blowdown angle*, θ_B. During this period the high-pressure exhaust gases blow down from the cylinder. After the blowdown period, the transfer ports open and the rest of the exhaust is driven out by the scavenging process. After the transfer closes, the exhaust remains open for the blow-up period, equal to the blowdown, so the exhaust angular duration is the transfer plus twice the blowdown. With a tuned exhaust, the exhaust duration is chosen to produce the desired exhaust pulse strength, because long duration means early opening when the cylinder pressure is higher. The transfer period is chosen independently, early opening being the criterion of choice, hence long duration. Typical timing would be 195° exhaust, 135° transfer for 30° of blowdown. However, for a simple expansion box silencer, or an unsilenced engine, the exhaust lead is shorter, and important in its own right, and the exhaust period is selected as the necessary transfer plus (twice) the necessary blowdown.

The blowdown angle may be rated as follows:

Blowdown Angle (Plain Silencer):

3°	Very small
6°	Small
9°	Medium
12°	High
15°	Very high

As exhaust lead (blowdown angle) is provided specifically to facilitate blowdown, a larger value is needed for best high-speed operation. The above table covers low-speed to very high-speeds. Therefore a low-speed engine could have a timing of 110°/122°, that is transfer timing 110°, blowdown 6°, exhaust 122°. A medium speed engine could be: transfer 120°, blowdown 9°, exhaust 138°. A high-speed engine could be transfer 130°, blowdown 12°, exhaust 154°.

4. Piston-controlled inlet

For classical piston skirt controlled inlet, the correct duration is not as clear cut as for the other ports, because the inlet tract length can be altered to compensate, altering the gas inertia. However, the inlet angular duration θ_1 can be classified as follows:

Piston Inlet Timing:

100°	Very short
120°	Short
140°	Medium
160°	Long
180°	Very long
200°	Extremely long

As usual, the longer values are associated with higher engine speeds. The extremely long value would apply only to a full-race engine.

5. Rotary inlets

Rotary disc and other rotary inlets are always asymmetrical about top dead centre, with much more period before tdc than after. Symmetrical timing about tdc would be equivalent to piston-controlled inlet. An inlet opening roughly at bdc and closing at tdc would be similar to a four-stroke type inlet.

The opening point may be specified as after bdc or before tdc. The closing point is always specified as after tdc. In practice it is expressed as btdc + atdc = duration, e.g. as 140° + 60° = 200°, or, in general,

$$\theta_{IO} + \theta_{IC} = \theta_I$$

The opening point of a rotary inlet is not usually critical, and is generally less important than the closing angle. A reasonable classification of the opening is:

Rotary Inlet Opening (Plain Silencer):

abdc	btdc	
35°	155°	Very early
40°	150°	Early
45°	145°	Medium
50°	140°	Late
55°	135°	Very late

The above figures apply only to non-resonant exhausts. Some tuned exhaust engines like very early inlet opening because the early and strong reflected suction wave pulls the crankcase pressure down much sooner than for a simple expansion silencer. Hence for tuned exhausts the inlet openings are as follows:

Rotary Inlet Opening (Tuned Exhaust):

abdc	btdc	
10°	170°	Very early
15°	165°	Early
20°	160°	Medium
25°	155°	Late
30°	150°	Very late

These timings apply to engines targeted at very high speeds. Where low exhaust timings are used for special purposes with tuned pipes, more normal opening angles around 45° abdc (135° btdc) may be appropriate

The closing angle for a rotary inlet is directly related to the engine speed and inlet dynamics. Keeping the inlet open beyond top dead centre is justified by two factors:

(i) as a side effect of minimising valve resistance earlier on,

(ii) deferred flow reversal, because of inlet gas inertia.

The first of these is sufficient to allow closing at 30° atdc even at low normalised rev/min, understandable in view of the fact that the piston fall is essentially related only to the cosine of the crank angle. For ultra high-speed engines, inlet gas inertia may allow beneficial closure as late as 70°, or even 80° in extreme cases. These figures are not directly dependent upon the type of exhaust system, but are indirectly so because only tuned exhausts will be run at the very highest normalised rev/min. Hence the closure classification, in degrees atdc, is:

Rotary Inlet Closure:

30°	Very early
40°	Early
50°	Medium
60°	Late
70°	Very late
80°	Extremely late

Considering the previous figures for opening and closing, the inlet total duration may be classified as:

Rotary Inlet Duration:

btdc	+	atdc	=	Duration	
130°	+	30°	=	160°	Very short
140°	+	40°	=	180°	Short
150°	+	50°	=	200°	Medium
160°	+	60°	=	220°	Long
170°	+	70°	=	240°	Very long

The very long value of 240° is remarkable in being some 2/3 of the whole revolution; this is only possible because the gas flow is being controlled to a large extent by the exhaust dynamics.

Schnürle-ported engines usually conform quite well to the guidelines given above. However, engines without Schnürle-ports often deviate considerably from them, sometimes because the form of porting simply cannot be made to conform. However, there is little advantage in deviating from the figures quoted, for the speeds intended. The right timing for a given job falls within quite narrow bands established by engine operators world-wide. In other words, exceptions to the above guidelines tend to be poor engines.

3.6 Timing Geometry

Figure 3.6.1 shows an end view of the engine, with the crank rotating clockwise. There is lateral symmetry. Coordinates are measured from the shaft axis, with X to the right and Y towards the cylinder head. The cylinder axis is considered to intersect the shaft axis. When it does not do so it is known as Desaxé. This is considered later. The crank throw is L_C, where the stroke is therefore

$$S = 2L_C$$

The length of the connecting-rod is L_R between the bearing centres. The relationship between the piston position, above bottom dead centre, as a fraction of the stroke, and the crank position, depends upon the ratio of rod length to crank throw:

$$f_R = \frac{L_R}{L_C}$$

with a value of around 3.6. The geometry is shown in Figure 3.6.2.

The crank position is θ_C, measured clockwise after bottom dead centre. The connecting rod angular position is θ_R measured clockwise from vertical. The defining line of the conrod is the line directly between centres.

The rod angular position θ_R is

$$\theta_R = \arcsin\left(\frac{L_C \sin \theta_C}{L_R}\right)$$

(The function arc sin x is also known mathematically as $\sin^{-1} x$. This is the angle with sin equal to x, accessed on some hand calculators as 2 keys INV SIN. In most computer languages it is called ASN or ASIN.)

The piston lift (piston position above bdc) is

$$H_P = L_C \left(1 - \cos \theta_C\right) - L_R \left(1 - \cos \theta_R\right)$$

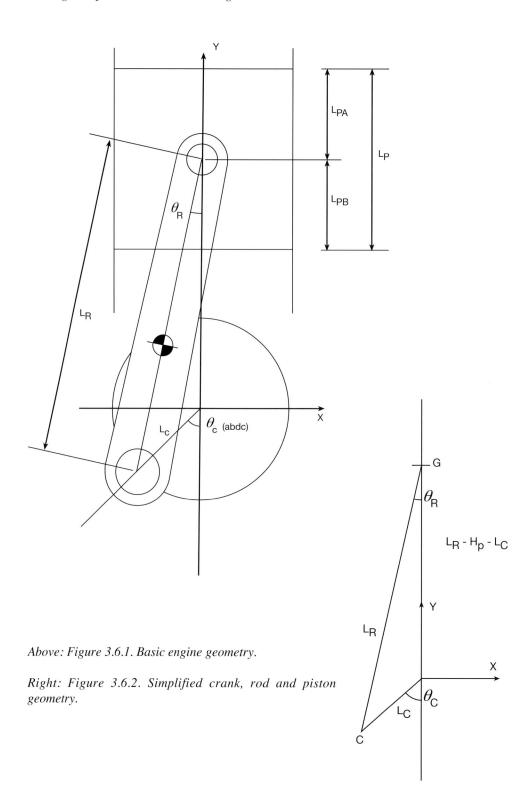

Above: Figure 3.6.1. Basic engine geometry.

Right: Figure 3.6.2. Simplified crank, rod and piston geometry.

The transfer and exhausts ports are open at bottom dead centre, of course, and each port closes at some particular position of the crankshaft. For an exhaust port angular duration θ_E, the port closes at a crank angle

$$\theta_{CE} = \tfrac{1}{2}\theta_E$$

from which the piston lift from bdc, and the position of the port top edge, can be calculated. The necessary port heights for a given timing are found from

$$\theta_R = \text{arc} \sin\left(\frac{L_C}{L_R}\sin\theta_C\right)$$

$$H_P = L_C(1-\cos\theta_C) - L_R(1-\cos\theta_R) \tag{3.6.1}$$

In analysing an existing engine, one must calculate the timing from depth gauge measurements of the piston lift at which the port closes. In that case, use

$$L = L_R - L_C + H_P$$

$$\theta_C = 180° - \text{arc}\cos\left\{\frac{L_C^2 + L^2 - L_R^2}{2L_C^2 L}\right\} \tag{3.6.2}$$

$$\theta_{portduration} = 2\theta_C$$

where the term in { } braces has a value about -0.2 to -0.3, i.e. is negative, usually giving a positive arccos angle of around 130° down to 120° for transfer ports and 120° down to 80° for exhaust ports. The port angular timing is, of course, $2\theta_C$, being θ_C on each side of bottom dead centre.

The example relates to the engine with stroke 50mm, connecting rod length 90mm and transfer timing 130°. To derive the necessary port height above bdc, using Equations 3.6.1:

$$\theta_T = 130°$$
$$\theta_{CT} = 65°$$
$$\theta_R = 14.581°$$
$$H_P = 11.536 \text{ mm}$$

To check, use Equations 3.6.2 to obtain the timing:

$$H_P = 11.536 \text{ mm}$$
$$L = 76.536 \text{ mm}$$
$$\theta_C = 180° - 115° = 65°$$
$$\theta_T = 130°$$

Inaccuracies are possible in the port height measurements. As a check, it may be useful to measure the port angular duration directly with a degree wheel, and to compare this with the calculated duration from the port top edge positions.

Although the bottom edge of a port is usually positioned at the piston edge at bdc, this is not universal, so the total port depth in the cylinder does not itself necessarily indicate the timing.

When working on an engine, it is useful to have a tabulation of timing against port edge position. With the foregoing equations this is easily computed and printed out. Tables 3.6.1 and 3.6.2 give results for the example engine.

Table 3.6.1. Port timing, $L_C = 25$ mm, $L_R = 90$ mm, $L_R / L_C = 3.60$

Port duration (deg)	Crank angle (deg)	Piston lift (mm)	Lift/stroke (–)
80.0	40.0	4.40	0.088
85.0	42.5	4.97	0.099
90.0	45.0	5.57	0.111
95.0	47.5	6.20	0.124
100.0	50.0	6.87	0.137
105.0	52.5	7.57	0.151
110.0	55.0	8.30	0.166
115.0	57.5	9.06	0.181
120.0	60.0	9.86	0.197
125.0	62.5	10.68	0.214
130.0	65.0	11.54	0.231
135.0	67.5	12.42	0.248
140.0	70.0	13.33	0.267
145.0	72.5	14.27	0.285
150.0	75.0	15.23	0.305
155.0	77.5	16.22	0.324
160.0	80.0	17.23	0.345
165.0	82.5	18.26	0.365
170.0	85.0	19.31	0.386
175.0	87.5	20.37	0.407
180.0	90.0	21.46	0.429
185.0	92.5	22.56	0.451
190.0	95.0	23.66	0.473
195.0	97.5	24.78	0.496
200.0	100.0	25.91	0.518
205.0	102.5	27.04	0.541
210.0	105.0	28.17	0.563

Table 3.6.2.   Port timing, $L_C = 25$ mm, $L_R = 90$ mm, $L_R / L_C = 3.60$

Port duration (deg)	Crank angle (deg)	Piston lift (mm)	Lift/stroke (−)
76.25	38.12	4.00	0.080
85.26	42.63	5.00	0.100
93.43	46.71	6.00	0.120
100.95	50.48	7.00	0.140
107.98	53.99	8.00	0.160
114.60	57.30	9.00	0.180
120.88	60.44	10.00	0.200
126.88	63.44	11.00	0.220
132.65	66.32	12.00	0.240
138.21	69.10	13.00	0.260
143.59	71.80	14.00	0.280
148.82	74.41	15.00	0.300
153.91	76.96	16.00	0.320
158.89	79.45	17.00	0.340
163.76	81.88	18.00	0.360
168.55	84.27	19.00	0.380
173.26	86.63	20.00	0.400
177.89	88.95	21.00	0.420
182.48	91.24	22.00	0.440
187.01	93.51	23.00	0.460
191.50	95.75	24.00	0.480
195.97	97.98	25.00	0.500
200.41	100.20	26.00	0.520
204.83	102.42	27.00	0.540
209.25	104.62	28.00	0.560
213.66	106.83	29.00	0.580
218.09	109.05	30.00	0.600

The normalised piston rise against crank angle is a function only of the ratio of conrod length to crank throw. Actual rise values are more useful. The tables show that the piston is below the mid-stroke point at 90° crank position, because of the connecting rod inclination. The very long rated exhaust timing of 196° occurs for a piston lift of 50% of the stroke, although there is nothing magical about this.

The inclination angle of the conrod has a maximum value of 15.5° at a crank angle of 105.5° abdc in this case. This occurs when the crank is perpendicular to the rod.

3.7 Angle Area
Actual computations of angle-area are not essential for tuning purposes. However an understanding of the effect of port width and angular duration on the angle-area

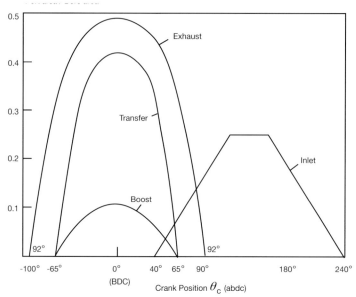

Figure 3.7.1. Port area variation with crank angle, showing flow capability of the port, which depends on the area under the curve for the particular port. Shorter transfer timing compared with exhaust means that the transfer angle-area is less than that of the exhaust, particularly for the long exhaust timing with a tuned exhaust. Hence a boost port helps the main transfer. The inlet shown will be restrictive, with poorer angle-area than the cylinder ports. Its duration is quite long (200°) but the maximum area is only 0.25 of the bore area. Opening and closing are rather slow (each covering 80°). Attention to the inlet would improve maximum power.

is helpful. It is illuminating to graph the dependence of port areas on crankshaft position.

From the widths of the ports (e.g. as in Figure 3.4.1) and the relationship between piston lift and crank angle, for any given crank angle there is a corresponding port area. Figure 3.7.1 shows an example graph of the effective port areas against crank angular position.

There are three curves symmetrical about bottom dead centre. The individual curves can be identified by the total open period. They are the exhaust, transfer and boost ports. Normally a pair of transfers would be taken as a pair with a total area, as here. Often the boost ports are included in a total effective transfer area.

A piston-controlled intake would appear as a curve symmetrical about top dead centre. A rotary intake is recognised by asymmetrical timing about tdc. In Figure 3.7.1, for any particular port, the angle-area is the area under the curve for that port. Mathematically this is the integral of the port area against crank angle. This can be evaluated by computer, or simply, and possibly more quickly, by drawing the graph and simply counting squares, unless one has a planimeter.

The ability of a port to admit air depends not just on the port area but also on the time for which it is open. For a given flow velocity, the quantity of gas flowed is proportional to the product of the area and time. With an area that varies with time, it depends on the integral of the port flow area with respect to time. For a given crankshaft speed, the curves of port area against time are the same as those against angle, as in Figure 3.7.1, but with a new time scale replacing the angle scale. The practical units of time-area are ms.cm^2 (millisecond cm^2) or µs.inch^2 (microsecond inches^2). The open time depends upon the angular duration and the crankshaft speed.

The angular speed of the crank is N_M rev/min, or N_S rev/s. This can be expressed in degrees per second as

$$N_{DS} = 360 \, N_S = 6 \, N_M$$

so the time-area and the angle-area are simply related by the shaft speed (in degrees/s) N_{DS}:

$$T_{AP} = \frac{A_{AP}}{N_{DS}}$$

The units of angle area are deg.m^2, or for practical use deg.cm^2 (or deg.in^2 in imperial units). For any given angle-area, the time-area is reduced by a high shaft speed, reducing the breathing ability of the engine. Therefore high-speed engines require large angle-area values, needing wide ports with long timing. Slow-speed engines can use short-duration ports.

In the graph of port area against crank angle, the angle-area integral is the area under the curve for the particular port. This can be derived manually by plotting the curve on graph paper, but if the exercise is to be performed many times then computer evaluation is recommended. The computation itself is then automatic, but data input for the specification of the port shape may be as time consuming as a simplified manual calculation of the integral.

The angle-area of a port is directly proportional to the width of the port. However, the timing has a much more dramatic effect because it increases both the angular duration and the maximum area. This is illustrated in Figure 3.7.2 for a realistic case (100 cm^3, 50 mm stroke, 90 mm conrod, port sharp cornered).

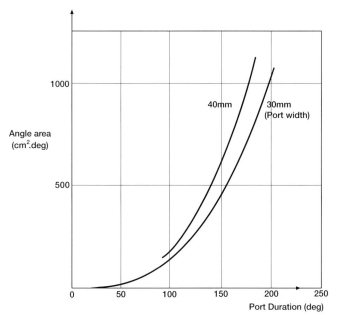

Figure 3.7.2. Variation of port angle-area with port duration for example 100 cm^3 engine at the stated port widths.

This rapid increase of angle-area with angular duration partly explains the limited range of port timings required for widely different design engine speeds. More pessimistically, it also means that for a given design speed, the optimum timing may be rather critical. Also, although a long port duration provides large angle-area, the useful (trapped) stroke is shortened, so wide ports are necessary to avoid the need for excessive duration.

If the bottom edge of an exhaust or transfer port is not as low as the piston at bottom dead centre, there is some loss of area. From the curve of Figure 3.7.2, however, it is apparent that, proportionally, the loss of angle area is less than the loss of maximum area. However, the port discharge coefficient is probably reduced, so there is no incentive to do this on exhaust or transfer ports if it can be avoided. However, it is frequently done on piston-controlled inlets because the piston skirt gives a poor port shape with high resistance. Reducing the port depth in this case reduces the angle area but improves the flow, potentially with some net benefit, or at least at no loss.

The product of port maximum flow area and port angular duration also gives a figure for deg.cm^2:

$$B_P = A_{Pmax} \theta_P$$

However, this is not the correct angle-area, and it does not indicate directly the flow capability of the port, since it takes no account of the shape of the port, for example difference between gradual and sudden opening. This B_P value is the area of a rectangle enclosing the true angle-area curve of Figure 3.7.1. For exhaust and transfer ports, the real angle-area is typically 65% to 70% of B_P depending on the exact port shape. A simple, although rather crude, method of estimating the true angle area is therefore to use 2/3 of the maximum area times the angular duration.

3.8 Head Volume

In the theoretical thermodynamic analysis of engine cycles, the equations for idealised performance are conveniently expressed using the compression ratio of the cycle, and, for this reason, 'compression ratio' is a term widely used. For two-strokes, this is also sometimes known as the secondary compression ratio to distinguish it from the (primary) crankcase compression ratio. The compression ratio is the ratio of volumes

$$R_C = \frac{V_S + V_C}{V_C} = \frac{V_S}{V_C} + 1$$

where V_S is the swept volume and V_C is the combustion volume (the volume above the piston at top dead centre).

The compression ratio is therefore an indirect way of relating the combustion volume to the swept volume. In fact it is quite satisfactory to work directly with such a ratio, the normalised combustion volume:

$$V_{NC} = \frac{V_C}{V_S}$$

from which

$$R_C = \frac{1}{V_{NC}} + 1$$

The combustion volume ratio can be expressed as a simple number (e.g. 0.12) or as a percentage (12%). One advantage of using this is that the volume is normalised in the systematic way, by dividing by the reference volume V_S. Another advantage is that by moving away from compression ratio, expectations regarding actual values are circumvented, and inappropriate comparison with four-stroke engines is avoided. However, the two variables V_{NC} and R_C do contain the same information.

The expression given for compression ratio is based on the full stroke of the engine, as for a four-stroke. It has become common of late to consider only the trapped swept volume V_{TS}, the swept volume above the exhaust closure point, which varies from about 0.5 V_S for a racing engine to 0.75 V_S for a low speed one. The trapped compression ratio is defined as

$$R_{TC} = \frac{V_{TS} + V_C}{V_C}$$

The practical significance of the compression ratio is that it governs the density and temperature of the gas just before combustion. In this respect the trapped compression ratio is nearer to reality than the full-stroke ratio, but it is still not exactly correct of itself, because the gas is not at ambient temperature and pressure when the exhaust closes, particularly when a tuned exhaust is used. Therefore, although the trapped compression ratio is more relevant to calculations, when comparing engines it is equally useful to compare the whole ratio, or simply the normalised combustion volume V_C / V_S.

The work done by combusted gas depends basically upon the expansion ratio up to the point when the exhaust opens, when the gas pressure drops sharply. For normal modern engine designs, the expansion ratio is nominally the same as the compression ratio:

$$R_E = R_C$$

and the trapped expansion ratio is

$$R_{TE} = R_{TC}$$

The equality of the expansion and compression ratios results from the fixed geometry of the ports. Engines have been built with considerably different ratios, e.g. by changing processes at part stroke. For a four-stroke engine, the fact that the inlet and exhaust valves do not open exactly at the ends of the stroke, having overlap, implies that calculated trapped compression and expansion ratios would, in general, have different values. Even on the two-stroke, the equality is based on the idea of instantaneous combustion at top dead centre, which is a considerable over-simplification.

Basic thermodynamic cycle analysis leads to the prediction that higher compression ratios always give more power and better thermal efficiency (lower fuel consumption for a given power output). However, this is based on adiabatic (zero heat transfer) analysis. In practice, a higher compression ratio means denser compressed gas, more rapid combustion before expansion cooling, and more heat transfer to the metal, so there is a practical upper limit to its use to improve power and efficiency. This is especially true of sustainable power rather than flash power. High compression ratio may also cause increased cooling problems. In any case, as discussed in Chapter 12, compression ratio may be limited by the fuel and by detonation problems.

The actual combustion volume is defined as the total volume in the cylinder when the piston is at top dead centre, Figure 3.8.1. Depending on the particular engine design, some of the following will be involved:

1. Head interior volume
2. Ignition plug cavity volume
3. Gasket clearance volume
4. Cylinder volume down to piston edge
5. Piston crown volume
6. Head-to-cylinder insertion volume
7. Squish clearance volume
8. Crevice volumes

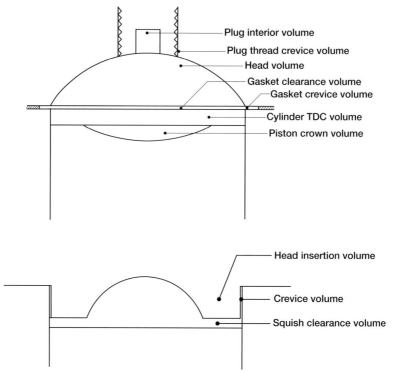

Figure 3.8.1. Head combustion volume analysis.

The combustion volume of an existing engine can be found simply by measuring the volume of liquid required to fill it. Fill a suitable burette with a paraffin/oil mixture. The principle is simply that the engine is positioned and locked at top dead centre with the plug removed, and the liquid is run in through the plug hole until the head is filled. A correction is then made for the plug hole and plug cavity volume. It is important to know the head internal shape to be sure that there are no air traps. These can sometimes be avoided by suitable positioning of the engine. If the head is to be removed, then it may be possible to measure head and cylinder tdc volumes separately, by bolting on a Perspex sheet with a small hole, and then allowing for the gasket clearance volume. To prevent liquid leakage around the piston and past the ring, the ring should be sealed with grease.

If the engine has a simple piston crown and head geometry, a few measurements are all that is needed to calculate the volume.

Alternatively, numerical integration may be used in a simple computer program. The bore area is divided up into numerous small areas, either in an x, y pattern or an r, θ pattern, it being better for the pattern to avoid being similar to the head style, e.g. for an axisymmetric head, use (x, y). The numerical integration is made of the incremental areas times the piston crown to head profile distance. This will give the volume. The piston shape and head shape must be specified in the program by suitable coefficients and conditional statements. Though a little time consuming to set up, this system works well.

Many modern heads are designed with a flat or nearly flat area very close to the piston (less than 1 mm away at top dead centre). This so-called squish area is intended to squeeze out the gas as the piston approaches, creating turbulence and accelerating combustion. It also concentrates the combustion into a more compact volume, and reduces the piston

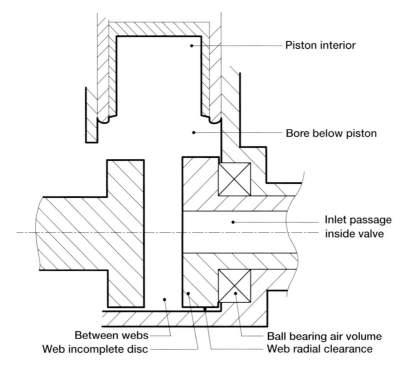

Figure 3.9.1. Crankcase interior volume analysis.

temperature under the squish area. The squish area is usually expressed as a normalised fraction of the bore area, as 'squish area 40%'.

The actual distance of the plug from the piston may be important, increasing the piston temperature if it is too close. With a squish head the plug can be further from the piston while retaining the correct volume.

3.9 Crankcase Volume

The crankcase interior volume (Figure 3.9.1) is important for gas flow dynamics in the inlet and transfer systems. A small crankcase volume increases the amplitude of pressure oscillations in the case, giving a higher maximum pressure and a lower minimum. The lower minimum pressure improves fuel atomisation in the crankcase, making the droplets smaller. With correct atomisation, the fuel becomes a fine mist. Improved vaporisation gives better combustion and reduced fuel consumption. The droplets need to be extremely fine, so the whirling crankshaft contributes little.

There are two effective crankcase volumes. One, V_{CT}, is at top dead centre. The other, V_{CB}, is at bottom dead centre. V_{CT} is primarily relevant for inlet dynamics, including the transfer passage volume but excluding any interior inlet passage volume (i.e. the passage volume on the crankcase side of the actual inlet valve). V_{CB} is at bottom dead centre, and is relevant for dynamics of the transfer action. It excludes the transfer passage volume but includes interior inlet passage volume. Hence the two volumes are related by

$$V_{CT} = V_{CB} + V_S + V_T - V_{II}$$

where V_T is the volume of the transfer passages, V_{II} that of the interior inlet passage and V_S is the swept volume.

It is convenient to define a reference case volume V_{CR} given by

$$V_{CR} = V_{CB} - V_{II} = V_{CT} - V_S - V_T$$

so that

$$V_{CB} = V_{CR} + V_{II}$$
$$V_{CT} = V_{CR} + V_S + V_T$$

Note that V_{II} is excluded from V_{CT} because V_{II} is then part of the active inlet-passage gas-flow inertia. Table 3.9.1 shows some example crankcase volume values for a 100 cm³ engine.

Table 3.9.1.   Example Crankcase Volume Values (100 cm³ engine)

			$V (cm^3)$	V / V_S
1.	Between crank webs		75	0.75
2.	Crank web edge clearance		10	0.10
3.	Incomplete crank discs		15	0.15
4.	Ball bearing internal volume		20	0.20
5.	Piston interior		50	0.50
6.	Below piston		30	0.30
7.	Below liner or barrel		25	0.25
	Total reference volume	V_{CR}	225	2.25
8.	Interior intake passage		40	0.40
9.	Transfer passage		30	0.30
10.	Swept volume		100	1.00
	Total bdc volume	V_{CB}	265	2.65
	Total tdc volume	V_{CT}	355	3.55

These volumes may be found by careful inspection and measurement, with calculations, but this generally requires some approximations for awkward shapes. As with head volume, measurement may be made by burette and liquid, again with precautions to avoid gas pockets. An old piston may be drilled in the centre, through which liquid is introduced with the crank at top dead centre. Drilling the piston skirt will ensure that all air can escape from the transfer passages. Also the inlet port will need to be sealed. Depending upon where this sealing is done, this will give the test volume

$$V_T = V_{CR} + V_{II} + V_S + V_T$$
$$= V_{CB} + V_S + V_T$$
$$= V_{CT} + V_{II}$$

Hence the case volumes can be found provided that the transfer passage volume and intake passage volume have been separately evaluated, by direct measurement.

If an old piston is not available, a plate may be bolted over the cylinder flange, and the resulting test volume adjusted for tdc piston crown height, piston material volume and con-rod volume. The material volumes can be derived from the component mass and material density (7.8 g/cm³ for steel and 2.8 g/cm³ for aluminium alloys). If there is doubt about the metal densities, then use direct measurement. Archimedes' principle is useful for awkward shape components. Simply measure the volume of liquid displaced by the component. If the weight is known, the density can also be calculated.

Because the air is first compressed in the crankcase, this is called the primary compression, with a primary compression ratio, and the cylinder head compression is called the secondary compression with secondary compression ratio.

The primary or crankcase compression ratio is based on the tdc case volume and the complete stroke, and is defined as

$$R_{CC} = \frac{V_{CT} + V_{II}}{V_{CT} + V_{II} - V_{S}}$$

Some people object to the use of case compression ratio, because, as with the combustion compression ratio, the inlet port does not close at tdc and the transfer port opens before bdc. The idea of trapped case compression is fair enough qualitatively, but is rarely calculated. On the whole, it is better to work in terms of the crankcase volume V_{CB} or normalised crankcase volume V_{CB} / V_{S}.

It used to be normal practice to minimise the crankcase volume for high-speed engines, but it is generally held nowadays that a primary compression ratio of 1.5 is sufficient, giving a case volume of about $2V_{S}$, which is low enough even for very high speed running. This is certainly worth experimenting with. Some say that the case volume is not critical, although the author once witnessed a 10% power change with a small change of case volume. The crankcase volume affects the natural Helmholtz frequency of the inlet and transfer processes, so the peak-power speed is affected. Changes in the inlet tract length can restore correct inlet resonance.

3.10 Desaxé Layout

The Desaxé layout is when the cylinder axis is offset from the shaft axis, or the gudgeon pin is offset, typically by ten per cent of the stroke (Figure 3.10.1). Desaxé was popular up to the 1960s. The arguments presented in its favour were:

1. During the power stroke, the inclination of the conrod can be reduced, hence reducing the side thrust on the piston due to gas pressure.

2. Asymmetry in timing. It was claimed the ports opened nearer to bdc and closed further from bdc.

The first reason is valid, but considers only the gas pressure forces. However, for high-speed engines the reciprocating inertia forces are very important. When these are considered, the offset layout is no longer helpful, and possibly even detrimental.

The argument of asymmetrical timing is specious, because the crankpin position A is no longer bottom dead centre for the piston, the true effective bdc being delayed. In short the Desaxé format may offer some advantage for low-speed engines, but none for high-speed engines and has largely been abandoned. The author owns one engine with negative Desaxé. The engine was originally designed positive, but to change the inlet porting system the manufacturer reversed the crankcase, with no apparent ill effects.

3.11 Effect of Timing

To better understand the effect of cylinder port timing, consider a simple engine with no exhaust system, scavenged by a scavenge pump providing constant pressure. Longer timing gives bigger ports and faster scavenging, so the peaking speed goes up. However, the

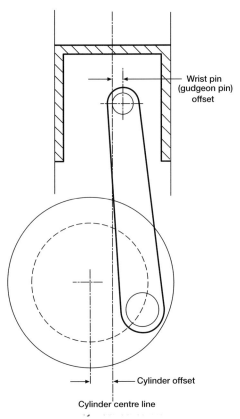

Figure 3.10.1 Desaxé layout (shown exaggerated).

trapped volume is reduced so the torque is reduced. The time taken to scavenge the cylinder depends on the total resistance of the ports (transfer and exhaust in series, with, to be more realistic, an additional series resistance representing the induction system). The maximum power is reached at the maximum speed, where the scavenging is complete. Above this speed the scavenging would deteriorate and the power begins to drop. The entire cylinder must be scavenged, but any mixture below the top of the exhaust port is squeezed out, and not trapped. Table 3.11.1, Figure 3.11.1 and 3.11.2 show the results of such an analysis.

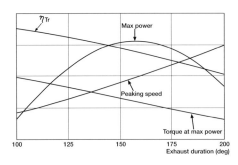

Figure 3.11.1. The effect of cylinder port timing (a).

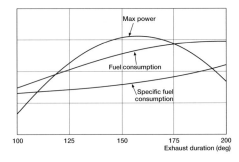

Figure 3.11.2. The effect of cylinder port timing (b).

Table 3.11.1. The effect of exhaust timing (transfer also varying)

Exhaust Timing (deg)	Trapped volume (cm³)	Geometric C. ratio (-)	Trapping effcncy (%)	Torque (Nm)	Peaking speed (rev/min)	Peak power (bhp)	Fuel cons (cc/s)	Specific fuel con (g/kW.s)
100	96.8	9.11	87.8	9.73	4133	5.64	0.731	0.127
110	93.6	9.39	85.2	9.13	4965	6.36	0.849	0.130
120	90.1	9.72	82.3	8.50	5861	6.98	0.964	0.135
130	86.3	10.10	79.2	7.83	6818	7.49	1.075	0.140
140	82.3	10.54	75.9	7.15	7834	7.86	1.177	0.146
150	78.0	11.07	72.3	6.46	8905	8.07	1.269	0.154
160	73.5	11.68	68.5	5.77	10027	8.11	1.347	0.162
170	68.9	12.40	64.5	5.09	11196	7.99	1.408	0.172
180	64.0	13.26	60.3	4.43	12406	7.70	1.451	0.184

Bore x stroke = 50.0 x 50.0 mm
Exhaust width = 40.0 mm
Transfer width = 40.0 mm
Intake area = 4.91 cm²
Trapped thermal efficiency = 20.0%
Scavenge pressure = 30.0 kPa
Transfer timing = 100 + 0.5*(Exhaust-100)
Trapped volume includes combustion volume
Constant trapped compression ratio = 8.0

The compression ratio for the trapped gas has been kept constant, so for longer timing the smaller trapped volume has a smaller combustion volume needing a higher geometric compression ratio.

The table and figures show how a short-timed engine has better torque, lower peaking speed and better fuel consumption. A long-timed engine has higher peaking speed, lower torque and worse fuel efficiency. In the example, the best power occurs for an exhaust timing of about 158 degrees (transfer 129 degrees). Underlying these results is the idea that a longer timed engine is a smaller engine because its trapped capacity is less. It has less torque, but it is capable of scavenging more quickly, so within limits it can provide more power.

CHAPTER 4

Kinematics

4.1 Introduction

The velocities of individual components are not necessarily of direct interest, but the velocity differences at points such as bearings are important for lubrication and frictional losses. For a given oil, the greater the sliding speed the greater the load capacity without reaching metal-to-metal contact. This affects the shaft main bearings, the two ends of the connecting rod, the piston in the liner, and the rotary disc or other rotary inlet.

The velocities of the parts then lead on to their accelerations, especially of the piston and connecting rod. Even for a high-speed competition engine the velocities are still modest. Velocities of internal parts may reach about 40 m/s, although gas speeds may be much higher. However, because of the high angular speeds the accelerations are enormous, thousands of g, so they require considerable forces and pressures to produce them. Kinematic analysis of velocities through to accelerations is necessary to predict the forces in the bearings and the stresses in the components so that they are designed correctly or can be safely modified.

The times involved in processes such as the gas exchange and combustion are extremely small. At 12,000 rpm, one full revolution takes just 1/200 s.

$$T_R = \frac{1}{N_S} = 0.005 \text{ s} = 5 \text{ ms}$$

This 5 milliseconds for one revolution allows only 0.014 milliseconds (14 microseconds) for each degree of crank motion. $180°$ of inlet takes 2.5 ms; $120°$ of transfer about 1.7 ms. An exhaust lead (blowdown) of $10°$ corresponds to 0.14 ms. An ideal combustion period of about $40°$ lasts one half of a millisecond. These short times show why the accelerations are so severe despite the modest speeds. And, of course, many engines run faster than 12,000 rpm. Although the individual processes, or even whole revolutions, are over so quickly on a human scale, they can still be analysed in detail.

It may help to imagine the engine slowed down by a factor of 1,000 to visualise the processes so that, at 12,000 rpm, one revolution takes five seconds.

4.2 Approximate Kinematics

The most accurate values for the velocities and accelerations call for a full algebraic solution of velocity and acceleration diagrams. However, a simplified approach still gives an accuracy of better than 1%.

The piston height above bdc has been solved in terms of crank angle abdc (after bottom dead centre) as

$$H_P = L_C(1 - \cos\theta_C) - L_R(1 - \cos\theta_R)$$

To express this exclusively in terms of the crank angle rather than the rod angle, use

$$\lambda = \frac{L_C}{L_R} \tag{4.2.1}$$

$$\sin\theta_R = \lambda \sin\theta_C \tag{4.2.2}$$

$$\cos\theta_R = \left[1 - (\lambda \sin\theta_C)^2\right]^{1/2} \tag{4.2.3}$$

The approximation expands this expression for the cosine of the rod angle as a series by the binomial expansion. The first two terms alone give adequate accuracy.

$$\cos\theta_R \approx 1 - \tfrac{1}{2}\lambda^2 \sin^2\theta_C$$

The piston position can now be written as

$$H_P \approx L_C(1 - \cos\theta_C) - L_R\left(\tfrac{1}{2}\lambda^2 \sin^2\theta_C\right) \tag{4.2.4}$$

The approximation for the rod angle shows how the presence of the connecting rod introduces harmonic frequencies to the piston reciprocation. The good approximation corresponds to including the first and second harmonics only, because the $\sin^2\theta_C$ term can be expressed in terms of $2\theta_C$ by the equality

$$\sin^2\theta_C = \tfrac{1}{2}(1 - \cos 2\theta_C)$$

which is mathematically exact for any crank angle, giving

$$\cos\theta_R \approx 1 - \tfrac{1}{4}\lambda^2(1 - \cos 2\theta_C)$$

The piston position is therefore

$$H_P \approx L_C(1 - \cos\theta_C) - L_R\left(\tfrac{1}{4}\lambda^2(1 - \cos 2\theta_C)\right)$$

or

$$\frac{H_P}{L_C} \approx (1 - \cos\theta_C) - \tfrac{1}{4}\lambda(1 - \cos 2\theta_C) \tag{4.2.5}$$

With this simplified approximate form, differentiation gives the piston velocity and acceleration.

$$\frac{V_P}{\Omega_C L_C} \approx \sin\theta_C - \tfrac{1}{2}\lambda \sin 2\theta_C \tag{4.2.6}$$

$$\frac{A_P}{\Omega_C^2 L_C} \approx \cos\theta_C - \lambda \cos 2\theta_C \tag{4.2.7}$$

This expression for the reciprocating accelerations shows the presence of the secondary, second harmonic, forces due to the rod inclination, with a relative amplitude governed by $f_R = L_R / L_C$ which is about 1/4.

Another useful approximation is that the connecting rod angular speed is

$$\Omega_R = \Omega_C \lambda \cos \theta_C \tag{4.2.8}$$

4.3 Crankshaft Speed

The crankshaft angular velocity is often referred to as N_M revolutions per minute. It is also N_S revolutions per second, with

$$N_S = \frac{N_M}{60}$$

For kinematic calculations it needs to be expressed as Ω_C radians per second with

$$\Omega_C = 2\pi N_S = 6.2832 N_S = 0.10472 N_M$$

The piston reciprocates, and its speed varies dramatically around one cycle. There is therefore varying kinetic energy in the piston and connecting rod. The resistive load on the shaft is generally roughly constant over a cycle, but the torque output from the gas pressure is cyclical so the end result is that there are small variations of the crankshaft angular speed over one cycle, even at a nominally constant speed. However, these variations are generally small enough to be neglected, so shaft speeds are taken as constant.

Given the shaft angular speed Ω_C and the shaft journal diameter D_{SJ}, for a plain journal bearing the shaft journal surface sliding velocity is simply the angular velocity times the radius, or

$$V_{SJ} = \frac{1}{2}\Omega_C D_{SJ}$$

This sliding speed is important for lubrication and friction. The example 25 mm diameter shaft at 12,000 rpm gives 15.7 m/s. Because of the scaling laws, in an homologous series of engines the operating speed is inversely proportional to the linear scale, so the journal sliding speed is independent of engine swept volume.

The position diagram is in Figure 4.3.1 (a repeat of Figure 2.6.1). The shaft rotates clockwise. The crankpin velocity, from Figure 4.3.2, is tangential with

$$V_C = \Omega_C L_C$$

The tangential velocity of the crankpin is around 35 m/s at peak power for a very highly tuned two-stroke, independent on scale. This is low enough for aerodynamic forces on the rod to be neglected. For the example engine at 12 000 rpm it is 31.4 m/s.

Figure 4.3.3 shows the complete velocity diagram. The origin O represents the zero speed of crankcase and of the shaft centre. Point C represents the crankpin velocity, on any suitable scale, at the angle θ_C. The crankpin velocity components are

$$V_{CX} = -V_C \cos \theta_C$$
$$V_{CY} = +V_C \sin \theta_C$$

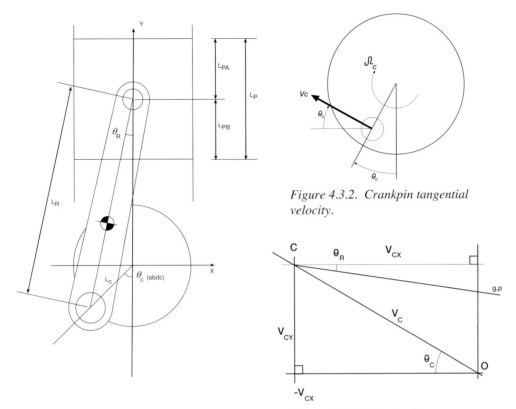

Figure 4.3.2. *Crankpin tangential velocity.*

Figure 4.3.1. *Basic engine geometry.*

Figure 4.3.3. *Velocity* diagram.

4.4 Piston Speed

The velocity of the gudgeon pin is directly upwards, so its *x*-component V_{GX} is zero. Therefore point g representing the gudgeon pin velocity must be on the vertical axis of the velocity diagram. Also, the velocity of G relative to C must be perpendicular to the rod itself. Therefore cg may be constructed at the rod angle θ_R as shown.

The gudgeon pin and piston velocity are given by

$$V_P = V_{CY} + V_{CX} \tan\theta_R$$

where V_{CX} is negative in Figure 4.3.1. The piston velocity can be expressed as

$$V_P = V_C \ \sin\theta_C - V_C \ \cos\theta_C \ \tan\theta_R$$
$$= \Omega_C \ L_C \left(\sin\theta_C - \cos\theta_C \ \tan\theta_R \right)$$

The approximate expression obtained in Section 4.2 was

$$V_P = \Omega_C L_C \left(\sin\theta_C - \tfrac{1}{2}\lambda\sin 2\theta_C \right)$$

73

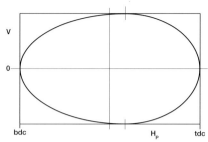

Figure 4.4.1   Piston speed v. position.

The rod angle θ_R depends on the ratio of rod length to crank throw, and on the crank angle. It is independent of scale. For homologous engines, the product $\Omega_C L_C$ is not dependent on scale, so the piston sliding speed is independent of scale. This is correct, because the gas speeds are independent of scale, and the ratio of piston speed to gas speed in scavenging will not depend on scale.

For an infinitely long conrod, or a Scotch Yoke mechanism, θ_R is effectively zero, and V_P varies simply sinusoidally. However, a real rod of finite length introduces an extra second harmonic term. Figure 4.4.1 shows how the piston velocity varies along the stroke for the example engine. For any piston position there are upwards and downwards velocities, equal in magnitude because of symmetry. The peak velocity occurs approximately at mid stroke, the exact position depending only on L_R / L_C. The maximum piston sliding velocity is close to the crankpin tangential speed. Variation of the piston speed near to tdc is of interest with regard to combustion, and in particular for squish effect.

4.5   Connecting Rod Speed

The centre of the connecting rod big end has the same velocity as the crankpin. The little end has the same velocity as the piston.

The rod tangential speed of one end centre relative to the other, clockwise positive, from the velocity diagram of Figure 4.3.3, is

$$V_{Rtan} = V_{C/G} = \frac{-V_{CX}}{\cos \theta_R}$$

The rod angular velocity, clockwise positive, is therefore

$$\Omega_R = \frac{V_{Rtan}}{L_R} = \frac{-V_{CX}}{L_R \cos \theta_R}$$

This conrod angular velocity is important because it gives the little-end journal bearing angular speed, and has a substantial effect on the big end journal speed. Also it gives an acceleration of the piston relative to the crankpin. For the example engine and position (30° abdc), the rod angular speed is 305 rad/s.

Zero conrod angular speed occurs when the crank and conrod form a right angle, which is above 90° crank angle. Nevertheless the extreme rod angular velocities, positive at bdc and negative at tdc, are equal in magnitude, since both are equal to

$$\Omega_{Rmax} = \frac{\Omega_C L_C}{L_R} = \frac{\Omega_C}{f_{RL}}$$

depending on the crank speed and the rod length factor L_R / L_C.

The rod maximum angular velocity as a fraction of the shaft speed depends only on the crank/rod length factor, with a value

$$\Omega_{Rmax} = \lambda \Omega_C$$

where $\lambda = 25/90$ for the example engine.

4.6 Little-end Journal Speed

Normally the gudgeon pin will effectively be fixed in the piston, with the motion occurring in the rod little-end eye. The piston and wrist pin do not rotate, so the little-end journal angular speed equals the rod angular speed. The actual sliding speed, relevant for lubrication, wear and friction, is simply

$$V_{LJ} = \tfrac{1}{2} \Omega_R D_L$$

where D_L is the diameter of the little-end bearing. This varies approximately sinusoidally, having maximum at tdc and bdc, so the velocity is relatively high when the load is high, although still small compared with big-end speed. For the example engine, the maximum little-end journal sliding speed is 2.6 m/s. The average little-end angular speed is about 1/6 of the shaft speed, and is why much less power is lost to friction at the little-end than at the big-end.

4.7 Big-end Journal Speed

The relative angular velocity Ω_B of the rod to the crankpin at the big-end is

$$\Omega_B = \Omega_C - \Omega_R$$

Using equation 4.2.8,

$$\Omega_B \approx \Omega_C(1 - \lambda \cos\theta_C)$$

The absolute rotational speed of the crankpin is equal to that of the shaft, and effectively constant. Therefore the big-end journal speed, Ω_B, varies as shown in Figure 4.7.1, with a maximum at tdc and a minimum at bdc. Fortunately the high sliding speeds, good for lubrication, occur around tdc when the rod bearing forces are high.

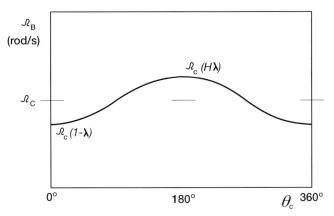

Figure 4.7.1. Big-end journal speed versus crank angle.

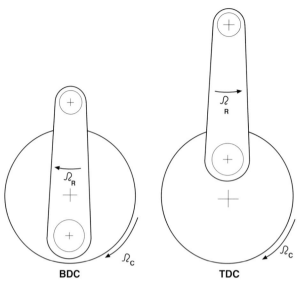

Figure 4.7.2. Extremes of big-end journal sliding speed occur at the ends of the stroke.

These extreme cases are easily investigated, as in Figure 4.7.2. At bottom dead centre,

$$\Omega_{Bb} = \Omega_C(1 - \lambda)$$

At top dead centre,

$$\Omega_{Bt} = \Omega_C(1 + \lambda)$$

The amplitude of variation of speed relative to the mean speed is simply λ, or about 28%. The ratio of minimum speed to maximum is

$$\frac{\Omega_{Bb}}{\Omega_{Bt}} = \frac{1 - \lambda}{1 + \lambda}$$

and is about 0.56, i.e. the big-end journal speed varies by a ratio of nearly 2:1, the ratio being more extreme, the shorter the rod/crank length ratio.

The big-end journal sliding speed is

$$V_{BJ} = \tfrac{1}{2}\Omega_B D_B$$

where D_B is the big-end journal diameter, i.e. the crankpin diameter, and varies in the same ratio. This sliding speed is important for lubrication and friction.

For the example engine, the mean big-end journal speed is 12.6 m/s. The extreme values are 9.1 m/s and 16.1 m/s, the ratio of extremes being 1.77.

4.8 Piston Acceleration

The high-revving nature of racing engines causes severe accelerations of the moving parts. These, even with the small masses involved, produce large forces. High stresses, bearing loads and vibration are one of the engine designer's problems. The vibration amplitudes are only a fraction the crank length, so may be neglected when evaluating the acceleration of internal components.

Finding true accelerations and forces requires full algebraic solution of the acceleration diagram. However, sufficiently accurate accelerations and internal inertia forces can be found from the piston acceleration approximation of Equation 4.2.7 with a simplified inertial representation of the connecting rod. This method avoids finding the linear and angular accelerations of the connecting rod as a solid body.

The shaft is considered to have constant speed, so the crankpin acceleration is simply a centripetal acceleration, Figure 4.8.1. The value is

$$A_C = \Omega_C^2\, L_C$$

which can easily be evaluated for any known speed. For the example engine it is a remarkable 39.5 km/s² or just over 4,000 *g*. Its direction is from the pin towards the shaft centre. The complete acceleration diagram is shown in Figure 4.8.2. Point C, representing the crankpin acceleration, may be drawn in the figure at any suitable scale, at the crank angle θ_C as shown.

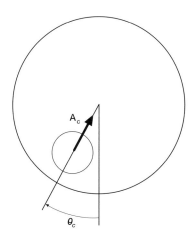

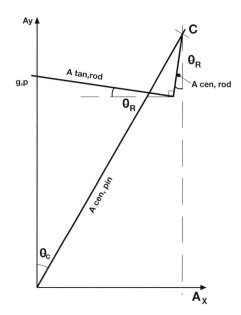

Above: Figure 4.8.1. Centripetal acceleration of the crankpin.

Right top: Figure 4.8.2. Acceleration diagram.

Right bottom: Figure 4.8.3. Piston acceleration versus crank angle.

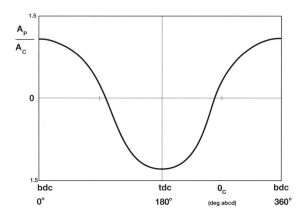

The simplified equation for the piston acceleration (Equation 4.2.7) was

$$A_P = \Omega_C^2 L_C \left(\cos \theta_C - \lambda \cos 2\theta_C \right)$$

The acceleration of the piston is shown for the example engine in Figure 4.8.3. The extreme values occur at bdc and tdc and are easily evaluated.

The centripetal acceleration of the rod, top end relative to the bottom end, is downwards, and therefore at bdc

$$A_{Pb} \approx A_C (1 - \lambda)$$

and at tdc

$$A_{Pt} = -A_C (1 + \lambda)$$

The piston acceleration is therefore much more severe at tdc than at bdc, owing to the action of the swinging rod which increases the piston acceleration at tdc and reduces it at bdc.

The ratio of the magnitudes of extreme accelerations is

$$\left| \frac{A_{Pb}}{A_{Pt}} \right| = \frac{1 - \lambda}{1 + \lambda}$$

which is the same ratio as was found for the extremes of big-end journal speed, with a value approaching 2:1 for maximum to minimum, and about 1.8 for the example engine.

In a high-speed engine, the reciprocating accelerations reach quite remarkable values. For the example engine the crankpin centripetal acceleration is

$$A_C = \Omega_C^2 L_C$$
$$= 39478 \text{ m/s}^2$$
$$\approx 4020 \text{ g}$$

The peak piston acceleration, at tdc, is

$$A_{Pt} = A_C \left(1 + \frac{L_C}{L_R} \right)$$
$$= 50,444 \text{ m/s}^2$$
$$\approx 5,142 \text{ g}$$

At bottom dead centre it is 28.5 km/s². These large accelerations underline the importance of light reciprocating components for a high speed engine.

The effect of scaling on acceleration is an interesting one. Scaling up in the linear factor K_L, with swept volume going with K_L^3 of course, the stroke goes with K_L and the operating rotational speed with $1 / K_L$. Therefore the accelerations scale as

$$K_{Acc} = K_L K_V^2 = \left(K_L K_L^{-2} \right) = \frac{1}{K_L}$$

Hence the accelerations are less for larger cylinders, and greater for small ones. Masses scale with K_L^3. Hence the reciprocating inertia forces basically scale with K_L^2, and maintain their relationship with the gas pressure forces. The gas pressures are proportionally somewhat higher for large engines.

Multi-cylinder engines have similar individual internal inertias but their several cylinders allows some internal forces to be balanced. Though reducing the external vibration, the loads internally are unchanged.

4.9 Vibration Kinematics

Vibration of single-cylinder engines is approximately sinusoidal in motion in any particular direction. At a vibratory (shaft) speed

$$\Omega_C = 2\pi N_S$$

and a vibratory amplitude X, the sinusoidal vibratory displacement is

$$x = X \sin\left(\Omega_C\, t\right)$$

where t is the time in seconds. By differentiation, the vibratory velocity is

$$v = \Omega_C\, X \cos\left(\Omega_C\, t\right)$$

so the amplitude of velocity is

$$V = \Omega_C\, X$$

By further differentiation, the acceleration is

$$a = -\Omega_C^2\, X \sin\left(\Omega_C\, t\right)$$

so the amplitude of acceleration is

$$A = \Omega_C^2 X$$

Even a small displacement amplitude X coupled with a large speed Ω_C gives a large acceleration amplitude. This means that at high frequency even large forces give only a small amplitude of motion.

4.10 Direction of Rotation

When the crankcase pressure is positive, as when the piston is descending, the crankcase mixture tends to leak up past the piston and out of the exhaust port. The rings are too high to provide a seal. If the direction of rotation is such that the positive gas pressure in the cylinder, pressing the piston down against the connecting rod, pushes the piston against the exhaust side of the cylinder, then the leakage is minimised. Inertia forces in the connecting rod due to piston acceleration in the bottom half of the stroke have the same effect. Leakage is often a problem with large piston-cylinder clearances as found in racing engines. This is why racing engines usually rotate in the direction that reduces leakage. For the usual motorcycle layout with the exhaust port at the front, the engine should rotate in the opposite direction to the wheels, requiring a change of the direction of rotation in the transmission.

CHAPTER 5:

Dynamics

5.1 Introduction

Though computer programs may provide a detailed and accurate analysis of the forces in an engine, simple algebraic analysis gives more insight into the consequences of design decisions.

The engine produces power because the combusted gas provides pressure that forces the piston down. In a high-speed engine the connecting rod can, surprisingly, still be in tension during part of the power stroke.

Connecting rod dynamics and friction complicate analysis of piston and connecting rod forces. In a simplified analysis, the frictional forces can be investigated assuming that the main forces are known.

Analysing connecting rod dynamics can be simplified by replacing the rod by a pair of masses, one at the small end and one at the crankpin, thus reducing the analysis to rotating and reciprocating masses.

Weigh the connecting rod in the horizontal position, independently at each bearing centre, while pivoting the other end on a knife edge. The big end should be between half and 70% of the total rod mass. For the example engine (Section 1.5) the rod masses are 36g at the big end and 24g at the little end (big end 60%). This inertial representation of the rod is not exact, because although the total mass and the centre-of-gravity position are correct, the rotational moment of inertia is not, but is acceptable for most purposes.

Piston (80g), gudgeon pin (35g) and the two rings (5g) gives a total of 120g. Add the little end mass to this, and the total reciprocating mass at the little end becomes 144g.

The previous chapter explained how to calculate approximate accelerations for various engine speeds and crank positions. Computer simulations may give greater accuracy, but they give less insight into what is happening.

The piston is subject to the gas pressures above and below it. These are not easy to calculate or to measure accurately, so most tuners make do with estimated values.

5.2 Basic Forces

Figure 5.2.1 shows the basic forces on the reciprocating mass (piston, rings, gudgeon pin and rod little-end). These are:

1. F_{PGC} piston force from cylinder gas
2. F_{PGCC} piston force from crankcase gas
3. F_{RC} connecting rod force (positive for compression)
4. F_{PS} piston side force from cylinder

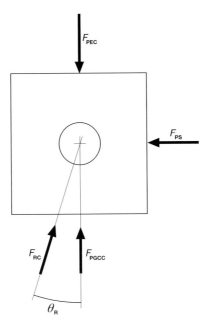

Figure 5.2.1. Basic forces on the reciprocating mass (friction omitted).

In principle the gas forces are the pressure times the bore area. Accurate pressure data requires serious instrumentation. However, estimates can be made.

The connecting rod angle is Ω_R, with the rod compressive force F_{RC}. The lateral component of this must be balanced by a side force from the cylinder, F_{PS}. Actually there is also a friction force from the cylinder, and one at the gudgeon pin.

To provide the known acceleration A_{PY}, the sum of the axial forces is

$$\Sigma F_Y = F_{RC} \cos\theta_R + F_{PGCC} - F_{PGC} = m_{ER} A_{PY}$$

where m_{ER} is the total effective reciprocating mass:

$$m_{ER} = m_P + m_R + m_{WP} + m_{RL}$$

The required connecting rod force is therefore

$$F_{RC} = \frac{m_{ER} A_{PY} - F_{PGCC} + F_{PGC}}{\cos\theta_R}$$

The piston side force then follows from

$$F_{PS} = F_{RC} \sin\theta_R$$

To find the gudgeon pin bearing force, this must be considered in X and Y components. The X component is simply $F_{WPX} = F_{PS}$. The Y component requires allowance for the little end inertia:

$$F_{WPY} = F_{RC} \cos\theta_R - m_{RL} A_{PY}$$

In some cases the gudgeon pin is locked to the connecting rod little end, and the bearing surface is in the piston. The mass of the gudgeon pin must then also be allowed for.

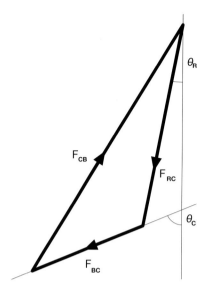

Figure 5.2.2. Forces at the crankpin bearing.

The previous expression for F_{WPY} can also be expressed as

$$F_{WPY} = \left(m_P + m_R + m_{WP}\right)A_{PY} - F_{PGCC} + F_{PGC}$$

The rod compression force is also applied, reversed, to the big end mass on the crankpin. Analysis of this gives the crankpin bearing force. Figure 5.2.2 gives the relevant triangle of forces, where F_{CB} is the bearing force obtained from the rod compression force plus the centrifugal force F_{BC} on the rod big end mass.

$$F_{BC} = m_{RB}\Omega_C^2 R_C$$

$$F_{CBX} = F_{BC}\sin\theta_C + F_{RC}\sin\theta_R$$

$$F_{CBY} = F_{BC}\cos\theta_C + F_{RC}\cos\theta_R$$

$$F_{CB} = \left(F_{CBX}^2 + F_{CBY}^2\right)^{1/2}$$

Top and bottom dead centres are simple cases. For the example engine (Section 2.6) the crankpin centripetal acceleration is 39.5 km/s^2. The vertical acceleration of the piston at bdc is 28.512 km/s^2 (upwards), and at top dead centre it is 50.444 km/s^2 downwards. So for a reduced reciprocating mass of 120 g (0.120 kg) the wrist pin bearing force due to reciprocation is 6,053 N (1,360 lbf) at tdc and 3,421 N (769 lbf) at bdc. If we include the little end mass of 24 g, this gives the corresponding connecting rod force as 7,264 N (1,633 lbf) tension at tdc and 4,106 N (923 lbf) compression at bdc. These large cyclic forces subject the connecting rod to high fatigue loads, and are the source of much of the vibration.

Now the rod cross-sectional dimensions and the rod stresses can be found.

For the crankpin bearing forces, the big-end mass of 36 g must be included. The associated centripetal force is 1,422 N. At tdc and bdc the big-end bearing forces are therefore 8,686 N (1,953 lbf) and 5,528 N (1,243 lbf).

At bdc the gas pressures are fairly small and the previous estimate is quite good. At tdc the gas pressure in the cylinder helps provide a downward acceleration to the piston. For a low speed engine, which has low inertial forces, this may be more than enough to accelerate the piston, and the connecting rod may remain in compression throughout the whole revolution. However, for a high speed engine the rod tension may be large. The calculated inertial force of 8,686 N on the crankpin bearing corresponds to a gas pressure of 4.42 MPa (641 psi) (bore area 19.63 cm^2). At tdc the combustion is incomplete, and compression pressure alone will be well below this value for any reasonable trapped compression ratio, probably around 1 MPa (150 psi).

5.3 Main Bearings
Modern engines have a double-shear crankpin with the big-end bearing loads shared between a symmetrically placed pair of main bearings, Figure 5.3.1 (a). Each associated bearing reaction is then equal to one half of the crankpin load. (Additional forces due to crank balance are discussed later.)

Some early two-stroke engines had a cantilevered crank, Figure 5.3.1 (b). In this case, the forward support force is in the same direction as the pin load, and the rear support force is larger.

Figure 5.3.1 Main bearings layout (a) symmetrical (b) cantilever.

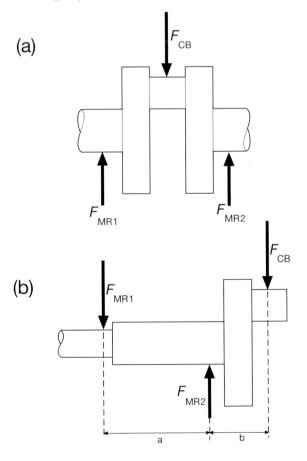

$$F_{MR1} = \frac{b}{a} F_{CB}$$

$$F_{MR2} = F_{MR1} + F_{CB} = \left(1 + \frac{b}{a}\right) F_{CB}$$

Vectorially, the sum of the main bearing forces equals the load, but friction in the bearings depends basically on the algebraic sum of the magnitudes

$$F_{MBM} = F_{MR1} + F_{MR2}$$

For the symmetrical layout, this also equals the load. For the cantilevered crank

$$F_{MBM} = \left(1 + \frac{b}{a}\right) F_{CB}$$

For a practical cantilevered crank, b/a is about 0.4 so the total main bearing reactions are 80 per cent greater than for the double-shear crankpin. This obviously gives greater frictional losses, and requires larger bearings with greater engine mass. In the early days this was felt to be an acceptable price for the advantages of easier manufacture and assembly. A further compensation is the compact big end and narrow crankcase. The basic crankcase diameter can be as small as 1.65 times the stroke.

However, the cantilevered load is not exclusive to the cantilevered crankpin. Even symmetrical cranks have asymmetrical loads, such as an external chain or gear power take-off, and a single-sided flywheel load. Inertial vibratory loads can be very severe.

5.4 Friction
Relevant forms of friction to consider are:

1. Dry (Coulomb)
2. Viscous
3. Rolling

Friction between unlubricated metal surfaces is denoted by the Greek letter μ, (mu) and relates the maximum friction force F_F to the force F_N acting at right angles to it

$$F_F = \mu F_F$$

where μ is effectively independent of F_N and of the sliding speed, provided the speed is not zero. Oil prevents this form of friction in a properly running engine. When lubrication fails microscopic metal asperities make contact, are briefly welded together and then break. The result is wear.

Viscous friction occurs when a lubricant fills a narrow gap, as in plain bearings and between piston and cylinder in a correctly operating engine. The viscosity of the oil or fuel/oil mixture keeps the metal surfaces apart. In theory the effective frictional coefficient μ of a plain journal bearing can be less than 0.01. In practice the bearings rarely operate correctly, due to mechanical distortion and imperfections of manufacture, so some metal-to-metal contact does occur, with consequent wear and increased friction.

Rolling friction occurs in ball journal bearings and roller bearings. These are generally commercial units of accurate manufacture with little scope for tuner intervention other than selection of clearances and quality. Claimed frictional coefficients may, again, be around

0.01, although it is unlikely that such low values are achieved in engines, and 0.02 may be more realistic. Rolling bearings are common for the big end, and ball bearings for the shaft main bearings. Ball bearing shafts have a good reputation, offering reduced wear and replaceability, and possibly better starting. Whether the actual performance is superior to a good plain bearing is questionable.

Frictional losses will occur at any bearing surface, specifically:

1. Piston to cylinder
2. Piston rings to cylinder
3. Gudgeon pin (connecting rod little end)
4. Crank pin (connecting rod big end)
5. Shaft main bearings

To deal with these in turn:

1. Piston-to-cylinder
At running temperature, there is a small diametral clearance between piston and bore. This is filled with hot oil, slightly diluted with fuel.

Excessive piston expansion due to overheating will increase viscous friction, and may be followed by direct metal-to-metal contact usually leading to seizure. This is a problem with aluminium pistons in iron cylinders due to the unfavourable difference of coefficients of thermal expansion. High-silicon low-expansion pistons help, particularly when combined with chromium plated aluminium cylinders. For road-going engines, the piston/cylinder clearance is limited by noisy piston slap, but this is not a problem for competition engines. The side force from the rod tends to move the piston out of centre in the bore, but this need not increase the viscous friction greatly because the reduced gap on one side is compensated on the other. Contact pressure is relatively low in most cases, because the lateral force is less than one quarter of the axial force and the bearing area is far greater than that of the connecting rod bearings.

2. Piston-rings-to-cylinder
The piston rings are forced against the cylinder by their natural spring, generally small, and by the gas pressure behind them, which is larger in the upper part of the stroke.

The feel of an engine when turned over slowly by hand is no guide because at such low speeds the rings penetrate the oil and make direct contact with the cylinder. The rings actually touch the cylinder near to tdc when the speed is low, lubrication worse and pressure high. We know this by the way that the upper cylinder wears.

3. Gudgeon Pin
Ideally the gudgeon pin is in properly lubricated viscous friction. The sliding speed is relatively low and the temperature may be high. Little ends generally give much less trouble than big ends, possibly because the low speed gives less frictional heating. A high quality finish to both gudgeon pin and little end is essential.

4. Crankpin
The basic big end is a plain bearing in fully lubricated viscous friction. Inadequate lubrication is the commonest problem as big ends often receive the minimum quantity of oil in the fuel/oil mixture. The method of air induction is important in directing cooling air and lubricant onto this bearing. Crankpin and big end quality are important. Problems often arise due to misalignment from out-of-parallel connecting rod bearing surfaces, lack of parallelism of the crankpin with the shaft main bearing centreline, and shaft distortion in cantilevered cranks. The very thin film of oil in the connecting rod bearings when under load is unforgiving of poor finish or misalignment.

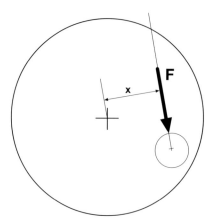

Figure 5.4.1. Conrod force and position for analysis of crankpin efficiency.

Big end lubrication problems are lessened by roller or needle bearing big ends. Pressure lubricated plain big ends are another possibility.

5. *Main Bearings*

Main bearings have used plain bearings, ball bearings, roller bearings, needle bearings and so on, usually one of the first two of these options. Plain bearings can perform well. Ball bearings are claimed to be better for starting because the low friction and low wear-rate is maintained at low speed, though starting friction is low in the engine sizes we are concerned with. Ball bearings can also take axial loads efficiently, which may be helpful for the axial load of helical gear output drives, although racing engines usually have spur gears without side thrust.

Figure 5.4.1 shows a crankpin of diameter d_P carrying a conrod force F on an effective moment arm x. The effective crankpin coefficient of friction is μ. The friction force is μF, giving a friction moment about the pin centre of

$$M_F = \frac{1}{2}\mu F d_P$$

The shaft driving input moment is Fx. The output moment is

$$M_O = M_I - M_F$$

The efficiency of the crankpin is therefore

$$\eta_{CP} = \frac{M_O}{M_I}$$

$$= 1 - \frac{\mu d_P}{2x}$$

With an average x of, say, $\frac{1}{4}S$, quarter of the stroke,

$$\eta_{CP} = 1 - \frac{2\mu d_P}{S}$$

For the example engine d_P is 20mm and S is 50mm, so considering a metal-to-metal coefficient of limiting friction of 0.3, then η_P becomes 0.76 (76%). This would obviously be disastrous, because, apart from the loss of output, with 24% of the power being dissipated, there would be immediate overheating and crankpin seizure, which is just what happens if the big end lubrication fails. Of course this analysis is not complete because the crankpin load also includes inertia loading. However, with the pin diameter d_p always being a large fraction of the stroke (0.40 for the example engine, with a usual range 0.3 to 0.4) the pin effective coefficient of friction must be kept very low to allow the engine to operate satisfactorily. In the example above, the coefficient of friction must not exceed 0.012 if losses at the crankpin are to be held down to 1%.

Considering Figures 5.3.1 and 5.4.1 with a crankpin force F_{CB} giving an input moment $M = F_{CB}x$, the friction moment due to the shaft main bearings is

$$M_{FM} = \mu_1 r_1 F_{R1} + \mu_2 r_2 F_{R2}$$

With the same approximations as before, the main bearing efficiency is

$$\eta_{MB} = 1 - \frac{\mu_1 r_1 F_{R1} + \mu_2 r_2 F_{R2}}{\frac{1}{4} F_{CB} S}$$

Considering the simplest case of a symmetrical crank with mainshaft diameter 25mm $(= \frac{1}{2} S)$ and $\mu = 0.3$,

$$\eta_{MB} = 0.70 \quad (70\%)$$

Again, with direct metal friction the efficiency is hopeless. At low engine speed, bearing lubrication is often ineffective, so low speed friction can cause starting problems and poor pick up even if the engine runs well at high speed. Some engines have better lubrication at lower speeds, some at higher speeds.

5.5 Balance

A single cylinder engine is always a vibrator, because there is no practical and economical means to oppose the reciprocating forces. However improving the balance can ease the problem. This is expressed as a percentage, with values ranging from 25% to 75%. The balance of an engine depends on the geometry and masses, rather than speed.

To calculate the balance factor we represent the connecting rod as two masses at the bearing centres, as previously explained.

The effective reciprocating mass, Figure 5.5.1, is

$$m_R = m_P + m_R + m_{WP} + m_{RL}$$

This has a value of 144 g (5.1 oz) for the example engine – about 1.5 kg/litre.

On the crankshaft itself (Figure 5.5.1), there is positive imbalance due to the rod big end mass m_{RB}, and the mass m_{CP} of the crankpin itself. This may be counterbalanced by:

1. Scalloped crank web sides
2. Other relief around crankpin
3. Tungsten inserts opposite the pin

The mass of the crankpin itself and big end are rotating rather than reciprocating, and can be perfectly balanced by counterbalancing. If exactly this balance is provided, then the balance factor is zero. Balance above this is positive. No attempt at balance would be a negative balance factor, not zero. The effective balance mass is then the mass beyond zero balance, considered to act at the crankthrow radius. A positive balance mass can be measured in the following way. With the shaft in free bearings, and the crankpin in the horizontal position for maximum sensitivity, add to the pin a sleeve having the big end mass

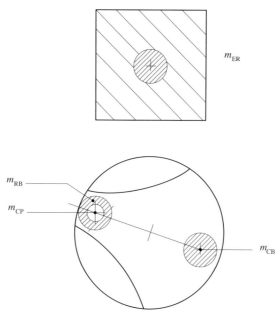

Figure 5.5.1 Balance masses.

as in Figure 5.5.1. Then measure the vertical force to hold the pin from rising, or, more practically, add further weights to the pin until it balances. These surplus weights, above that of the big end, give the value of the positive effective counterbalance mass of the shaft, m_{CBE}. The counterbalance factor is then

$$f_{CB} = \frac{m_{CBE}}{m_{ER}}$$

usually multiplied by 100 to make it a percentage.

The effect of such counterbalancing is as follows. With positive balance, at tdc when the reciprocating-mass inertia-force effectively pulls up on the shaft, the counterbalance pulls down. At bdc, when the reciprocating mass pushes down, the balance mass pulls up. Hence the vertical vibratory force is reduced by a percentage equal to the value of the balance factor. The price paid for this benefit is that the balance mass actually creates imbalance laterally, proportional to the balance factor.

Negative balance factor, arising from the crankpin mass and rod big-end mass with no crank web balance, has nothing to commend it other than simplicity and cheapness. With some web balance, at zero balance factor, the vibration is purely aligned with the cylinder. A 100% balance factor entirely eliminates the vibration along the cylinder, but introduces harsh lateral vibration. The best value to use depends on the sensitivity of the particular installation to vibration in different directions. A minimum workable value for many purposes is 25%. This is not difficult to achieve. A value of 50% is obviously a compromise value giving equal force amplitudes in the two directions (incidentally, and oddly, with the imbalance force vector rotating in the opposite direction from the engine rotation), and 70% as a maximum value for special cases. Careful analysis, with computer simulation, will minimise bearing forces and reduce frictional losses and wear.

With multi-cylinder engines one cylinder can be balanced against another. The external vibration of such engines can be much lower than for single cylinders, though this creates a false impression of the engine internals. The stresses and bearing forces on the connecting rod are not reduced by multi-cylinder balancing, although the shaft main-bearing forces are reduced.

5.6 Mountings

Depending on the installation, the engine is attached by mounting lugs to the vehicle frame or test block, by rigid connection or by compliant rubber mounts (Figure 5.6.1). The parameters are:

1. F_E, the effective vibratory force on the engine (generated internally)
2. m_E, the engine mass
3. K_M, the mounting stiffness
4. m_M, the mounting mass
5. F_M, the force in the mounting (in the engine lugs)

If the mounting stiffness K_M is very low, the engine can vibrate freely, limited only by its own inertia. The mounting force will then be very small, being the motion displacement times the small stiffness.

If the mounting is very stiff the mounting mass and engine will tend to move together. If the mounting mass is small relative to the engine, the vibration amplitude will be large, with the mounting force proportional to the mounting mass.

If the mounting mass m_M is large and the mounting stiffness K_M also great, then the engine and mounting (vehicle frame, air frame, test block) must move together, and the large total inertia will make the engine movement small. The force in the mounting lugs must therefore be more or less equal and opposite to the vibratory force, and therefore will be large.

For large engine vibration amplitudes, the mass of the shaft itself affects the main bearing forces significantly.

The system shown can also resonate. For a large mounting mass there is little

Figure 5.6.1. Vibratory force, engine mass, mounting stiffness and mounting mass diagram for single-degree-of-freedom vibration analysis.

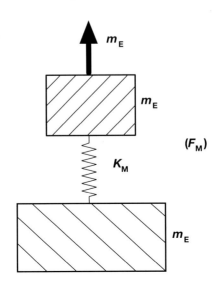

movement of the mounting, so the natural frequency of vibration, at which resonance will occur, is

$$f_N = \frac{1}{2\pi} \sqrt{\frac{K_M}{m_E}}$$

in hertz (cycles per second). More generally, with a mounting mass m_M that is not large relative to the engine,

$$f_N = \frac{1}{2\pi} \sqrt{\frac{K_M (m_E + m_M)}{m_E m_M}}$$

The result of a small mounting mass is therefore a higher natural frequency.

If the engine runs at the natural frequency then resonance will occur, with very large, even catastrophic vibration (Figure 5.6.2). This must be avoided. The natural frequency must be kept outside the normal engine operating speed range.

Mounting compliance reduces the transmission of engine vibration to the vehicle structure. This is more comfortable for passengers, reduces structural stress and noise radiation from the structure. Ideally, the mounting must be soft to keep the natural frequency below the normal operating speed range. Momentary resonance may occur at engine start-up or shut-down.

There are, however, some serious disadvantages in flexible engine mountings. Engine location is less precise, and the engine will vibrate more. Vibration of the engine itself will be least when the engine is rigidly mounted to a rigid massive frame. Engine vibration can be a serious problem, affecting power transmission, and possibly overloading the engine bearings, as explained in the next section. Hence, competition engines are frequently given rigid mountings.

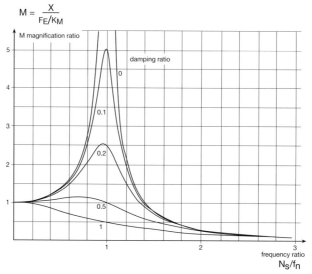

Figure 5.6.2. Magnification ratio for a single degree of freedom system. This is the oscillatory response amplitude of the engine to forces applied to the engine: Vibratory response amplitude divided by F/K versus frequency. An important feature is the existence of resonance. The response is also dependent on the damping ratio of the system.

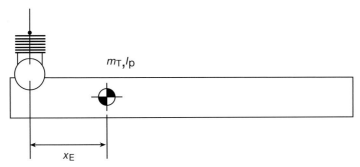

Figure 5.6.3. Engine mass mounted on vehicle mass, offset from centre of gravity. Vertical linear oscillatory force at the engine causes linear vibration plus rotational vibration unrelated to engine torque or torque variations.

The effective inertia (mass) of the vehicle as seen at the engine mountings may be much less than the total vehicle mass, and indeed less than that of the engine itself. For the 'vehicle' of Figure 5.6.3, with total mass m_T and total pitch inertia, about the centre of the mass, I_P (kg.m^2), the engine is positioned at a distance x_E in front of the centre of the mass. A vertical upward force F applied there causes a vertical acceleration F/m_T at the centre of mass but there is also a moment Fx_E which causes a pitch angular acceleration

$$\alpha_P = \frac{Fx_E}{I_P}$$

with a resulting additional vertical acceleration at the engine with value $\alpha_P x_E$. The effective total inertia at the engine is therefore only

$$m_{eff} = \frac{m_T}{1 + \dfrac{x_E^2 m_T}{I_P}}$$

Even a heavy vehicle may contribute little inertia at the engine because of the engine distance x_E from the centre of mass.

The total inertia (engine plus mounting) at the engine will be effectively equal to or greater than the basic engine mass. For a rigid mounting, the greatest engine vibration amplitude will occur for the engine mass alone. To simplify analysis, consider a sinusoidal force variation of amplitude F_V. The vibratory force is not exactly sinusoidal because of the connecting rod geometry, but the approximation is good enough. The peak acceleration (vibratory acceleration amplitude) is

$$A_V = \frac{F_V}{m_T}$$

The vibratory peak velocity (velocity amplitude) is

$$V_V = \frac{A_V}{\Omega_C}$$

and the displacement amplitude is

$$X_V = \frac{V_V}{\Omega_C} = \frac{A_V}{\Omega_C^2}$$

Again, for this simplified analysis, consider the effective force to be due to the reciprocating mass moving sinusoidally, so the force amplitude is

$$F_V = m_{ER} \Omega_C^2 L_C$$

Combining the above, the vibratory displacement amplitude becomes

$$X_V = \frac{F_V}{m_T \Omega_C^2} = \frac{m_{ER} L_C}{m_T}$$

Hence for a non-compliant mounting, the vibratory displacement does not depend on the engine speed, but only on the crank throw L_C ($= \frac{1}{2}S$), the reciprocating mass and the total inertial resisting mass m_T ($\geq m_E$). This result can also be obtained directly from conservation of momentum for the complete engine.

For the example engine (Section 1.5):

$$m_{ER} = 0.144 \text{ kg}$$

L_C	$= 0.025$m	(S = 50mm)
Ω_C	$= 1{,}257$ rad/s	($N_M = 12{,}000$ rpm)
m_T	$= 10.0$ kg	(m_E = 7.0 kg)

giving

F_V	$= 5{,}688$ N	(1,279 lbf)
A_V	$= 569$ m/s^2	(58 g)
V_V	$= 0.453$ m/s	
X_V	$= 0.36$ mm	

Vibration approaching 60 *g* is severe. The motion amplitude of about 0.40 mm is roughly what actually happens. It can only be reduced by reducing the reciprocating mass (lighter piston, gudgeon pin, little end) or by adding weight to the crankcase – not an attractive option for competition use. The small amplitude of 0.40mm shows how rubber bushes can deflect at low stiffness to allow an engine to vibrate in isolation from the vehicle.

With the engine rigidly mounted on a massive test bed, the mounting lugs will be severely loaded, being subject to force F_V to restrain the engine. This could cause distortion or even fatigue failure. The most realistic test conditions occur when the bed mountings simulate the real installation in inertia and stiffness.

5.7 Vibratory Load Forces

The effect of engine vibration on main bearing loads often causes premature failure.

Consider an engine carrying a flywheel or clutch outside its main bearings. This may be perfectly balanced so that its rotation causes no vibration or dynamic forces. The engine bearings support the flywheel weight, but this is a small force relative to the dynamic loads, and is not a problem. In the ideal case of a perfectly balanced electric motor, the motor could now spin up to high speed without additional loads on the bearings. However, a reciprocating engine will vibrate, according to the mountings and inertias, as seen in the previous section. For the example single cylinder engine the vibratory acceleration amplitude was 1,422 m/s^2 and the displacement amplitude was 0.9mm. The flywheel is attached to the shaft, and must vibrate with the engine. The force required to provide the vibrational acceleration of the flywheel is of amplitude

$$F_{FV} = m_F A_V$$

The enormous vibratory acceleration $A_V = 1,422$ m/s^2 must be transmitted to the flywheel by the shaft main bearings. The cantilevered external flywheel makes the individual main bearing forces even worse. Soft mounts make this problem worse by reducing the effective inertia to that of the engine alone, increasing the vibration amplitude.

This is a special problem for single cylinder engines, as multi-cylinders can be balanced to reduce the crankcase vibration. The flywheel's asset is its rotational inertia. Its deficit is its mass – so, where packaging permits, a large diameter for a given mass will help. An unbalanced load causes its own problems, but a perfectly balanced one doesn't eliminate them.

5.8 Torsional Vibration

Linear vibration of the engine along or traverse to the cylinder arises from the mechanical imbalance of the components. As the gas pressure in the cylinder head acts on both the piston and the head, there is no net force on the engine to cause linear vibration, other than a very small effect due to the mass and acceleration of the gas itself.

The gas pressure does, however, produce an output torque on the shaft, which is the purpose of the engine. This torque is highly cyclical in nature, being a large positive effect on the power stroke and generally small (sometimes negative) elsewhere. So, for a single-cylinder engine, there is a strong stimulus at engine frequency to torsional vibration of the complete engine on its mountings, around an axis along the crankshaft. That the two-stroke engine fires every revolution in contrast to the alternate revolution of a four-stroke is a significant advantage. The reciprocating inertia accepts and releases kinetic energy twice per revolution, so a high-speed engine also has a twice-per-revolution torsional reaction vibration.

Resonance must be avoided. Obviously, the problems are specific to the rotational inertia and torsional stiffness of the particular installation.

5.9 Pumping Losses

Crankcase pressure traces for one revolution are shown in Section 7.1.3. Obviously the details vary for different operating speeds. Modelling the crankcase pressure as sinusoidal with amplitude P_{CS}, and with the peak pressure preceding bottom dead centre, by crank angle ϕ, the pressure at crank angle θ_C is

$$P_C = P_{CM} + P_{CS} \cos(\theta + \phi)$$

The total pumping work per cycle, by use of integration, is

$$W_P = \frac{1}{2} \pi \sin(\phi) P_{CS} V_S$$

The loss of bmep against pumping can be expressed as

$$\Delta P_{BMEP} = \frac{1}{2} \pi P_{CS} \sin\phi$$

For $\phi = 0$, there is no pumping loss, which occurs only for the pressure component which leads the piston position by 90°. Realistically, for the example engine, the pressure amplitude P_{CS} is about 40 kPa (6 psi) at an effective angle ϕ of around 50° to 60°. Using 60° gives the bmep loss as about 54 kPa (8psi), which is substantial in relation to the probable total bmep of around 700 kPa (100psi). The pumping work per cycle is 5.3 J, and pumping power 1,060 W (1.42 bhp).

The crankcase pressure variation is not actually sinusoidal. It has higher harmonics, but relatively little work is done against these. The mean crankcase pressure has no effect on the work over a whole cycle.

The pumping work (1,060 W) is dissipated as heat, heating the air by about 50°C, less any heat transfer losses.

The air drawn into the crankcase expands through the throttle and inlet system. Expansion through a valve does not of itself cool a perfect gas, in contrast to expansion against a piston where the gas does work.

5.10 Compression Stroke

The compression work is the work done in compressing the gas trapped in the cylinder, notionally up to top dead centre.

In a nominally polytropic process

$$P = P_1 \left(\frac{V_1}{V} \right)^n$$

where n is the polytropic index, realistically in the range 1.3 to 1.4 for engine compressions. The work done in compression is

$$W_C = \frac{P_2 V_2 - P_1 V_1}{n-1}$$

Our example engine has a trapped swept volume of 54.37 cm^3 and a combustion volume of 10.91 cm^3 for a compression ratio of 10.0. Trapped conditions P_1 and T_1 are 130 kPa and 320°C. Then $V_1 = 65.28$ cm^3 and $V_2 = 10.91$ cm^3, for a compressed $P_2 = 1330$ kPa (193 psi). The compression work is 20.1 J, with a bmep decrement of 204 kPa (30 psi). The averaged power used in compression is 4,020 W (5.4 bhp).

If the engine failed to fire most of this would be recovered in the subsequent expansion, so compression work doesn't usually count as pumping work. As we will see, the assumed trapped pressure of 130 kPa is too small for a very powerful engine, because it requires too much pressure rise at combustion.

The temperature after compression is given by

$$T_{K2} = T_{K1} \left(\frac{V_1}{V_2} \right)^{n-1}$$

where the temperatures must be in absolute values, kelvin in the SI system, otherwise degrees rankine. In kelvin, to convert from celsius,

$$T_K = T_C + 273.15K$$

Hence the compression process has, on the basis of the above figures,

$$T_{K1} = 593.1K$$
$$T_{K2} = 1014.3K$$
$$T_{C2} = 741°C$$

5.11 Power Stroke

For the example engine, the shaft power output is given as 21 kW at 12,000 rpm, a shaft energy yield of 105 J/rev. The mechanical efficiency is stated as 85%, so the indicated power P_I, from

$$P_S = \eta_M P_I$$

is 24.7 kW, yielding an indicated 123.5 J/rev, and the mechanical losses are 18.5 J/rev, a mechanical power dissipation of 3,706W (5.0 bhp) doing the pumping work of 1,060 W plus 2,646 W of frictional heating of the various rings and bearings.

The indicated power is that corresponding to the cylinder pressure and motion of the piston. As the pressures and work done while the ports are open are small, the power stroke from tdc to exhaust opening must yield 143.6 J, to allow the 20.1 J for the compression, leaving 123.5 J indicated output.

For the expansion stroke, after combustion (State 3), from tdc to exhaust opening (State 4),

$$V_3 = 10.91 \text{cm}^3$$

$$V_4 = 65.28 \text{cm}^3$$

$$R_{CT} = 5.98$$

$$n = 1.3$$

$$W_X = 143.6 \text{J}$$

also

$$P_4 = P_3 \left(\frac{V_3}{V_4} \right)^n$$

$$W_X = \frac{P_3 V_3 - P_4 V_4}{n - 1}$$

$$= \frac{P_3 V_3}{n - 1} \left(1 - R_{TC}^{1-n} \right)$$

$$\frac{T_4}{T_3} = \left(\frac{V_3}{V_4} \right)^{n-1}$$

Knowing the work output W_X then the initial pressure must be

$$P_3 = \frac{W_X (n - 1)}{V_3 \left(1 - R_{TC}^{1-n} \right)}$$

which evaluates to

$$P_3 = 9,510 \text{ kPa (1,380 psi)}$$

$$P_4 = 929 \text{ kPa (135 psi)}$$

The pressure at the end of compression came out at 1,330 kPa so, to obtain the required power output, combustion would have to raise the pressure by a factor of 7.15 at tdc. This is much more than is normally achieved in an engine. Therefore the exhaust system must create considerably more pressure before mechanical compression begins. Table 5.11.1 shows the numbers for an assumed trapped pressure of 300 kPa (about 3 atmospheres, so requiring a very active exhaust system). In this table the compression work is allowed to depend on the trapping pressure, so the mechanical efficiency is no longer constant at the assumed value of 0.85. Table 5.11.2 shows how the required combustion pressure ratio varies with the trapped pressure.

Of course, the combustion process lasts for many degrees of crank angle, and the power stroke is not so clearly defined as is assumed for the simplified analysis here. Combustion proceeds simultaneously with the early stages of expansion, so the peak pressures do not reach those indicated by this simple calculation. Also, very high temperatures are not possible because chemical dissociation of the products of combustion further delays the process.

Table 5.11.1. Engine combustion pressure analysis

DATA:

Engine type	=	Demo 98
Engine swept volume	=	98.200 cm^3
Trapped swept volume	=	54.370 cm^3
Combustion volume	=	10.910 cm^3
Shaft power	=	21.000 kW
Shaft speed	=	12.000 krpm
Mechanical efficiency	=	0.850
Trapped pressure	=	300.000 kPa
Trapped temperature	=	400.000 K
Polytropic index compr	=	1.300
Polytropic index expan	=	1.300

ANALYSIS:

Swept vol	=	98.200 cm^3
Combustion vol	=	10.910 cm^3
Capacity	=	109.110 cm^3
Trapped stroke vol	=	54.370 cm^3
Trapped capacity	=	65.280 cm^3
Speed	=	12.000 krpm
Speed	=	0.200 krev/s
Speed	=	1.257 krad/s
Power – shaft	=	21.000 kW
Power – shaft	=	28.112 bhp
Power – indicated	=	24.706 kW
Power – indicated	=	33.073 bhp
Energy/rev – indicated	=	123.529 J

Air specific gas const	=	287.103 J/kg.K
Trapped volume	=	65.280 cm^3
Trapped pressure	=	300.000 kPa
Trapped temp	=	400.000 K
Trapped density	=	2.612 kg/m^3
Trapped mass nominal	=	0.171 g

Compression:

Comp ratio	=	5.984
Polytropic index	=	1.300
Compressed volume	=	10.910 cm^3
Compressed pressure	=	3070.176 kPa
Compressed temp	=	684.143 K
Compression work	=	46.372 J

Combustion:

Compression work	=	46.372 J
Indicated output work	=	123.529 J
Required expansion work	=	169.901 J
Combusted pressure	=	11,248.743 kPa
Combusted temp	=	2,506.613 K
Combustion press ratio	=	3.664

Expansion:

Polytropic index	=	1.300
Expanded pressure	=	1,099.163 kPa
Expanded temp	=	1,465.550 K
Expansion work	=	169.901 J

Table 5.11.2. Variation of required combustion pressure ratio with P1

P1 (kPa)	P3/P2	P4 (kPa)
100.0	8.992	899.2
150.0	6.328	949.2
200.0	4.996	999.2
250.0	4.197	1,049.2
300.0	3.664	1,099.2
350.0	3.283	1,149.2
400.0	2.998	1,199.2

While the mixture is in the closed cylinder, from trapping to exhaust opening, the pressure changes from P_1 to P_4. The exhaust system receives a pressure pulse created by the blowdown from the initial pressure P_4 and must use this to create P_1, the cylinder trapping pressure.

CHAPTER 6:

Fluid Dynamics

6.1 Introduction

The power an engine produces depends largely on the amount of air it consumes. This in turn depends on the flow resistance of the inlet and transfer passages, ports and valves. Carburettor fuel suction is calculated from Bernoulli's equation, flow curvature, compressibility and so on. The effectiveness of the exhaust system depends on pressure pulses.

This chapter presents a brief overview of fluid dynamics relevant to engine operation. That it looks quite mathematical is inevitable, but understanding what is happening and how to calculate for improvements is the key to winning races.

6.2 Air and Exhaust

The basic physical properties of air are its density and viscosity. Thermodynamically, it has specific thermal capacity (specific heat). Gas also has compressibility. Chemically air comprises oxygen and nitrogen, as shown in Table 6.2.1. The gas in the crankcase and transfer passages is laden with fuel vapour and liquid fuel mist. On combustion, the chemical

Table 6.2.1. Standard Properties of Dry Air at Sea Level

Constituents by mass	Nitrogen	(N_2)	0.7553
	Oxygen	(O_2)	0.2314
	Argon	(Ar)	0.0128
	Carbon dioxide	(CO_2)	0.0005
Temperature	T_C	15	°C
	T_K	288.15	K
Pressure (absolute)	P	101,325	Pa
Density	ρ	1.2256	kg/m³
Dynamic viscosity	μ	17.83×10^{-6}	Ns/m²
Kinematic viscosity	ν	14.55×10^{-6}	m²/s
Molar mass	m_m	28.965	kg/mol
Specific gas constant	R_A	287.05	J/kg K
Specific heats	C_P	1,005	J/kg K
	C_V	718	J/kg K
Ratio of specific heats	γ	1.400	-
Thermal conductivity	k	0.02534	W/m K
Speed of sound	V_S	340.6	m/s

Table 6.2.2. Chemical constitution by mass of engine gas (ideal combustion of n-heptane in dry air)

	Intake (air)	Exhaust
Nitrogen	0.7553	0.5500
Oxygen	0.2314	0.0000
Argon	0.0128	0.0116
Carbon dioxide	0.0005	0.2987
Water vapour	0.0000	0.1397

Constituents by volume or mole proportions:

	Intake (air)	Exhaust	MW (molecular mass)
Nitrogen	0.7809	0.5697	28.014
Oxygen	0.2095	0.0000	31.998
Argon	0.0093	0.0084	39.948
Carbon dioxide	0.0003	0.1969	44.009
Water vapour	0.0000	0.2250	18.015

Table 6.2.3. Properties of Water (H_2O)

Constituents by mass:	Hydrogen	0.1119	
	Oxygen	0.8881	
Freezing point	T_F	0.0	°C
Boiling point (1 Ata pressure)	T_B	100.0	°C
Density of water at 4°C	ρ	1,000.0	kg/m^3
Density of water at 15°C	ρ	999.2	kg/m^3
Density of water at 30°C	ρ	995.7	kg/m^3
Dynamic viscosity at 15°C	μ	1.139	MNs/m^2
Kinematic viscosity at 15°C	ν	1.140	Mm^2/s
Molar mass	m_m	18.015	kg/kmol
Specific gas constant	R_W	461.51	J/kg K
Specific thermal capacity at (50°C)	c_P	4,178	J/kg K
Thermal conductivity of water (50°C)	k	0.643	W/m K
(Latent) Energy of boiling (100°C)	h_{fg}	2,257	kJ/kg

constitution is changed, so the exhaust gas is rather different. Table 6.2. gives the results of the ideal combustion of n-heptane, equivalent chemically to gasoline.

The exchange of oxygen for CO_2 and H_2O, of molecular mass 44 and 18, respectively, has a fairly balanced effect on the total average molecular mass, depending on the relative quantities of carbon and hydrogen in the original fuel, and on the completeness of combustion.

Engine power is sensitive to the condition of its intake air. Power corrections are controversial (Appendix E). The simplest concept is that the power depends on the mass of oxygen ingested, which is obviously reduced by low air density due to high temperature or low pressure, or by a high humidity.

There are substantial variations in the temperature and pressure of air, and therefore in its density. Dry air, considered as an ideal gas, obeys the perfect gas equation.

$$P = R_A \rho T_K$$

where $R_A = 287.05$ J/kg K is the specific gas constant for air, ρ is the density and T_K is the absolute (kelvin) temperature:

$$T_K = T_C + 273.15$$

Thus the density is proportional to the pressure and inversely proportional to the absolute temperature. The ambient pressure varies typically ±3 kPa from the mean, or about 3%. The ambient temperature varies by typically 15 K from the mean, 5% of the absolute temperature. Thus at sea level the density can vary by 8% or more, with more variation with altitude, and with temperature. The standard conditions should be seen in this light.

Appendix A gives an accurate method for calculation of density and other properties of air. Where an approximate density will suffice, then it is usual to neglect the water vapour content and to treat the air as a simple ideal gas, giving, in SI units,

$$\rho = \frac{P}{R_A T_K}$$

Within the ambient temperature range the dynamic viscosity is often taken as having a constant value, for example $\mu = 17.8 \times 10^{-6}$ Ns/m^2. The speed of sound, if required, is often taken as constant at $V_s = 340$ m/s.

6.3 Viscosity

The oil content of the fuel provides lubrication. Its most important property is its viscosity at the prevailing temperature. In the bottom end of the engine the oil is cool, possibly even below ambient, but diluted by the fuel. In the upper cylinder, the temperature is high but most of the fuel is vaporised out from the lubricant. The actual operating conditions are therefore uncertain. In general the oil has a viscosity at reference temperature (15°C), and its viscosity index indicating how the viscosity falls as temperature increases. There is a 'flash' temperature above which the oil will oxidise causing lubrication failure.

Table 6.3.1 Example Oil Properties (Basic Mineral Oil)

1.	Density	ρ	≈	800	kg/m^3
2.	Viscosity	μ	≈	40	mPas
3.	Expansion coefficient	$(-d\mu dT)/\rho$	≈	0.1	%/°C
4.	Viscosity index	$(d\mu dP)/\mu$	≈	-2	%/°C
5.	Viscosity-pressure sensitivity	$(d\mu dP)/\mu$	≈	3	%/MPa
6.	Compressibility	$(d\rho/dP)/\mu$	≈	0.04	%/MPa
7.	Thermal capacity	c_P	≈	2.5	kJ/kgK
8.	Thermal conductivity	k	≈	0.15	W/m K

The viscosity of a fluid is its resistance to laminar shearing motion. The viscosity of oils depends on the molecular structure, and is also sensitive to temperature, which can cause problems.

Because of this, the size and nature of the molecular structure determines viscosity. In fact, for oils generally, larger molecules generally mean high viscosity, and also higher density. Viscosity and density are related.

The kinematic viscosity is the dynamic viscosity divided by the density. It is called 'kinematic' simply because its units are m^2/s. The term viscosity alone always means dynamic viscosity.

Over a limited temperature range, the effect of temperature on dynamic viscosity may be represented approximately by:

$$\mu = \mu_1\left[1 - k_{\mu T}\left(T - T_1\right)\right]$$

with $k_{\mu T}$ having value around 0.02/°C or 2%/°C. Typically, a 10°C temperature increase reduces viscosity by 20%.

Because of the large viscosity variation, this is not accurate for the wide range of temperatures relevant to engine use. The viscosity of a liquid over a wide temperature range is typically represented by the de Guzmann Carrancio equation:

$$\mu = \mu_1 e^{E/(RT)}$$

where E is characteristic energy value (in practice 1/3 to 1/4 of the latent heat of vaporisation), R is the universal gas constant, and T is the absolute temperature. This may also be expressed as

$$\log(\mu) = A + \frac{C}{T}$$

This model predicts that the logarithm of viscosity plotted against $1/T$ is a straight line, which proves to be a fairly good approximation for most real oils.

6.4 Continuity

The Principal of Continuity is really a statement of the conservation of mass for a fluid. In steady state the mass flowing into a set space equals the mass flowing out. In unsteady state, the rate of increase of mass inside the control volume is equal to the mass inflow rate minus the mass outflow rate. In other words, mass is not created.

This is the basis of many assumptions in fluid flow analysis, including the idea that in steady state flow the mass flow rate along the inside of a pipe is the same at all transverse sections of the pipe.

A common assumption in many fluid flow problems, often justified, is that the density is constant. With this assumption, the Principle of Continuity can easily be expressed in terms of volume flow rate rather than mass flow rate; the volume of fluid is then conserved, and the volumetric flow rate at each section of the pipe will be the same.

The airflow within an engine is severely unsteady, being cyclical in nature, with large accelerations, and also with significant density variations due to the variations of pressure. The Principle of Continuity as applied to engines in a quantitative sense therefore generally appears as conservation of mass over given processes. For example, the mass of gas transferred from the crankcase to the cylinder through the transfer ports must either appear in the cylinder or be lost elsewhere, such as directly out of the exhaust port.

In a qualitative way, the principle is also applied to volumetric flow within any given passage, such as an inlet or transfer, implying that the flow velocity at any section, for constant density at least, is inversely proportional to the passage cross-sectional area.

Perhaps most importantly, for a flow area A, perpendicular to the flow direction, and a mean flow velocity U, the volumetric flow Q through the section is

$$Q = UA$$

and the mass flow rate is

$$\dot{m} = \rho Q$$

where ρ is the density. In practice, these may be applied in reverse, with an estimated volumetric flow being used to estimate the flow velocity, allowing estimates to be made of frictional pressure losses.

6.5 Reynolds Number

Flow can be laminar (smooth) or turbulent (erratic) depending on the shape and size of the flow passage, the mean flow speed, the fluid properties, and the entry state of the fluid. The Reynolds number predicts the type of flow. For a circular pipe this is given by

$$N_{Re} = \frac{\rho U D}{\mu}$$

where ρ and μ represent the fluid density and viscosity, D is the pipe inner diameter and U is the mean flow speed over the cross-section. For the example engine a representative passage diameter is 20 mm, and gas speeds can be over 100 m/s. For air, with density $\rho = 1.2$ kg/m^3 and viscosity $\mu = 1.8 \times 10^{-6}$ Pa.s, then N_{Re} based on that diameter is over 133,000. Turbulent flow is expected for Reynolds numbers exceeding the much smaller number 4,000, based on pipe diameter. Therefore variations of density or the presence of fuel, or variation of passage cross-sectional shape for a given area, will have no effect on the conclusion that flow can be treated as turbulent.

6.6 Bernoulli's Equation

Bernoulli's equation is a way of expressing the conservation of energy for a flowing fluid. In a steady state condition it may be applied to a series of points along a streamline, provided that the losses are negligible. First, then, the streamline. The relevant two points or sections must be specified.

Bernoulli's equation may then be expressed as

$$P_1 + \frac{1}{2}\rho U_1^2 + \rho g h_1 = P_2 + \frac{1}{2}\rho U_2^2 + \rho g h_2$$

which is a relationship between pressures. For engine gas flow analysis, the potential pressure term $\rho g h$ does not change significantly, so this term may be omitted. Bernoulli's equation then simplifies to

$$P_1 + \frac{1}{2}\rho U_1^2 = P_2 + \frac{1}{2}\rho U_2^2$$

The pressure terminology is:

1. Static pressure P,

2. Dynamic pressure $q = \frac{1}{2}\rho U^2$ at fluid speed U,

3. Stagnation pressure $P_{St} = P + q$

Bernoulli's equation therefore gives a relationship between the static pressure and the flow velocity. The static pressure is the pressure actually experienced by the liquid, including, for example a small bubble being swept along with the fluid. It is also the pressure exerted by the fluid on the walls of a parallel-sided pipe.

Considering flow from a reservoir (i.e. a region of zero or negligible velocity) to a point where there is a velocity U_2, then neglecting losses, Bernoulli's equation gives

$$P_1 - P_2 = \frac{1}{2}\rho U_2^2$$

$$U_2 = \sqrt{\frac{2(P_1 - P_2)}{\rho}}$$

Considering a pressure difference $P_1 - P_2$ equal to 10 kPa (1.5 psi), as may be found in an engine crankcase relative to the cylinder, at a density of 1.2 kg/m^3 the resulting calculated velocity is $U_2 = 129$ m/s (424 ft/s), or about Mach 0.38.

From Bernoulli's equation, a high velocity at a given section is associated with a low static pressure at that section, so for a pipe with a given mass flow rate the sections of small cross-sectional area have a high velocity and a low static pressure. This is the basis of the venturi for carburettor suction of fuel.

Bernoulli's equation may be extended to allow for energy losses between the two sections being analysed:

$$P_1 + \frac{1}{2}\rho U_1^2 = P_2 + \frac{1}{2}\rho U_2^2 + \Delta P_{St}$$

where ΔP_{St} is the loss of stagnation pressure arising from friction at the walls, energy dissipation due to extra turbulence at bends, etc.

The pressure loss ΔP_{St} is normally related to some particular dynamic pressure

$$q = \frac{1}{2}\rho U^2$$

by the loss coefficient K:

$$\Delta P_{St} = Kq = K\frac{1}{2}\rho U^2$$

Obviously the loss coefficient in any particular case depends not just on the pressure loss but also on the particular reference dynamic pressure, which must be specified. For a pipe or other channel of uniform cross-sectional area, this is based on the mean speed at that cross-sectional area. With gas velocities around 100 m/s there is potential for large frictional losses.

6.7 Pipe Flow

Fluid flow in simple circular pipes has been extensively studied, and this provides some guidance on flow in passages of more complex cross-sections, such as inlet and transfer passages or exhaust pipes.

As explained in 6.5, there are two types of flow, laminar and turbulent. The criterion for this is the Reynolds number

$$N_{Re} = \frac{\rho U D}{\mu}$$

with, for circular or approximately circular section,

$$N_{Re} < 2,000 \quad \text{Laminar flow}$$
$$N_{Re} > 4,000 \quad \text{Turbulent flow}$$

Whether the flow is laminar or turbulent between 2,000 and 4,000 depends on whether it is already turbulent at the entrance to the pipe, or whether the pipe contains bends or other abnormal shaping.

For turbulent flow, the pressure drop along a pipe is approximately proportional to the square of the mean velocity. Therefore the following parameters are useful. The volumetric flow rate is Q in a passage of cross-sectional area A.

The mean speed is

$$U = \frac{Q}{A}$$

The reference dynamic pressure is

$$q = \frac{1}{2}\rho U^2 = \frac{\rho Q^2}{2A^2}$$

The stagnation pressure loss is

$$\Delta P_{St} = Kq$$

where K is the pressure loss coefficient. The pressure loss is a loss of stagnation pressure, but for a pipe of constant cross-sectional area ΔP_{St} is seen directly as the change of static pressure, because the dynamic pressure is constant.

The pressure loss coefficient K associated with a straight run of pipe is related to the pipe friction factor by

$$K = f\frac{L}{D}$$

The value of f may be obtained from various equations or charts.

In turbulent flow, the loss coefficient is sensitive to both Reynolds number and surface roughness. The latter factor is expressed by an effective roughness for the surface, and by relative roughness e/D for a particular pipe. Values of surface roughness vary considerably. For good machining, the effective value should be better than 5×10^{-6} m. Drawn metal tubing is typically 1.5×10^{-6} m, whilst sandcast surfaces can be 100×10^{-6} m or even worse.

The dependence of friction factor f on N_{Re} and e/D may be read from a Moody diagram (Figure 6.7.1). Alternatively, several equations are available to evaluate f, all simply empirical, unlike laminar flow analysis.

Moody's equation is adequate for most purposes, giving the friction factor as

$$f = 0.0055\left[1 + \left(20000\frac{e}{D} + \frac{10^6}{N_{Re}}\right)^{1/3}\right]$$

As a matter of interest, to avoid the static pressure loss consequent upon the stagnation pressure loss due to friction, a pipe with slight outward taper may be used. This requires a diametral increase x given by

$$\frac{x}{L} = \frac{1}{4}f$$

so the taper required is a total included angle of about half a degree.

The Moody diagram (Figure 6.7.1) implies that surface roughness values, especially for sand castings, could create significant additional resistance. Practically speaking, polishing of passages to increase power output remains controversial.

For non-circular cross-sections with turbulent flow, the concept of the hydraulic diameter is used. This is defined as

$$D_H = \frac{4A}{C}$$

where, for a gas, A is simply the pipe cross-sectional area and C is the circumference. The earlier analysis for turbulent flow then proceeds using D_H instead of a circular D. In other

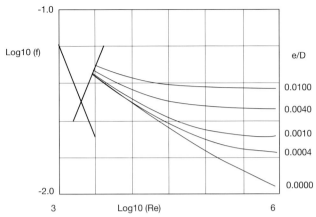

Figure 6.7.1. Pipe friction factor. (Moody diagram)

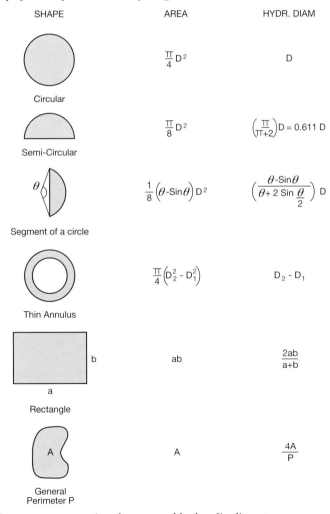

SHAPE	AREA	HYDR. DIAM
Circular	$\frac{\pi}{4}D^2$	D
Semi-Circular	$\frac{\pi}{8}D^2$	$\left(\frac{\pi}{\pi+2}\right)D = 0.611\,D$
Segment of a circle	$\frac{1}{8}\left(\theta - \sin\theta\right)D^2$	$\left(\frac{\theta - \sin\theta}{\theta + 2\sin\frac{\theta}{2}}\right)D$
Thin Annulus	$\frac{\pi}{4}\left(D_2^2 - D_1^2\right)$	$D_2 - D_1$
Rectangle	ab	$\frac{2ab}{a+b}$
General Perimeter P	A	$\frac{4A}{P}$

Figure 6.7.2. Passage cross-sectional areas and hydraulic diameters.

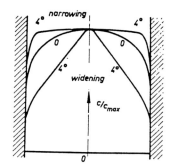

Figure 6.7.3. Change of turbulent velocity profile (0°) caused by the flow acceleration of a convergent pipe (4° narrowing) or flow deceleration (4° widening). Excessive widening causes the flow to separate from the wall, with the formation of a jet within the pipe. (Jante, SAE 660468).

words, the non-circular section is assumed to behave like a circular section of diameter D_H. Figure 6.7.2 gives some example sections.

For a circular section, $D_H = D$.

For a rectangle a by b

$$D_H = \frac{2\,ab}{(a+b)}$$

For a square side of a,

$$D_H = \frac{4a^2}{4a} = a$$

For other values see fluid dynamics handbooks such as Blevins (1984).

For a given cross-sectional area, the least loss is obtained by the greatest hydraulic diameter, which means a circular passage. However, this is often impractical, as in the case of transfer passages.

The mean velocity profile of turbulent flow in a pipe is typically given by

$$\frac{V}{V_{max}} = \left(\frac{y}{R}\right)^{1/7}$$

where V_{max} is the centreline mean velocity, and y is the distance in from the pipe wall towards the centre. The 1/7 factor is purely empirical. The exact value actually depends on the Reynolds number. For a pipe tapering in or out this profile is considerably modified, as shown in Figure 6.7.3.

6.8 Other Losses
Apart from the basic friction loss at the walls of a passage, additional pressure losses arise from:

1. Entry
2. Bends
3. Change of section
4. The exit

These are dealt with by obtaining a *K* value for each feature, and summing the pressure losses for the complete passage, including basic pipe friction. Information on these extra losses may be found in handbooks, frequently under the title of 'minor losses'. They may indeed be minor losses for a long pipeline, but they are very important for the passages in engines. The *K* values themselves can only be added if they are based on the same velocity.

1. Entry loss
Additional entry loss arises from two possible causes. The stable velocity profile has to develop from an initial uniform velocity, with high surface shear stress. Also there may be flow separation due to entry shape. There is, therefore, a minimum entry *K* of about 0.1 for a bellmouthed entry with edge radius *r* not less than *D*/6. Other shapes are worse, depending on the details, Figure 6.8.1. A conical entry is easy to machine consistently, and usually quite effective. A radiused entry is best of all.

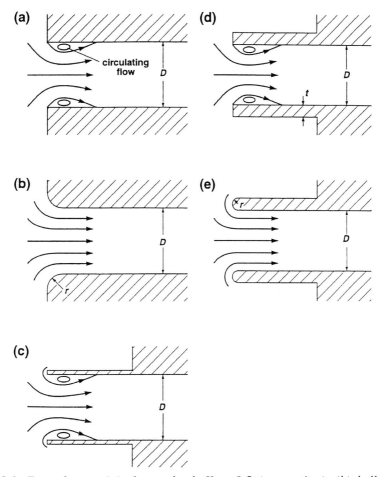

Figure 6.8.1. Entry losses. (a) sharp-edged, K = 0.5 (separation), (b) bell-mouthed, r>= 0.14D, K= 0.10 (no separation), (c) sharp, re-entrant, K= 1.0 (separation), (d) sharp, thick-edged, re-entrant, t > 0.05D, K = 0.5 (separation as in (a) above), (e) rounded, re-entrant, r > 0.14D, K = 0.10 (no separation).

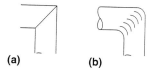

(a)   (b)

Figure 6.8.2. Sharp corner losses. (a) K = 1.1, (b) K= 0.2.

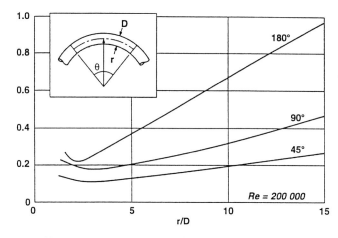

Figure 6.8.3. Loss coefficient for smooth bends.

2. *Bends*
A sharp ('mitred') bend has K = 1.1, Figure 6.8.2. This is greatly reduced by a smooth radius, Figure 6.8.3.

3. *Change of section*
A sharp-edged contraction from A_1 to A_2, as in Figure 6.8.4, gives

$$K = 0.50\left(1 - \frac{A_2}{A_1}\right)$$

$$\Delta P_{St} = Kq_2$$

The above is a purely empirical equation for K, usually accurate to within 0.03.

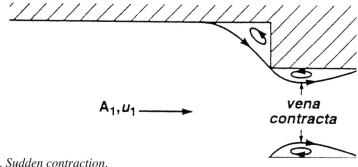

$A_1, u_1 \longrightarrow$

vena
contracta

Figure 6.8.4. Sudden contraction.

A sharp-edged sudden expansion, as in Figure 6.8.5, gives

$$K = \left(1 - \frac{A_1}{A_2}\right)^2$$

$$\Delta P_{St} = K q_1$$

This result is obtained from a theoretical analysis including continuity, momentum and energy, and is quite accurate. Although there is a stagnation pressure loss, the static pressure increases, and is easily found by the extended Bernoulli equation, giving

$$P_2 - P_1 = \eta_R q_1$$

Where η_R is the static pressure recovery coefficient, i.e.

$$\eta_R \equiv \frac{P_2 - P_1}{q_1}$$

with

$$\eta_R \equiv 2\left(\frac{A_1}{A_2}\right) - 2\left(\frac{A_1}{A_2}\right)^2$$

or

$$\eta_R = 1\left(\frac{A_1}{A_2}\right)^2 - \left(1 - \frac{A_1}{A_2}\right)^2$$

Considered as a static pressure recovering stepped diffuser, the diffuser recovery coefficient η_D, to be distinguished from η_R, is defined as

$$\eta_D \equiv \frac{P_2 - P_1}{q_1 - q_2}$$

$$= \frac{\eta_R q_1}{q_1 - q_2}$$

$$= \frac{\eta_R}{1 - q_2/q_1}$$

$$= \frac{\eta_R}{\left(1 - \left(\frac{A_1}{A_2}\right)^2\right)}$$

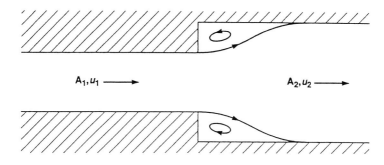

Figure 6.8.5. Sudden expansion.

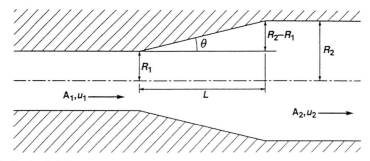

Figure 6.8.6. Conical diffuser.

A conical, or other smooth shape, gives the most efficient pressure recovery, as in Figure 6.8.6. The stagnation pressure loss is

$$\Delta P_{St} = K q_1$$

$$= \left(1 - \frac{A_1}{A_2}\right)^2 \varepsilon \, q_1$$

where ε is called the diffuser loss factor. It has a value of 1.0 for a sharp step, but not much less for a good diffuser design. Therefore

$$K = \left(1 - \frac{A_1}{A_2}\right)^2 \varepsilon$$

For a reasonably good conical diffuser, the conical half angle θ is in the range $2°$ to $10°$, in which case

$$\varepsilon = 0.140 + 0.0066 \left(\theta - 3.5°\right)^2$$

Actually the optimum θ ($3.5°$) and minimum ε (0.140) are somewhat dependent upon Reynolds number and surface finish.

The recovery coefficient, from Bernoulli's equation, becomes

$$\eta_R = 1 - \left(\frac{A_1}{A_2}\right)^2 - K$$

$$\eta_R = 1 - \left(\frac{A_1}{A_2}\right)^2 - \varepsilon \left(1 - \frac{A_1}{A_2}\right)^2$$

4. Exit Loss

At the exit plane of a pipe, entering a large area 'reservoir', the fluid has the specific flow kinetic energy per unit mass $\frac{1}{2}U^2$ (J/kg) and kinetic energy per unit volume $\frac{1}{2}U^2$. This energy is then dissipated by turbulence of the jet into the bulk of fluid in the reservoir, with the fluid eventually reaching negligible speed and kinetic energy. The exit mechanical kinetic energy per unit mass $\frac{1}{2}U^2$ is therefore lost, becoming thermal energy. However, whether it appears as a loss in the application of the extended Bernoulli equation depends upon the choice made for the end of the streamline or steamtube under analysis. If Section 2 is at the exit plane then the energy has not yet been lost, it is merely the $\frac{1}{2}U_2^2$ term of the final stagnation pressure, and should not be included in the losses. On the other hand, if the streamline is chosen to pass into the bulk of fluid in the reservoir, then it appears as lost energy. The final speed is then $U_2 = 0$, with $\frac{1}{2}U_2^2 = 0$, and the dissipated energy must be included in the losses. In that case, the loss coefficient based on exit speed is $K = 1.0$. This condition arises, for example, for inlet flow to the crankcase, and for transfer flow into the cylinder. These are not true reservoirs, and the exit energy may not be fully dissipated.

When a pipe is extremely short, less than ten diameters in length, as for most engine passages, the so-called 'minor' losses dominate. Indeed a simple hole of notionally zero length has only 'minor' losses. Such a single hole or short pipe is called an orifice.

Data for some cases may be found in fluid dynamics handbooks, e.g. Blevins (1984) or Idelchik (1986), but the range of possible geometries is very great and complete design data is not available.

For an orifice of cross-sectional area A and pressure difference P flowing an incompressible zero-viscosity fluid of density ρ, the theoretical ideal speed realised is given by

$$U = \sqrt{\frac{2P}{\rho}}$$

The actual volumetric flow rate is

$$Q = C_d A \sqrt{\frac{2P}{\rho}}$$

where C_d is the discharge coefficient. Alternatively, the dynamic pressure loss coefficient K is given by

$$\Delta P_{St} = K\frac{1}{2}\rho U^2 = K\frac{1}{2}\rho\left(\frac{Q}{A}\right)^2$$

Therefore

$$K = \frac{1}{C_d^2} \quad \text{and} \quad C_d = \frac{1}{\sqrt{K}}$$

In the above equations, K includes the exit loss. Published investigations of orifice flow may be expressed in terms of K or C_d, which depend on the geometry and Reynolds number.

Transfer and inlet passages have a length equal to several hydraulic diameters, so a very useful investigation is that by Licharowicz, Duggins and Markland [1965], of the discharge coefficient of circular cylindrical sharp-edged orifices with L/D ratios of 0.5 to 10 and Reynolds numbers from 10 to 10^5. One notable result is that the discharge coefficient increases from 0.61 to 0.81 (at $\mathrm{Re} > 2 \times 10^4$) as L/D increases from zero to 2; thus in this range the resistance falls considerably as the length increases, because there is a diffuser effect with reattachment and pressure recovery.

For Reynolds number $> 2 \times 10^4$, C_d is given, within about 2 per cent, by

$$C_d = 0.61 + 0.16(L/D)^2 \qquad \text{for } 0 < L/D <= 1$$
$$C_d = 0.730 + 0.040(L/D) \qquad \text{for } 1 < L/D < 2$$
$$C_d = 0.827 + 0.0085(L/D) \quad \text{for } L/D >= 2$$

The discharge coefficient C_d tends to be unstable for L/D around 0.5. The above C_d values reduce substantially as Reynolds number decreases.

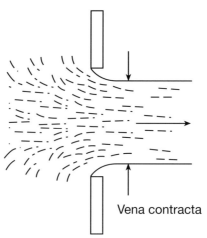

Vena contracta

Figure 6.9.1. The 'vena contracta'.

Figure 6.9.1 shows how fluid emanates from an orifice. There is a section called the *vena contracta*, at which the flow cross-sectional area is a minimum and the mean speed is a maximum. The cross-sectional area of the *vena contracta* is

$$A_{VC} = C_A A_O$$

where A_O is the orifice area and C_A is called the area coefficient. The velocity at the *vena contracta* is

$$V_{VC} = C_V V_{Th}$$

where V_{Th} is the basic theoretical speed

$$\sqrt{2P/\rho}$$

from Bernoulli's equation for constant density, and C_V is called the velocity coefficient. The discharge coefficient is therefore

$$C_d = C_A C_V$$

To obtain the greatest flow, both C_A and C_V need to be maximised, for example, by suitable radiusing of the entry. Figure 6.9.2 gives some example discharge coefficients.

The effective area A_E of a port is the area that would have the actual pressure loss with ideal flow. Therefore

$$\frac{1}{2}\rho\left(\frac{Q}{A_E}\right)^2 = K\frac{1}{2}\rho\left(\frac{Q}{A}\right)^2$$

$$A_E = \frac{A}{\sqrt{K}}$$

$$A_E = C_d A$$

For two or more ports in parallel (as with transfer ports), the total effective area is just the sum of the individual effective areas:

$$A_E = A_{E1} + A_{E2} + ...$$

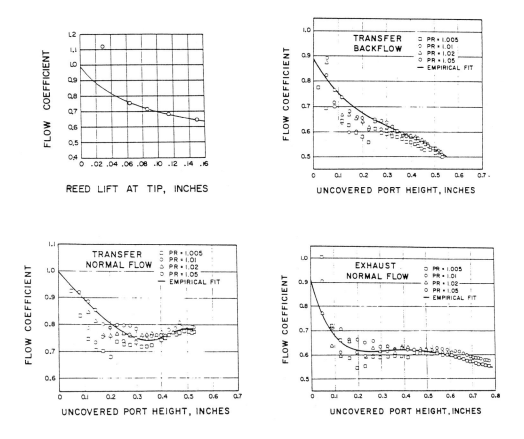

Figure 6.9.2. Example port discharge coefficients (Krieger, Booy & Uyehara, SAE 690135, 1969).

For two or more ports in series, there is a single effective area that gives the same total pressure loss. The pressures are

$$\frac{1}{2}\rho\left(\frac{Q}{A_E}\right)^2 = \frac{1}{2}\rho\left(\frac{Q}{A_{E1}}\right)^2 + \frac{1}{2}\rho\left(\frac{Q}{A_{E2}}\right)^2 + ...$$

So the effective area is given by

$$\frac{1}{A_E^2} = \frac{1}{A_{E1}^2} + \frac{1}{A_{E2}^2} + ...$$

This is sometimes applied to transfer and exhaust ports to obtain an effective combined size during scavenging.

6.10   Jets

Fluid issuing at high speed from a hole forms a turbulent jet, as shown in Figure 6.10.1. Unconstrained jets of this kind are called free jets. The transfer streams in an engine cylinder are similar, but partially constrained by cylinder walls.

113

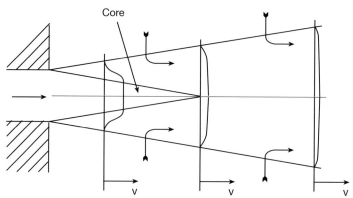

Figure 6.10.1 Turbulent free jet diverging at 15 degrees total included angle, with velocity profiles.

Figure 6.10.2 Spreading and thinning of a free jet striking a solid surface.

Figure 6.10.3. Coanda effect. A jet tends to deflect around a convex surface.

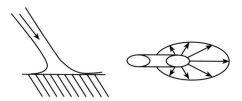

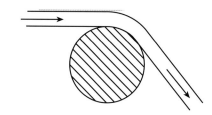

The jet of Figure 6.10.1. has certain characteristics, including:

1. Expansion at total included angle of about 15°.
2. A tapering pure core with a length about six times the inlet hole width.
3. A mixed region with purity varying from 100% at the core to zero at the outer edge.
4. Velocity profiles as shown, becoming wider and shallower.
5. Exterior entrainment into the jet as shown by arrows.

A jet striking a solid surface tends to spread over the surface, becoming a thin wide sheet, as shown in Figure 6.10.2.

A jet passing close to a convex curved surface is deflected around the curve. This is called Coanda effect. It occurs because the jet itself pumps ambient air away from the inner side of the jet, lowering the pressure there. The resulting pressure difference across the jet causes it to bend.

6.11 Pressure Steps

In Figure 6.11.1, a graph of pressure against position for gas in a pipe, there is a step change of the pressure, propagating to the right. Something like this is produced in the exhaust header pipe during blowdown. On the right of the step is stationary gas with the following initial conditions: velocity $U_1 = 0$ absolute pressure R, absolute temperature T_1, and density ρ_1. Behind the step are new conditions, subscript 2, with, in particular, a velocity U_2 towards the step, necessary to provide the extra mass as the step, with its increased density, propagates forwards.

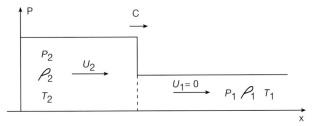

Figure 6.11.1 A propagating pressure front.

For a small pressure step (i.e. $P_2 - P_1 \ll P_1$), the velocity of pulse propagation is the velocity of sound or sonic velocity, given by

$$V_S = \sqrt{\frac{\gamma P_1}{\rho_1}} = \sqrt{\gamma R T_1}$$

where γ is the ratio of specific heats of the gas, 1.4 for air, and R is the gas constant, 287.05 J/kg K for air. These are obviously equivalent expressions, because, for an effectively perfect gas, $P = \rho RT$. For air in standard conditions (Table 6.2.1) the speed of sound is 340.6 m/s (1,117 ft/s). For the exhaust, the gas constant may be somewhat different because the relative molecular mass (molecular weight) of the exhaust products depends somewhat on the particular fuel and on the degree of completion of combustion to CO_2 rather than just to CO. However, the velocity of sound in the exhaust depends more critically on the temperature there. At 600°C, which is 973.1 K, the speed of sound for air becomes 592 m/s. The temperature varies significantly through the exhaust.

For a large pressure step, i.e. $P_2 - P_1$ large in relation to P_1, the speed of the pulse is greater than the speed of sound. In fact, the speed depends on the conditions behind the step rather than those in front of it. A small wavelet of pressure on top of the high-pressure region will have its own local speed of sound, depending on the conditions behind the step. This proves to be the speed of the step itself so

$$C = \sqrt{\frac{\gamma P_2}{\rho_2}} = \sqrt{\gamma R T_2}$$

which happens to be virtually equal to the value in front of the step for sonic (small step) conditions only. The step itself is an adiabatic compression (zero heat transfer), with PV^{γ} constant, so

$$\frac{P_2}{\rho_2^{\gamma}} = \frac{P_1}{\rho_1^{\gamma}}$$

$$\frac{C}{V_{S1}} = \sqrt{\frac{P_2/\rho_2}{P_1/\rho_1}} = \left(\frac{\rho_2}{\rho_1}\right)^{(\gamma-1)/2} = \left(\frac{P_2}{P_1}\right)^{\frac{\gamma-1}{2\gamma}}$$

For air with $\gamma = 1.4$,

$$\frac{\gamma - 1}{2\gamma} = \frac{1}{7}$$

so the pulse velocity increases with the seventh root of the pressure ratio. Exhaust pulses can easily have a pressure ratio of 1.5 with a velocity increase of 6%. The factor of 1/7 is mathematically exact for $\gamma = 1.4$, but this gamma value is itself a slight approximation.

115

The flow velocity U_2 behind the step may be evaluated as follows. The pipe cross-sectional area is A. In time t the front advances $x = Ct$. Therefore a volume

$$V = Ax = ACt$$

requires a density increase from ρ_1 to ρ_2, and requires a mass inflow.

$$m = V(\rho_2 - \rho_1) = ACt(\rho_2 - \rho_1)$$

The actual mass inflow due to velocity U_2 is

$$m = \rho_2 A U_2 t$$

Equating the expressions for the mass inflow gives

$$U_2 = \left(\frac{\rho_2 - \rho_1}{\rho_2} \right) C$$

Therefore, for a sonic step with small density change, the physical flow velocity is a correspondingly small fraction of the velocity of sound. For a realistic exhaust pulse with $\rho_2 - \rho_1$ equal to 30% of ρ_1 then U_2, the actual gas velocity, is about 100 m/s.

The propagating front causes a temperature increase due to the adiabatic compression, for which

$$\frac{T_2}{T_1} = \left(\frac{\rho_2}{\rho_1} \right)^{\gamma-1} = \left(\frac{P_2}{P_1} \right)^{\frac{\gamma-1}{\gamma}}$$

For air, $(\gamma - 1) / \gamma = 0.286 \ (= 2/7)$. The above equation applies to absolute temperature. Therefore the above pressure step of 30% density increase will give an 11% increase of absolute temperature, say by 60 degrees K or Celsius (Centigrade).

As a matter of interest, Wallace and Mitchell give the particle velocity of a plane wave as

$$U = 5C \left[\left(\frac{P}{P_0} \right)^{1/7} - 1 \right]$$

and the wave propagation velocity as

$$C = C_0 \left[6 \left(\frac{P}{P_0} \right)^{1/7} - 5 \right]$$

When a shock front forms, this has a velocity

$$C_S = C_0 \sqrt{ \frac{6 \left(\dfrac{P}{P_0} \right) + 1}{7} }$$

6.12 Pressure Pulses

When exhaust gas enters the exhaust system from the cylinder, it creates a wave which then moves along the system, with various reflections. This may interact with residual pressure effects of the previous cycle. However, the basic model of exhaust action is based on the solitary wave, or pulse, and its reflections, in contrast to the periodic waves normally considered in acoustic theory.

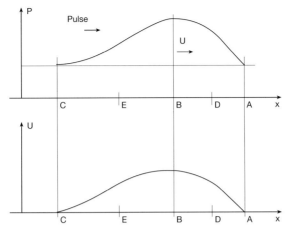

Figure 6.12.1 Propagation of a pressure pulse.

Figure 6.12.1 shows a propagating pulse, with its associated physical flow velocities, which follow from a similar line of argument to that of the wave front of the previous section.

At the instant shown, between A and B the pressure at a fixed point such as D is rising as the pulse advances. At E, between B and C, the pressure is falling with time.

For the density to rise at any point, the local mass inflow rate must exceed the outflow rate. By analysing a short section of length dx, the local rate of density change can be shown to be

$$\frac{d\rho}{dt} = \frac{d}{dx}(\rho U)$$

To simplify this, consider a small amplitude pulse (sonic pulse) with nearly constant density ρ.

$$\frac{d\rho}{dt} \approx \rho \frac{dU}{dx}$$

$$\frac{dU}{dx} \approx \frac{1}{\rho} \frac{d\rho}{dt}$$

The sonic wave propagates at velocity C, assuming constant shape, so

$$\frac{d\rho}{dt} = C \frac{d\rho}{dx}$$

so finally

$$\frac{dU}{dx} = \frac{C}{\rho} \frac{d\rho}{dx}$$

The local flow velocity gradient therefore varies with position x in proportion to the density gradient in the wave.

The velocity profile of the wave is therefore similar in shape to the pressure and density profiles. The peak velocity occurs at the peak density.

Pressure pulses of significant amplitude (non-sonic) do not actually propagate with constant shape. Because the propagation velocity is greater at higher local pressures, the peak of the wave will catch up with the front edge. This is apparent from consideration of the velocity of small wavelets, having a speed dependent on the local speed of sound. Points A and C will propagate at sonic velocity but point B will be faster by the seventh root of the pressure ratio. Therefore the peak advances faster, and the front edge will become steeper, and the rear edge shallower, and in due course a shock wave will form at the front (an essentially instantaneous change of pressure). For a 10% higher speed at B, this will occur whilst A propagates ten times the initial length of AB. This is of practical significance in exhaust systems.

In contrast, a solitary suction wave will have a peak that moves slowly, so the front edge will be softened, but the rear edge will become steeper as it propagates.

As the wave of Figure 6.12.1 passes a given point, the velocity varies in time, and there is a cumulative displacement of gas to the right. After the wave has passed, conditions have returned to the start as far as P, ρ, T and U are concerned, but there has been a displacement of material, to provide the extra mass of gas within the solitary wave. This extra mass in the wave is

$$m_{\mathrm{w}} = \int_{A}^{C} (\rho_2 - \rho_1) A \, dx$$

where A is the pipe cross-sectional area. The resulting final displacement x_{w} is given by

$$x_{\mathrm{w}} A \rho_1 = m_{\mathrm{w}}$$

$$x_{\mathrm{w}} = \int_{A}^{C} \left(\frac{\rho_2}{\rho_1} - 1 \right) dx$$

6.13 Pulse Reflections

In exhaust systems, the primary solitary exhaust wave gives rise to reflections of positive (pressure) and negative (suction) waves due to changes of pipe cross-sectional area. In general, the wave energy incident at any section of an exhaust system will be transmitted, reflected or dissipated. These three energy factors are usually represented by (τ, ρ, δ) (tau, rho, delta) respectively, with the principle of conservation of energy being expressed by

$$\tau + \rho + \delta = 1$$

(6.13.1)

Wave reshaping and other complex behaviour often takes place. Silencers (mufflers) are designed to reduce the sound finally emitted, by introducing multiple reflections and dissipations. Power-improving exhaust systems are generally intended to have low dissipation with maximum efficiency of controlled reflections.

A pulse propagating along a pipe is normally considered to be uniform across the cross-section. Obviously this is an approximation because of friction and heat transfer at the walls. Reflections occur because of changes of cross-sectional area. The usual method of computer simulation is to assume uniform conditions across the section, but this neglects the important fact that the flow can become non-parallel in a tapered section. A taper is commonly treated as equivalent to a series of small steps of diameter, with the reflection and transmission dependent on the area ratio for the incremental step, assuming the pressure wave remains planar.

But this is wrong for two reasons:

1. In the case of a pipe into a conical diffuser, the pressure front converts from planar to spherical, centred on the apex. Further propagation of the correct spherical wave then gives no further reflection in a cone.

2. For a convergent cone, this reflection is not axially back towards the source from the whole plane, as assumed, but occurs at the wall only, i.e. around the edges of the cross-section. These edge reflections at any one section act as the effective source of a new ring (toroidal) wave, which travels in all directions away from its source. The combination of all these toroidal waves and their subsequent reflections form the reflected pulse. The whole pulse reflection therefore only occurs after multiple local reflections.

Various types of pipe area variation are given in Figure 6.13.1.

Figure 6.13.1. Pipe area variations.

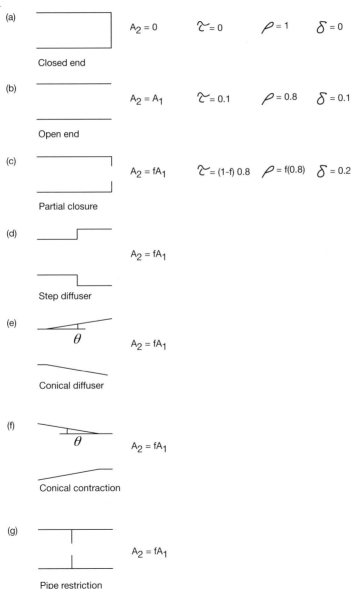

(a) Closed end — $A_2 = 0$ $\tau = 0$ $\rho = 1$ $\delta = 0$

(b) Open end — $A_2 = A_1$ $\tau = 0.1$ $\rho = 0.8$ $\delta = 0.1$

(c) Partial closure — $A_2 = fA_1$ $\tau = (1\text{-}f)\,0.8$ $\rho = f(0.8)$ $\delta = 0.2$

(d) Step diffuser — $A_2 = fA_1$

(e) Conical diffuser — θ $A_2 = fA_1$

(f) Conical contraction — θ $A_2 = fA_1$

(g) Pipe restriction — $A_2 = fA_1$

1. Closed End

The most basic reflection occurs at a solid flat end. This gives a highly efficient positive reflection ($\delta = 0$) of the wave in the original form. The flat end experiences a pressure equal to twice that of the approaching wave, this being, notionally, the sum of the approaching and reflected waves.

2. Open End

The open end reflects a wave of reversed sign, a positive pressure approach wave being reflected as a suction wave, and vice versa. For a practical engine pulse the energy reflection is 80% to 90%. The remainder is dissipated or transmitted, some as noise if this is a tail pipe. The reflection occurs because the incident wave, on reaching the end, can over-expand, thereby drawing excess gas out of the pipe and creating the reversed-sign return wave.

In steady flow, the corresponding behaviour is a simple exterior dissipation in a jet, with the static pressure before the exit being equal to the exterior static pressure. The radial over-expansion of the pulse is therefore associated with its static pressure rather than with the axial velocity of its contents.

3. Partially-closed End

The end of a pipe can be partially closed, either by welding on a washer or by fishtailing it. The ratio of exit area over pipe cross-sectional area is

$$f = \frac{A_2}{A_1}$$

The solid part tries to reflect a positive wave and the open area tries to reflect a negative wave, these two reflections interfering. Some results seem to confirm that at an area ratio of about 0.5 the total reflection is eliminated. However, other results indicate that the reflected negative wave is slightly delayed, so there is then a reflected wave with a leading positive section and a trailing negative section, which can further separate as it propagates because of the 1/7 pressure-velocity relationship, Figure 6.13.2.

4. Stepped Diffuser

The area ratio is $f = A_2 / A_1$. There is a reflected reversed-sign wave with intensity dependent on the area ratio. At $f = 1$ there is no step and all energy is transmitted. At $f = \infty$ it becomes an open end. For $f > 2$ it is practically equivalent to an open end.

5. Conical Diffuser

The incident planar wave becomes a spherical wave, the transformation process creating a reflection wave with pressure of reversed sign. The spherical wave then proceeds down the cone without creating any further reflection. Transformation is notionally never complete, but practically occurs for an axial distance x large relative to the entry diameter. The intensity of reflection depends on the effective rate of change of area with length, and on the mismatch between the flow direction and the wall angle, and is most intense in the entry area, diminishing as the flow adapts. In practice the entry shape is critical, especially due to sharpness of the edge and manufacturing faults, as found for steady state diffusers. Flow separation at the entry causes poorer performance, so the diffuser angle of a simple cone must be fairly small, at most 6 degrees.

6. Radiused-profile Diffuser

The smooth entry discourages flow separation. The continuing expansion due to the local cone angle continuously stresses the flow giving continued expansion and reversed-sign reflection. Therefore the reflection is more widely spread in time and position than for the conical diffuser. The smooth shape is generally more efficient than a discontinuous wall angle, so energy dissipation is less.

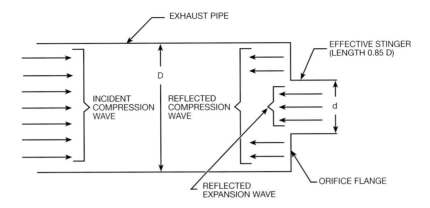

Wave reflection from an orifice

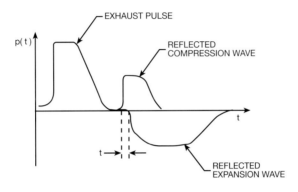

Reflected wave shapes from an orifice

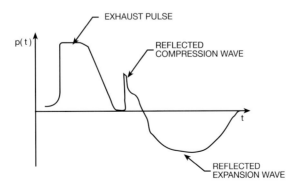

Compression and expansion waves combined

Figure 6.13.2. Reflection of a pressure pulse from a partially closed end. (Murphy and Margolis, SAE 780708).

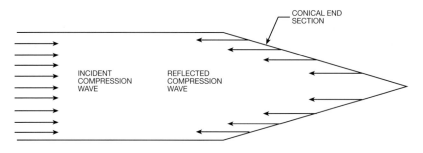

Continuous reflection from a cone

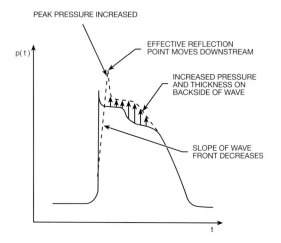

Effect of decreasing cone angle (180° - 40°)

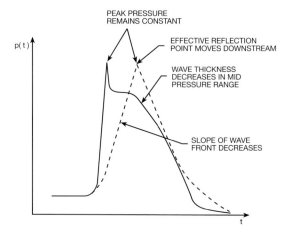

Effect of decreasing cone angle (40° - 10°)

Figure 6.13.3. Pressure pulse reflection at a converging cone. (Murphy and Margolis, SAE 780708).

7. Conical Contraction

The conical contraction reduces the diameter, possibly to zero. This can be considered to be a variation of the flat closed end. The actual mechanism of reflection is highly complex because where the wave edges strike the wall and are reflected, they act as a source of a new wave, and do not reflect directly back towards the source. There are complex multiple reflections, with a great deal of wave refraction. The end result is efficient energy reflection of a same-sign wave but spread-out somewhat in space, being spread more for smaller cone angles. Significant spreading requires a cone half angle of less than 15 degrees.

8. Obstructed pipe

An obstruction, generally a flat disc with one or more holes, may be inserted into a pipe, with free area A_2 and area ratio $f = A_2 / A_1$. Provided that f is not too close to 1 (not too open) this reflects similarly to the partially open end. An area ratio of 0.5 may give relatively little reflection. The purpose of such an insert is to create dissipation. It may also spread and delay the transmitted pulse.

When pressure waves are superimposed the results are difficult to predict accurately because of the complex interactions and mutual refractions. However, some equations are available. Wallace and Mitchell give the following for superposition of two high-pressure waves:

$$\left(\frac{P}{P_0}\right)^{1/7} = \left(\frac{P_1}{P_0}\right)^{1/7} + \left(\frac{P_2}{P_0}\right)^{1/7} - 1$$

For a closed-end reflection they give

$$\left(\frac{P_R}{P_0}\right)^{1/7} = \left(\frac{P_1}{P_0}\right)^{1/7}$$

where R is reflected and I is incident, i.e. no losses, and for an open-end reflection

$$\left(\frac{P_R}{P_0}\right)^{1/7} = 2 - \left(\frac{P_1}{P_0}\right)^{1/7}$$

Sudden changes of section naturally dissipate more energy than smooth changes, so exhaust systems intended to have a considerable silencing (muffling) effect are characterised by numerous sudden changes of section. In contrast, power-improving exhausts are smooth in profile to give controlled desirable pressure reflections.

Finally, Figure 6.13.4 gives information on reflection at an orifice obstructing a pipe.

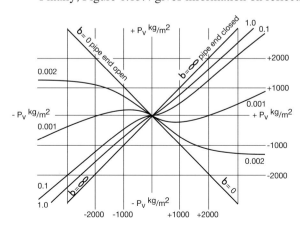

Figure 6.13.4. Reflection pressure relationship for an orifice obstruction in a pipe, according to Pischinger. (Leiber, SAE 680470). Parameter b is a function of several variables including the area ratio.

123

CHAPTER 7

The Inlet System

7.1 Introduction

The inlet, or induction system, comprises all parts involved in bringing air into the crankcase. Especially with a tuned exhaust, the inlet process is by no means independent of the transfer process, although a study of the intake system alone is still highly informative.

Figure 7.1.1 shows the essential parts of the inlet system. The volume and pressure in the case change with the reciprocating movement of the piston. Gas enters through the inlet pipe, usually of varying diameter, then through a carburettor, with a valve at some point such as the entry to the case.

The crankcase bdc volume is approximately twice the swept volume. Not all the inducted air leaves the case immediately. Some remains behind and leaves on a later cycle,

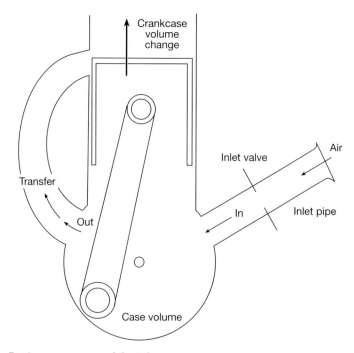

Figure 7.1.1. Basic components of the inlet system.

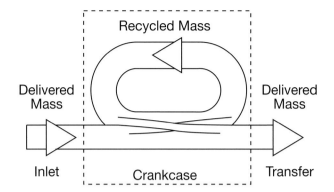

Figure 7.1.2. Passage of gas through the crankcase.

as in Figure 7.1.2. In other words, the transfer gas is taken partially, a fraction *f*, from the most recent intake of air; the rest from air that has been in the crankcase for some cycles.

When the valve is open or partially open the inlet pipe permits inlet gas to flow, but with some resistance. This resistance is high when the valve is barely open but should be small when fully open.

Intake type and inlet valve timing vary from engine to engine, depending on the transfer ports and exhaust system. Figures 7.1.3, 7.1.4 and 7.1.5 give some experimental results.

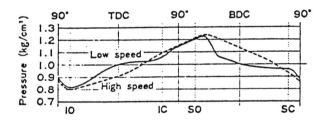

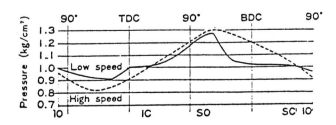

Figure 7.1.3. Variation of crankcase pressure through the cycle as found by Naito and Taguchi. (SAE 660394, 1966).

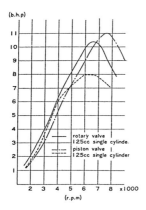
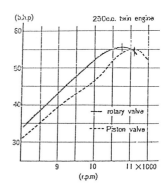

Figure 7.1.4. Variation of power output with intake system: (a) from Naito and Taguchi (SAE 660394), (b) Naitoh and Nomura (SAE 710084).

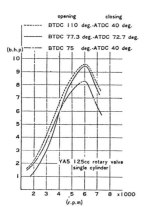
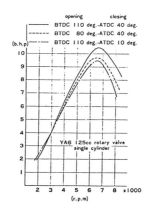
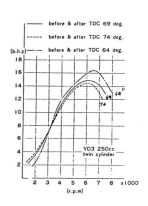

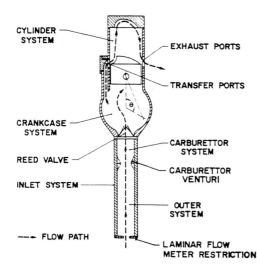

Above: Figure 7.1.5. Variation of power output with intake timing as found by Naito and Taguchi (SAE 660394).

Left: Figure 7.1.6. Illustration of engine model for analysis of the intake system. (Krieger et al, SAE 690135).

Intake systems are classified by the type of valve, of which there are at least twelve types in three main groups, plus some oddities. The three main groups are:

1. Flexure valves
2. Piston valves
3. Rotary valves

Probably the simplest inlet valve of all is a disc guided on a pin, with free movement out to a stop. However, the high frequency impacts at closure would be too violent for engine work.

7.2 Flexure Valves

These are valves activated by the gas pressure and momentum, opening by flexure. Their opening and closing points therefore vary with engine speed and load. Their position in the crankcase is less restricted than that of a mechanical valve. They may be placed anywhere on the crankcase, at any angle. This is useful for multi-cylinder engines, and historically this is where they have found most favour, especially for marine engines, and on some in-line-four racing motorcycle engines.

There are three main variants of the flexure valve:

1. The coil spring disc valve
2. The coil spring poppet valve
3. The reed valve

The lightest, and fastest responding, is simply a thin disc held by a coil spring. However, this really needs some guidance for its movement. If the disc is fixed to a sliding rod the result is a poppet valve. The sprung poppet valve (Figures 7.2.1 and 7.2.2) goes back to the earliest two-strokes, such as the Day engines. Because of its weight it is suitable only for low engine speeds. If the spring is strong enough to close it quickly then it is too stiff for adequate opening, and actuating by a valve mechanism defeats the simplicity of the two-stroke. The sprung poppet valve has been superseded by reed and rotary valves, which are more effective.

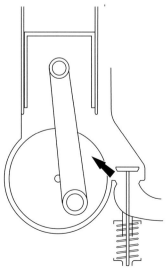

Figure 7.2.1   Sprung poppet valves as on early Day engine.

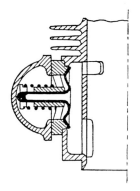

Figure 7.2.2   Sprung poppet valve in the transfer passage of an early DKW engine.

Figure 7.2.3.   Early simple double-inlet reed valve with backing plate (Sachs) of the type known as a petal valve.

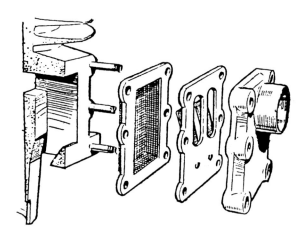

Figure 7.2.4. Early Austrian Titan engine inlet with metal gauze to prevent the ingress of broken reeds.

The basic reed valve (Figures 7.2.3 onwards) comprises a thin flexible membrane, which bends away from the passage to admit air. This bending characterises the reed valve in which the sealing member and the stiffness member are combined. Reed fatigue can be a problem. The early Titan engine had a metal gauze to prevent broken reeds from entering the engine and causing damage. A double-layer reed is sometimes used so that interleaf friction provides damping. Reed valves are sometimes known as petal valves when rounded like a flower petal and particularly when the several separate parts form a radial array, like a complete flower. However, this is rarely used in reciprocating engines, so the terms reed and reed valve will be used here.

Long periods at high engine speeds can cause fatigue in the reeds. Twelve thousand rpm for ten hours is 7.2 million cycles, so best quality spring steel or beryllium copper are needed. A rigid backing plate is sometimes provided to limit bending stresses.

With a simple reed valve, limiting lift makes it hard to achieve sufficient exit flow area for the highest performance. Multi-finger reeds (Figure 7.2.5) were developed to reduce

128

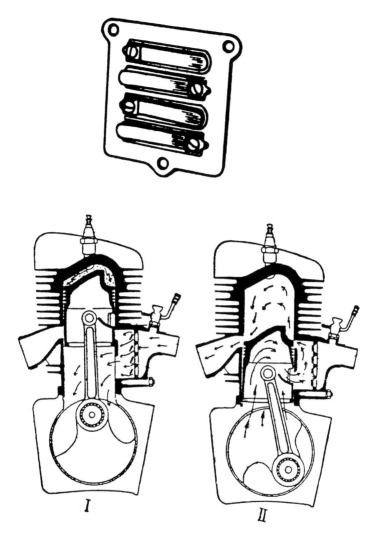

Figure 7.2.5. Early multi-finger reed valve by DKW, placed on a transfer passage (circa 1920).

resistance. However, reed valves fell from favour until improved designs appeared in the 1970s. Part of the problem was the change of flow angle around the reed. This was reduced by angling the reed relative to the flow channel, as in Figure 7.2.6, or by rotating either the channel or the reed. The other problem was the small exit flow area compared with a good rotary valve. Several reeds in parallel, resulting in a reed block (Figure 7.2.6) gave satisfactory performance.

If a thin and flexible reed is used to improve lift, then it strikes the seat hard when closing, soon causing damage. A slightly stiffer reed actually closes more gently because the bending stiffness overcomes the momentum of the gas. Early reed valves had a serious trade-off problem between performance and reliability. This was eased in 1972 by providing the seat with a thin layer of neoprene or other rubber-type material which softened the landing of the reed.

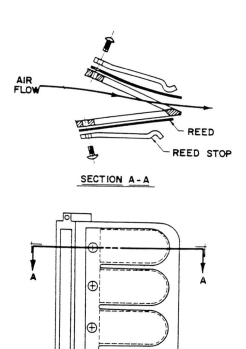

Figure 7.2.6. Eight-reed marine engine block (Krieger, SAE 690135).

As seen in Figure 7.2.7, for a reed thickness t and a bending radius of curvature R according to the backing plate, the maximum bending strains are

$$\varepsilon = \pm \frac{t}{2R}$$

with stresses

$$\sigma = \pm \frac{Et}{2R}$$

where E is the Young's modulus. Hence for a design stress, considering fatigue properties of the material, the minimum radius is

$$R = \frac{Et}{2\sigma} = \frac{t}{2\varepsilon}$$

For a given radius of curvature, a thin reed will have lower bending stresses. For example, a working stress $\sigma = 200$ Mpa, $E = 200$ GPa, $\varepsilon = 0.001$, and $t = 0.3$ mm gives $R = 150$ mm. The design must also take account of the stresses when the valve is closed, as well as the reversed pressure difference then across it, which is the maximum crankcase pressure, around 50 kPa (7 psi) plus some possible dynamic suction on the inlet side. Hence the reed may benefit from a supporting bar on the atmosphere side.

Reed lift is determined dynamically and is not easy to predict. The angle-area is not readily calculable. Reed block design must be based on requirements for maximum flow area. The duration θ and angle-area requirement A_A of a rotary valve for comparable duty will be known; assuming continuous maximum reed valve lift over the same duration as the rotary valve, the reed flow area will need to be A_A / θ. Assuming a linear opening to maximum, and an immediate linear reversal to closing, the maximum flow area of the reed valve must be $2A_A / \theta$. As a guide, and as with the rotary valve, the reed exit area will need to be between the same area and twice the area. Knowing that the rotary valve for maximum output of a high-speed engine requires a cross-sectional area of as much as half of the bore area, then the maximum reed-valve opening may even need to be as large as the bore area.

In Figure 7.2.7, by the intersecting chords theorem, for a modest lift,

$$e = \frac{l^2}{2R}$$

and the effective lift is

$$h = e \cos\theta = \frac{l^2 \cos\theta}{2R}$$

This illustrates how a longer reed allows higher lift for a given radius, thickness and stress. The assumption of constant radius of curvature is, of course, a basic approximation, but may be controlled by the shape of the backing plate.

The lift requirement may be minimised by using the maximum width w of reed block (i.e. into the paper in Figure 7.2.7) since the flow area for one reed is

$$A = wh$$

Therefore, the width, lift, thickness, length and backing plate radius along with the number of reeds in parallel must be juggled for a suitable combination. A very wide reed cannot resist the back pressure, so supporting bars are needed, and then multiple independent reeds can be used.

In principle, a large enough reed block can be made to have a more-or-less arbitrarily low flow resistance, but there are practical limits to installation in the crankcase, and the interior case volume may be increased compared with a rotary valve, because the space for reed opening is left as bdc case volume where the reeds are closed. However, with these modern design approaches, the reed valve can perform extremely well, offering better low-speed behaviour than a very late closing rotary valve.

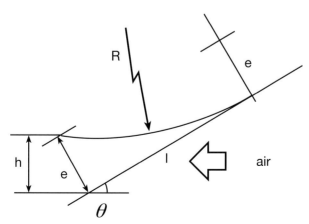

Figure 7.2.7. Reed valve bending analysis.

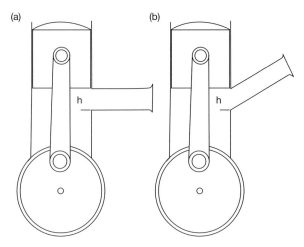

Figure 7.3.1. Piston-controlled inlet port (a) horizontal, (b) inclined.

7.3 Piston Valves

The piston-controlled inlet is perhaps the simplest and lightest of all, requiring no additional valve parts, Figure 7.3.1 (a), possibly inclined as in (b). Although the flow must turn up inside the case to follow the piston, so far no one has advocated a drooped inlet. The timing is controlled by the lower edge of the piston skirt, and is necessarily symmetrical about tdc, which is a disadvantage. To prevent excessive resistance losses the flow velocity must be modest and the port large. This demands long timing which affects the average effective pressure reduction producing the flow, and also reduces crankcase compression to produce transfer flow. Port timing is therefore a delicate compromise. To obtain the largest inlet area, the port should be as wide as possible. Because of connecting rod inclination, at 90° crank angle the piston lift is only about 0.43 of the stroke. Therefore a 180° exhaust port has height 0.43 S, but a 180° piston inlet port has depth 0.57 S.

The lower edge of the piston is bad for flow resistance, Figure 7.3.2 (a), giving a small *vena contracta* area with a high effective resistance. Therefore the top edge of the port can be positioned below the tdc position of the piston skirt, so that the port is fully open for a period, as in Figure 7.3.2 (b). This reduces the total angle area of the port (Figure 7.3.3) but with a possible slight increase of performance. A port depth of about 2/3 of the piston fall at closure is suitable – $h / f = 2 / 3$ (Figure 7.3.2 (b)). Hence, for lengthening the inlet timing it is generally better to shorten the piston skirt than to deepen the port.

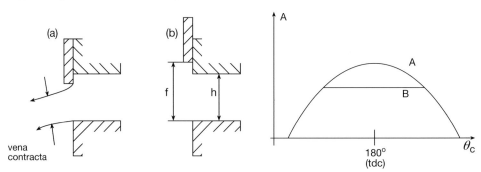

Figure 7.3.2. Piston skirt interference with air flow.

Figure 7.3.3. Area variation of the ports of Figure 7.3.2.

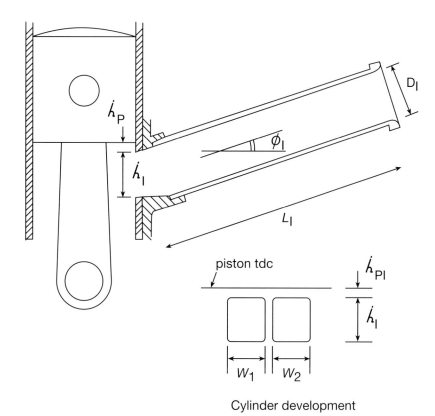

Cylinder development

Figure 7.3.4. Geometry of a piston-controlled inlet. Resonant tuning (Helmholtz type) is important for this type of intake. Wide torque band engines need short timing with smaller cross-sectional area having good oscillation damping. High-speed high peak-power engines need long timing (as much as 200° total inlet) with large area low-damped resonant inlet for maximum peak air charging, but this gives poor low-speed behaviour.

With a long inlet duration, this type of inlet port can cause flow reversal and is very sensitive to the inlet pipe dynamics. A correctly dimensioned resonant inlet is essential for optimum performance. Figure 7.3.4 gives the geometry of a piston inlet. Resonance is controlled mainly by the inlet pipe length and area, in conjunction with the timing.

This type of intake is characterised by the following variables:

1. Inlet pipe length L_1
2. Inlet pipe diameter D_1
3. Inlet pipe inclination $\emptyset_1$
4. Cylinder port height h
5. Cylinder port effective width w
6. Angular duration

For a racing engine, the port height h may be about half of the stroke. For an inlet port covering 90° of cylinder circumference, the port width is 0.71 B. The port area is then about 0.35 BS or about 0.45 times the bore area. This is a good area, comparable with rotary valves. However, the opening and closing characteristics of the piston valve are worse, with the piston skirt partially blocking the port for most of the time, increasing resistance pressure loss.

Inclining the inlet may improve the flow shape at the piston, when the piston obstructs the flow, with the *vena contracta* depth being a greater fraction of the port depth. However, it reduces the effective basic flow depth of the port by a factor cos Ø, so the angle must be fairly modest, e.g. cos 20° = 0.94. A flow area reduction by factor k will give an exit velocity increase by factor k and a pressure loss increase by k^2. Really it is required to maximise the *vena contracta* area.

One disadvantage of the piston-controlled inlet is that it is best positioned opposite the exhaust port, so it occupies space that could otherwise be used for a boost transfer port. In principle a piston-controlled inlet could be placed under the exhaust, but this is not convenient for packaging the inlet pipe and exhaust system.

With correct resonant inlet dynamics the piston-controlled inlet has good performance potential, although generally with a narrower power band than a rotary inlet, which also has a more glamorous image.

Figure 7.3.5 shows several possible shapes for the port. Ports (a), (b) and (c) have the same area, but (b) is wider, having shorter timing, and (c) is wide with long timing and has a low top edge with less piston skirt interference. Port (d) is bridged to prevent ring bowing with a widened port, whilst (e) has bridge tongues for less bridge interference. Ports (f) and (g) have progressive opening on the bottom edge, which reduces intake noise. Progressive opening at the top eases piston ring passage.

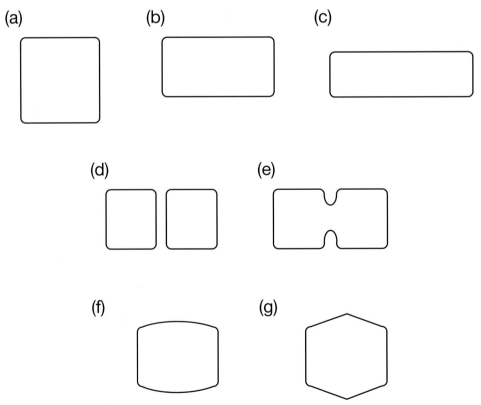

Figure 7.3.5. Port shapes for piston inlets.

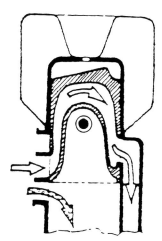

Figure 7.3.6. Bekamo engine with cooling inlet flow also directed through the piston.

Figure 7.3.6 shows the early Bekamo piston-controlled inlet, a historical oddity, where the flow was also channelled through the piston to improve cooling, making for a heavier piston.

A relatively recent development is to combine piston and reed inlets, giving some of the advantages of each. Basically, these can be in series, as in Figure 7.3.7, or in parallel as in Figure 7.3.8. In the former case it is possible to have the piston valve effectively permanently open (as actually seen in Figure 7.3.7) reducing inlet gas friction but reducing crankcase compression.

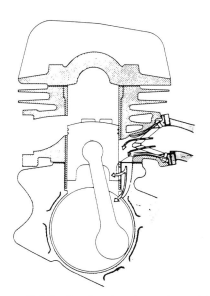

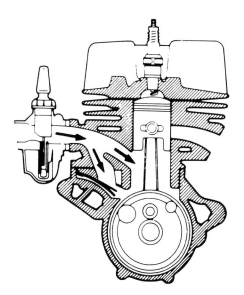

Figure 7.3.7. Reed valve in series with piston-controlled inlet, in this case also with permanently open port in parallel with the piston.

Figure 7.3.8. Reed valve in parallel with piston-controlled port.

The total port angular duration for piston-controlled inlets ranges from 120° for low speed engines to 200° for racing engines. Obviously, such long timing allows considerable flow reversal at low speed, limiting the low speed torque, which is why the series reed valve can be helpful in this case. On the other hand, a short timed inlet will be poor at high speed, in which case a parallel reed valve will allow the induction of extra air after the piston valve closes. Inlet dynamics are analysed in detail later.

7.4 Rotary Valves

Rotary valves have a long history in two-stroke engine design. The mechanically simpler ones with a rotational axis coaxial with the crankshaft are considered first. The more recent remote drive types are considered later.

The basic types of axial rotary valve are:

1. Shaft
2. Web
3. Interior disc
4. Remote disc
5. Drum
6. Pipe
7. Bell

Rotary valves have the advantage that the opening and closing times can be set independently, which has proved better than the symmetrical timing of a piston-controlled inlet. Asymmetrical timing allows good inlet with relatively early closing, giving better crankcase compression to drive the transfer action. The angular durations normally used are about 2/3 before tdc and 1/3 after tdc for a high speed engine, e.g., 140° btdc to 70° atdc. Low speed engines, if using a rotary disc valve, may still open at around 140° btdc but will close much earlier than a high speed engine, e.g. at 30° atdc. Early opening may reduce pumping energy loss.

The physical installation of rotary valves is not very flexible with regard to positioning, in contrast to reed valves. If a rotary valve is not coaxial with the crankshaft, it needs additional drive arrangements, as on the Rotax 454 in Figure 2.3.5.

7.5 Shaft Valves

The shaft rotary valve goes back to the early days, as for example the Ixion of Figure 7.5.1. This system utilises an axial gas hole with a gas port in the side of the shaft to match up with

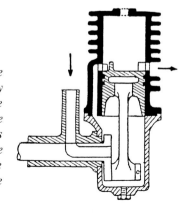

Figure 7.5.1. Early Ixion-Fahrrad-Hilfmotor motorcycle engine, circa 1900, with cantilever crankshaft, shaft rotary valve, and transfer passage over the crankshaft, with the exhaust port opposite. This alignment of ports is sensitive to thermal distortion. Also, the cantilever crankshaft is subject to mechanical stress distortion affecting the alignment of the crankpin. This configuration is unsuitable for high speed, and rarely used nowadays. However, the shaft rotary inlet port still has some advantages.

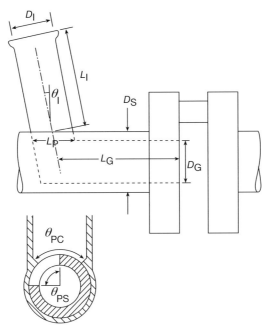

Figure 7.5.2. Shaft valve inlet geometry.

a passage in the crankcase. The normal size of crankshaft permits only a rather small gas passage, and the gas port seriously weakens the shaft. Therefore a considerably oversized shaft diameter is required for good breathing, which has the disadvantages of increasing the main bearing friction (overall mechanical efficiency down by 1% to 2%) and the weight. One big advantage is that the inducted cold mixture flows over the big end, providing excellent cooling and lubrication. Figure 7.5.2 shows the geometry of a shaft valve.

The shaft intake is characterised by several main variables as follows:

1. Shaft journal diameter D_S
2. Gas passage diameter D_G
3. Interior gas passage length L_G
4. Gas port angular width in shaft θ_{PS}
5. Gas port angular width in case θ_{PC}
6. Gas port axial length L_P
7. Exterior inlet pipe length L_I
8. Exterior inlet pipe diameter D_I
9. Inlet pipe inclination $\emptyset_I$

Many of these are actually not constant, e.g. diameter variations of passages.

The shaft wall thickness depends on the service that the engine will see, but typically a shaft outer diameter of about 80% of the cylinder bore would be used, with a gas hole of 60% of the cylinder bore, as a minimum for high performance on a tuned-exhaust engine. For the example engine this would be a 40 mm diameter shaft with a 30 mm gas hole, and 5 mm wall thickness. This is a gas hole cross-sectional area of 36% of the bore area. Even more is needed for absolutely maximum power with a tuned exhaust, whilst a shaft as small as 50% diameter with a gas hole diameter of less than 40% of the bore is suitable for a low-speed lightweight engine.

This kind of inlet port does have the advantage that any required angle-area can be achieved by lengthening it. However, the angular bend of 40° to 90° plus the shaft diameter problem mean that other forms of rotary valve, particularly the rotary disc valve, are usually considered preferable.

As a matter of interest, in one case, the early Dolf-motor, a shaft-valve was used with the shaft conically tapered in the valve region, presumably to reduce the turn angle required of the gas, reducing the flow resistance.

The crankshaft can also be used to control an inlet port without restricting the gas to flow through the main journal bearing, by using the crank web. Such web valves are a great rarity. The first type, with axial flow, has the valve on the front face of the crank web. A segment of the front of the web is relieved to admit the air. For best compatibility with shaft balance, this relief is distributed equally on each side of the crankpin position. This then determines the position of the crankcase hole for correct timing, and hence the intake pipe which must be at the crankpin when this is at about 45° btdc. Alternatively the web cut-out can lead the crankpin by 45° to bring the inlet pipe immediately in front of the cylinder. For balance without affecting the valve, there must be a relief on the inner face of the web, trailing the pin. The inlet pipe could also be positioned elsewhere, with suitable attention to crank web design.

The other type of web valve admits air radially, or semi-tangentially (as on the 247 cm^3 Alpha twin of 1964). Again, the valve position should take account of shaft balance requirements. With this type, sealing may be a problem. Web valves are not competitive with modern disc valves.

7.6 Disc Valves

The axial-flow disc valve is generally the preferred method of intake control for competition engines. There are two main types, interior and remote. The former type resides within the crankcase and acts against its inner surface.

With a double shear crankpin and double webs, this disc position is not very satisfactory. The Gerard engine of 1906 (Figure 1.3.1) had a disc of the interior type, but it

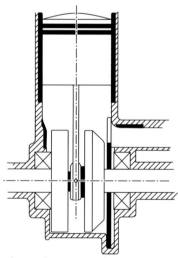

Figure 7.6.1. Interior rotary disc valve. Large diameter is essential to clear the crank web. The disc, unsupported on the internal side, must be thick and stiff, requiring shaping for balance at high speed.

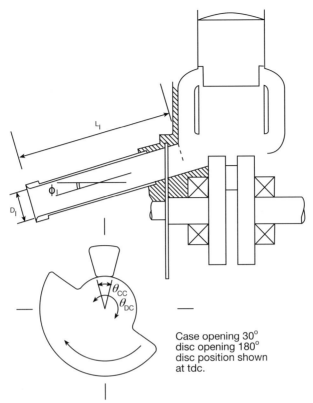

Case opening 30°
disc opening 180°
disc position shown
at tdc.

Figure 7.6.2. Geometry of the remote disc. The total inlet period is the sum of the case cut-out and disc cut-out angles. A smaller case cut-out gives quicker opening and closing. With a limited disc size relative to the desired inlet pipe size, the case cut-out may become rather wide, e.g. 80°, with worse characteristics than could be achieved with a larger disc. Disc-controlled intakes can work well with a short inlet pipe, unlike piston inlets.

was of small diameter, barely equal to the stroke, feeding air to a relieved section in the centre of the web flywheel. With such a small diameter, the potential port area is inadequate for modern high speed engines. The web can be cut away to allow better air flow, but this is still not very satisfactory.

Disc effectiveness can be improved by moving the disc away from the crank webs, giving a remote disc (Figure 7.6.2). In 1949 E. Ansorg made an engine with the intake rotor in a remote chamber. The concept was brought to fruition by Zimmermann for MZ, who introduced two additional innovations. First was a disc of thin steel sheet, about 0.8 mm, operating in a chamber about 1.4 mm wide, the thinness allowing the rotor to flex and seal against whichever side of the chamber was at low pressure. The second innovation put the rotor on splines on the shaft giving it axial float and facilitating assembly and set-up. As the metal removed for the timing sector of the thin disc was slight, rotor imbalance was not a problem.

A very thin flexible rotor cannot be used for an internal disc, which must be rigid and strong enough to withstand the pressure across it. For these, many materials have been used including aluminium, paper or cloth reinforced phenolics, nylon, graphite-leaded nylon, delrin, glass-reinforced nylon, steel and so on. The thickness provides stiffness, and allows machining to improve balance. In contrast, the remote disc is supported on both sides, needing sufficient strength to cover the port area only. At high speed, the thin disc is greatly stiffened by centrifugal action, but it may have problems at low speed, as when starting.

There is an interesting difference between internal and remote discs. Internal discs are found to be best with approximately equal sizes of port in the rotating and stationary parts, as for most shaft valves, whereas for remote discs the disc is given a larger cut-out than the crankcase, which has a modest passage angular size. Considering, for example, a total duration of 200°, the former method would have two sectors of 100°, whilst a remote disc would have a sector of 170° and the passage size would be about 30°. The resulting $A(\theta)$ graph is as in Figure 7.6.3. The remote disc is open for 170°+30°=200°, and fully open for 140° (200° – 2 × 30°) but has much less angle-area, barely 50% of that of the equal-sector valve.

The remote disc, being fully open for so long, will have less resistance from interference by the disc edges than does an interior disc, which is a major advantage. The differences may also be related to the existence of the internal passage, on the crankcase side of the remote disc. Although this gives a greater crankcase volume, it gives an opportunity for a diffuser shape to give some pressure recovery. The internal disc cannot benefit from this. However, by maximising the angle-area of the internal disc the pressure recovery may be better than the loss from disc edge interference. Therefore each design may actually be best for its disc position.

Physically, a thin remote disc is mounted on the shaft, its radial load from mechanical imbalance being carried on the shaft bearings. Axial loads are supported by pressure of the case on the disc.

Rotary disc induction works well with a short intake, but some benefit may still be gained by tuning of the size of the intake pipe. However, in some installations this creates packaging problems. On a motorcycle the engine axis is normally transverse, so a long piston intake packages well, behind the engine, but a disc intake protrudes sideways, making a long intake inconvenient.

The remote disc will have a diameter of up to 2.8 times the stroke, which, with some suitable shaping of the near crank web, allows a very large inlet passage.

Some useful relationships can be stated about the inlet area, disc size and bore area. The inlet pipe area over bore area (the normalised pipe area) may be up to 0.5, or a diameter ratio

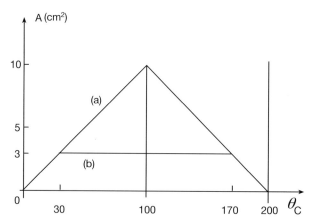

Figure 7.6.3. A(θ) curves for disc valves: (a) equal sector sizes (100°) (b) large disc sector (170°) and small passage (30°).

of 0.7. The case opening at the disc may be circular (e.g. the MZ 125 engine of Figure 2.3.3), but is usually squared out to make the most of the sector. The case opening cut-out area is then

$$A_{CC} = C_{CCI} A_1$$

with a factor of about 1.2. A sector angle of about 40° gives the easiest transformation from a circular inlet. A smaller angle (30° in Figure 7.6.2) becomes rather narrow, but opens and closes very quickly. A larger sector angle allows a smaller disc diameter, or allows a larger inlet pipe area on an existing disc size. The outer radius of the case cutout can be up to about 0.95 times the disc radius, and the inner radius can be 0.5 of the disc radius or a little less. Allowing for the corner radii, the case cut-out area can then be about 0.7 of the sector area, so

$$A_{CC} = 0.7 \frac{\theta_{CC}}{360} A_D = \frac{\theta_{CC}}{500} A_D$$

where A_D is the total disc area, and the cut-out angle is in degrees.

Also, the disc area related to the bore area simply depends on the diameters:

$$\frac{A_D}{A_B} = \left(\frac{D_D}{B}\right)^2$$

For example, as a design process, with say a bore of 50 mm, bore area 19.63 cm², an inlet area of 9.62 cm² is required (inlet diameter 35 mm). At the valve this will increase to about 11.5 cm². The disc area must be

$$A_D = \frac{500}{\theta_{CC}} A_{CC}$$

For a 40° case-inlet sector angle, this is 144.3 cm². The disc diameter is then 136 mm, or 2.71 times the bore.

For the engine tuner, the disc size is probably predetermined, and the case sector angle is to be found. Given a disc diameter of, say, only 100 mm (2.0 B), area 78.5 cm², then

$$\theta_{CC} = 500 \frac{A_{CC}}{A_D}$$

which is 73.2°. Because this disc is rather small for this inlet area, the case sector angle is rather wide, with poorer shape transformation from the circular pipe, and much slower opening and closing.

7.7 Other Axial Valves

The pipe valve (Figure 7.7.1) is a geometrically reversed shaft valve, with the flow entering axially, then diverting and passing through the port, then through a further passage and finally emerging into the case under the piston. The interior passage can allow some divergence and pressure recovery. It may even have a superior basic performance to the disc valve. It is easier to balance and perhaps somewhat easier to manufacture. Its flow characteristics are similar in general to those of the shaft valve. The valve diameter can easily be increased above that of the shaft, so there is no need for an enlarged shaft bearing. Also, the valve can be lengthened to give any required angle area, so its flow characteristics are potentially very good. However, big end cooling and lubrication are not as good as for a shaft valve.

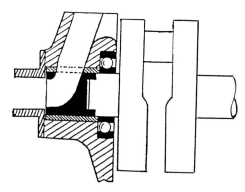

Figure 7.7.1. Pipe valve on early Gillett motorcycle engine.

If the pipe valve diameter is made much greater than its length, the result is the bell valve. This is significantly different, permitting a straight steeply-angled intake, ideal for resonant tuning effect, directed up under the piston, with a large radius at the valve permitting a very long fully-open period even better than the remote disc. Thus the bell valve seems to offer a good combination of features. The rotary bell itself requires balancing because of the large cut-out. Removing material on the front face of the bell can do this, although this leaves dynamic imbalance. A possibly better method would be to use a thicker rim with eccentric turning to thin the wall for balancing.

7.8 Other Rotary Valves

Other rotary valve arrangements are belt or gear driven so that the designer is freer to choose their position. Figure 7.8.1 shows, conceptually, a disc valve with offset axis, but still parallel to the main shaft, thus easily driven by gears or a belt.

Another possibility is a rotary pipe valve of parallel axis driven by gears or a belt, as in Figure 7.8.2. A long pipe-valve has been used successfully for in-line multi-cylinder engines, feeding conveniently from a single carburettor.

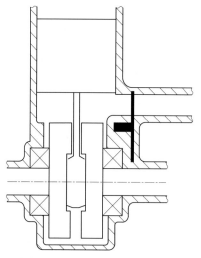

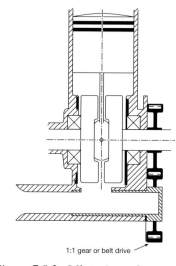

1:1 gear or belt drive

Figure 7.8.1. Offset disc valve.   *Figure 7.8.2. Offset pipe valve.*

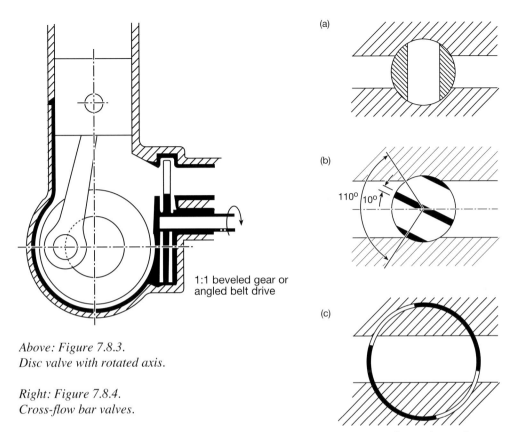

Above: Figure 7.8.3.
Disc valve with rotated axis.

Right: Figure 7.8.4.
Cross-flow bar valves.

With more complex belt or gear arrangements, the valve rotary axis can be made non-parallel to the shaft, as in Figure 7.8.3. This is the type used on the Rotax twin (Figure 2.3.5) with a bevel gear drive.

A further variation is the cross-flow bar valve, Figure 7.8.4 (a) or (b). This opens twice per revolution and therefore runs at half shaft speed. Unfortunately it exhibits a high flow resistance because of the more-or-less continuous intrusion of sharp edges. The addition of a centre bar on (b) improves the flow somewhat, but the result is still not good enough for very high performance. A variation on the above, the bar sleeve valve, has a fixed core with a rotating sleeve, as in Figure 7.8.4(c). This also opens twice per revolution and must rotate at half speed. With a generous sleeve diameter, the valve can be briefly fully open, but the flow is still subject to the resistance of two effective valves.

These alternative valve designs do not generally offer a performance improvement over the usual systems, in fact rather the opposite. However, they may be useful where packaging is a problem, and especially with multi-cylinder engines, as seen in Chapter 2.

Other unusual forms of inlet valve have performed well but have not achieved wide acceptance. One is the connecting-rod timed inlet by Ivanko, where the face of the rod passes over the inside of the inlet pipe. The rod has a small integral plate on its front face to give the correct timing.

7.9 Helmholtz Resonance

Inlet resonance is most easily understood in the case of piston-controlled induction. The rising piston reduces crankcase pressure to below atmospheric. The inlet port is then

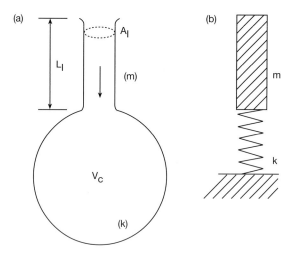

Figure 7.9.1. The Helmholtz Resonator (a) physical configuration, (b) solid mechanical analogue of mass and spring, in vertical motion only.

suddenly opened, forming a chamber and pipe arrangement (Figure 7.9.1) known as a Helmholtz Resonator.

In 1938, U. Schmidt published results on tests of a two-stroke engine, confirming that Helmholtz theory gave a reasonable prediction of the inlet natural frequency.

Figure 7.9.2 shows how crankcase pressure will vary for this idealised case, for zero frictional losses, given an initial depression in the case at the moment when the valve opens. In principle, with zero friction it is possible to obtain an overpressure equal to the opening depression, which would give a considerable power improvement compared with a simple pressure increase up to atmospheric.

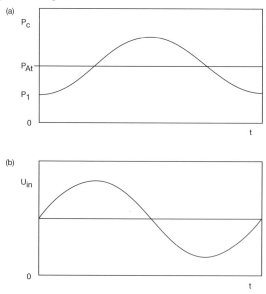

Figure 7.9.2. Idealised pressure variation in the crankcase due to Helmholtz oscillation of the inlet system, for zero energy losses (a) pressure in crankcase, (b) velocity in inlet pipe.

Physically, when the inlet opens, the pressure difference causes the air in the inlet pipe to accelerate inwards. The speed continues to build up, in the idealised absence of frictional loss, until the pressure difference is zero, at which point the speed is at maximum. The inertia of the air then resists attempts to slow it down. The air overshoots, giving the pressure rise. The behaviour is similar to that of a mass on a spring, with the air in the pipe being the mass, and the compressibility of the air in the crankcase being the spring. If the intake is left open too long, the air motion will reverse and the air will begin to flow out again. To obtain maximum torque or power, the designer needs to tune the system to close the intake port at the right moment.

It may seem surprising that the inertia of the air is so important. The mass of air in an intake pipe of diameter 30 mm and length 300 mm is only 0.25 g, less than 0.01 oz. However, because of the high frequencies involved, which need large accelerations, even this small mass can be of an enormous influence on the inlet dynamics. For example, the velocity in the intake pipe can exceed 80 m/s which must be reached in only about 0.001 s, with an acceleration of the air around 80,000 m/s^2 or 8,000 g. The 0.25 gram mass then requires a force of 20 N, which, on the inlet cross-sectional area of 7.07 cm^2 corresponds to a pressure of 28.3 kPa (4.1 psi).

Figure 7.9.1 shows the essential features of a Helmholtz resonator, for an engine, with crankcase volume V_{CT} (at top dead centre), and an inlet pipe of cross-sectional area A_I and length L_I. This behaves like the mass on a spring in vertical motion. Appendix C gives a full analysis. The equivalent mass is the mass of air in the inlet pipe

$$m = \rho \, A_I \, L_I$$

where ρ is the density of air, about 1.2 kg/m^3. The equivalent stiffness is

$$k = \frac{\gamma \, P_0 \, A_I^2}{V_{CT}}$$

where γ is the ratio of thermal capacities for air, or adiabatic index, about 1.4, and P_0 is the ambient atmospheric pressure, about 101 kPa.

The simple linear equivalent mass and spring has a natural frequency

$$f_N = \frac{1}{2\pi} \sqrt{\frac{k}{m}}$$

which gives an inlet natural frequency

$$f_{NI} = \frac{c}{2\pi} \sqrt{\frac{A_I}{V_{CT} L_I}}$$

(7.9.1)

where c is the velocity of sound (340 m/s or 11,400 in/s as appropriate). This is the essential equation for a resonant intake.

In practice, the parameters A_I and V_{CT} are chosen first, and the appropriate intake length must then be found. For design purposes, the Helmholtz equation must be rearranged to

$$L_I = \frac{A_I}{V_{CT}} \left(\frac{c}{2\pi \, f_{NI}} \right)^2$$

(7.9.2)

To apply this equation it is necessary to choose a suitable design natural frequency for the intake.

The intake opens with low pressure, which will convert to a maximum high pressure in one half natural oscillation, as shown in Figure 7.9.2. This is a simple cosine curve with the equation

$$P = P_0 - P_1 \cos(2\pi f_{NI} t)$$

For an engine rotational speed N_S rev/s, the time for one revolution is

$$T_R = \frac{1}{N_S}$$

The time of the inlet period for inlet duration θ_I degrees is

$$T_I = \frac{\theta_I}{360} T_R$$

$$= \frac{\theta_I}{360 N_S}$$

For the example engine, the speed is 200 rev/s so the time of one revolution is 5 ms. With inlet duration angle 200°, the inlet open period time is 2.78 ms. For highest pressure when the inlet closes this time must be one half of an inlet oscillation. Therefore one inlet oscillation should have a natural period

$$T_{INP} = 2 T_I = \frac{\theta_I}{180 N_S}$$

The natural frequency of the inlet must therefore be

$$f_{NI} = \frac{180}{\theta_I} N_S$$

(7.9.3)

The required inlet frequency is therefore similar to the engine rotation speed, but modified by the actual inlet period. This is the second design equation.

The two design equations, 7.9.2 and 7.9.3, may be combined to give

$$L_I = \frac{c^2 A_I \theta_I^2}{4\pi^2 180^2 V_{CT} N_S^2}$$

$$= \frac{A_I}{V_{CT}} \left(\frac{c\theta_I}{360\pi N_S} \right)^2$$

(7.9.4)

To consider a particular case, take the example engine at 12,000 rpm:

$$N_S = 200 \ \text{rev/s}$$

$$V_{CT} = 200 \ \text{cm}^3 = 200 \times 10^{-6} \ \text{m}^2$$

$$\theta_I = 200°$$

$$D_I = 25 \ \text{mm} = 0.025 \ \text{m}$$

Then

$$A_I = \frac{\pi}{4} D^2 = 491 \times 10^{-6} \text{m}^2$$

$$L_I = \frac{491 \times 10^{-6}}{200 \times 10^{-6}} \left(\frac{340 \times 200}{360 \times 314 \times 200} \right)^2$$

$$= 0.159 \ \text{m} \approx 160 \ \text{mm}$$

For imperial units, insert all dimensions in inches, and use a speed of sound of 13,400 in/s, giving 6.3 inches design length.

The applicable range of the above theory must be considered. Really the air in the pipe does not move as a solid plug, but has pressure waves passing through it, transmitted from the inlet port. The Helmholtz theory is acceptable from this point of view if the inlet pipe is short enough for the pressure wave to traverse the length of the pipe several times during the inlet period i.e., if

$$L_1 << T_1 c$$

Substituting this into the Helmholtz equation, the criterion becomes

$$V_I << 4\pi^2 V_C$$

This means that the equation should be applicable if the inlet pipe volume V_I is less than the case volume:

$$V_I < V_C$$

The inlet volume is

$$V_I = A_I L_I$$

which, for the example given, is 78 cm³. This would be less than half of the case volume for an engine, of 100 cm³ of swept volume.

The Helmholtz equation indicates that the inlet area and length may both be varied, giving resonance for a complete range of combinations of values. If the area and length are too large, however, the theory will cease to apply, as stated above. If the area and length are too small, or if the shape is bad, the gas frictional pressure losses will be high, and the simple theory above (neglecting friction) will be unsatisfactory. It will still predict the natural frequency roughly, but the actual results in terms of power will be disappointing because the resonant overshoot of the gas will be prevented by the friction, as considered in more detail later.

For zero resistance, the flow could fully reverse. Figure 7.9.3 shows how this would

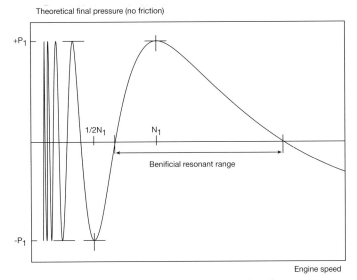

Figure 7.9.3. Idealised variation of crankcase pressure at inlet closure, versus engine speed, due to frictionless oscillation of intake air.

affect the closing pressure in the crankcase as a function of engine speed. This curve shape follows from Figure 7.9.2. Lower rpm also allows more time for inlet flow oscillation.

The results for the torque curve would be a similar shape, but with zero torque at zero net gas flow. The effective power band, by racing standards, is not too bad, and wider than that created by a tuned length exhaust. Complete loss of torque at one half of the peak-torque speed, with no net air entry at all, would obviously be unacceptable. In practice this is offset by fluid friction effects, so some inlet resistance can be advantageous.

Helmholtz theory cannot predict the best actual peak torque speed or peak power speed to aim for. In principle, resonance could be arranged at any desired speed. In practice, of course, the engine has its preferences, because of the transfer, combustion and exhaust, so the inlet will be tuned to suit the rest of the engine.

7.10 Resistance

For high power the inlet system must have a low resistance to air flow. Figure 7.10.1 shows the primary contributory factors, which are:

1. Entry loss
2. Pipe friction
3. Throttle plate
4. Fuel suction restriction
5. Area changes
6. Bends
7. Inlet valve
8. Diffuser (pressure recovery)
9. Exit 'loss'

Of the losses listed, one is deliberate: the throttle is intended to restrict the flow and control the power. Obviously, for greatest flow at fully open throttle, the internal form should be the smoothest possible. With good design, a throttle in this position can blend almost perfectly with the inlet shape.

The carburettor restriction, distinct from the throttle, is there to give a suitably low pressure for suction of the fuel. Normally this involves providing adequate consistent suction

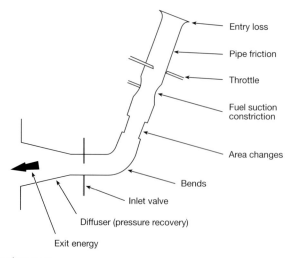

Figure 7.10.1. Inlet resistances.

to draw in the fuel. This may dictate the basic diameter and cross-sectional area of the inlet tract. The basic diameter is the dominant factor, because the pressure losses are roughly proportional to the air velocity squared. The area is proportional to the diameter squared, so for a given mass or volumetric flow rate, the pressure losses go inversely with diameter to the fourth power, or even the fifth power for a pipe, as discussed in Chapter 6.

The biggest single factor in the resistance of the inlet is therefore the basic diameter, or cross-sectional area, of the system. If this is too small, the resistance will be too high and the highest outputs will never be achieved. For the engine tuner the inlet system is frequently undersized, so any reduction of resistance by slight increase of size or improvement of details is valuable. For high performance engines, the inlet cross-sectional area needs to be one quarter to one half of the bore area.

The inlet resistance must be considered in total, and is most easily dealt with when there is a well-defined reference diameter. However, because the various components will have different diameters the total loss, and their comparative importance, are best evaluated by considering the actual expected pressure loss for a given realistic flow rate. This flow rate can be estimated as the swept volume times the peaking rev/s:

$$Q_{ref} \approx V_S \, N_{SP}$$

For the example engine a suitable round number is

$$Q_{ref} = 0.020 \text{ m}^3/\text{s} = 20 \text{ litre/s}$$

The example engine inlet dimensions are

$$D_1 = 25 \text{ m}$$
$$L_1 = 160 \text{ mm}$$
$$A_1 = 4.909 \text{ cm}^2$$
$$V_1 = 78.5 \text{ cm}^3$$

The actual flow is unsteady of course; so this particular choice is just for comparative purposes. The engine may breathe less air than this, but it does so in a short part of the cycle, so the peak air flow rate may actually be higher.

For a pipe of area A, carrying air at volumetric flow rate Q, the mean velocity is

$$U = \frac{Q}{A}$$

The dynamic pressure based on mean speed is

$$q = \tfrac{1}{2} \rho U^2$$

For the example engine these are 40.7 m/s and 996 Pa (133 ft/sec and 0.145 psi).

Pressure losses P_L are based on the dynamic pressure according to the loss coefficient K:

$$P_L = Kq$$

Chapter 5 gives information on K values.

1.Entry losses

The shape of the entry to a pipe is important. To keep K to a low value of 0.1, there must be an edge radius not less than 1/6 of the pipe inner diameter. There is an irreducible minimum to the entry loss because even with an ideal shape there must be an initial development of the boundary layer and pipe velocity profile. Hence K cannot go far below 0.10 for the entrance.

2. Pipe friction

The pipe pressure loss can be found from the information in Chapter 6. This requires an estimate of flow rate, and evaluation of Reynolds number, friction factor and loss coefficient. For differing diameters or cross-sectional areas, the pipe must be considered in a series of sections, and account also taken separately of the effect of the area changes themselves.

A fairly good internal finish will render the pipe effectively smooth. A good shape is more important than an extremely high polish. At a Reynolds number of 50,000 the friction factor is about 0.02. At a length/diameter ratio of 10 the pipe loss coefficient would be $K = 0.2$.

3. Throttle plate

For analysing the full throttle losses, this is of course fully open, but there may nevertheless be some perturbations of the pipe shape.

4. Carburettor restriction

Ideally this does not give any local restriction, but it probably dictates the basic pipe diameter, so the choice of carburettor size is of great practical importance.

5. Area changes

The effect of longitudinal variations of cross-sectional area may be estimated from information in Chapter 6.

6. Bends

Bends are better avoided. A close bend may give $K = 1.0$, large smooth bends much less. A bend is a significant disadvantage for shaft and pipe valves, which may, by compensation, be lengthened to give very large angle-area values. Piston valves, of course, can have a perfectly straight pipe.

7. Inlet valve

The inlet valve itself, when not fully open, is a major resistance. The timing disc edge, or other timing component, causes major disruption to the flow, which must accelerate through the reduced area, but will then have a turbulent expansion with large losses. It is the reduction of these losses, because of the rapid opening and closing that makes the remote disc attractive. For the piston-controlled inlet the controlling edge is the piston skirt. It is not practical to have a subsequent diffuser.

8. Diffuser and exit loss

If the inlet pipe discharges into the crankcase at its uniform diameter, one dynamic head of pressure is effectively lost by turbulent flow dissipation.

This can be reduced by a gradually tapering diffuser, which slows the exit velocity, and gives some pressure recovery. Details of diffuser performance are given in Chapter 6 and in some fluid dynamics handbooks.

It is evident from the above that the total pressure loss for the inlet pipe varies considerably with the valve opening. For the fully open position it varies with the detailed design, but average values of K in the range 0 to 5 are of interest to analyse, based on the mean area.

With a loss factor K, the pressure loss from gas friction is

$$P_f = \tfrac{1}{2}\rho U^2 K$$

and the effective friction force for the equivalent spring-mass system is this pressure times the pipe area:

$$F_f = P_f A_I$$
$$= \frac{1}{2} \rho U^2 K A_I$$

This force is proportional to velocity squared, not simply to the velocity, so normal linear damping theory is not applicable. Appendix C gives details. The analysis proceeds in terms of the quadratic damping coefficient C_Q, where

$$F_f = C_Q U^2$$

with

$$C_Q = \frac{1}{2} \rho K A_I$$

and in terms of the quadratic damping ratio ζ_Q (c.f. damping coefficient C_Q) where,

$$\zeta_Q = \frac{K}{2\gamma} \left(\frac{P_I}{P_{At}} \right) \left(\frac{V_C}{V_I} \right)$$

Here P_I is the initial gauge pressure in the crankcase, i.e. the initial crankcase pressure difference from atmospheric.

The quadratic damping ratio ζ_Q is directly proportional to the initial pressure difference P_I, and is reduced by a large ratio of inlet volume to case volume, V_I / V_C. The atmospheric pressure P_{At} and ratio of thermal capacities γ for air are not under the designer's control. Practical example values are

$$\zeta_Q = \frac{K}{2 \times 1.4} \left(\frac{30}{100} \right) \left(\frac{200}{78.5} \right) \approx 0.3 \, K$$

Hence realistic ζ_Q values are likely to be in the range zero to 2.0.

Figure 7.10.2 shows the free motion for various ζ_Q values, the effect of which is considerable. This is shown for a negative initial position which can be considered to be crankcase pressure depression from atmospheric. Even at $\zeta_Q = 1.0$ it is possible to obtain a significant overpressure. The dependence of the maximum overpressure on quadratic damping ratio, expressed as a fraction of the initial underpressure, is shown in Figure 7.10.3.

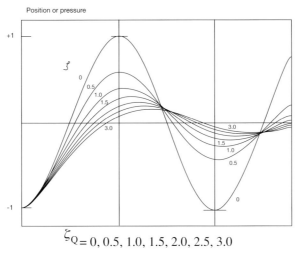

$\zeta_Q = 0, 0.5, 1.0, 1.5, 2.0, 2.5, 3.0$

Figure 7.10.2. Free motion for various quadratic damping ratio values.

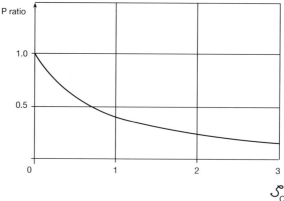

Figure 7.10.3. Effect of overpressure on quadratic damping ratio as a fraction of initial underpressure.

At low engine speed, with an inlet tuned for high speed, the flow can reverse. This reversed flow will generally have a somewhat different loss coefficient, but can be treated as the same for simplicity. The effect on the volumetric efficiency for various engine speeds is shown in Figure 7.10.4. Lower damping boosts the peak torque but with a loss of low speed performance. The torque at one half of the tuned speed is low, but not as bad as when undamped. Of course, real torque curves are also influenced by other dynamic gas behaviour of the engine, especially the exhaust, but the analysis here gives a good understanding of the influence of inlet tuning with damping, especially for piston-controlled inlets.

7.11 Inlet Inertia Model
The concept of the inlet inertia used in the Helmholtz model can be extended by creating a time-stepping computer numerical model in which the inlet gas accelerates according to the

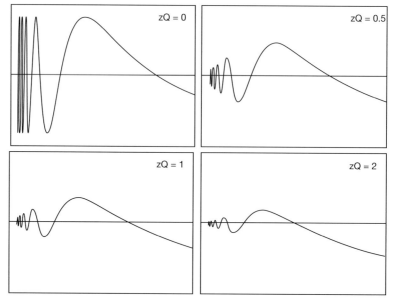

Figure 7.10.4. The effect on the volumetric efficiency for various engine speeds

instantaneous crankcase pressure and the instantaneous resistance. This can be done as part of a complete engine simulation, or by assuming an initial crankcase pressure. This latter form of simulation will not produce accurate quantitative predictions, but gives an excellent indication of influences and trends, and provides a useful way to study the effect of detail changes to the inlet system. In particular, this model can be applied to asymmetrical timing, and so is suitable for studying rotary valves, and permits the inlet resistance to vary in time, so the opening and closing of the valve can be represented with good accuracy. The pressure in the case depends upon the initial case pressure, the motion of the piston and the inflow from the inlet system. Rotary valve timing, resistance effects, inlet pipe sizes and so on may be studied. This simple gas inertia model can easily include frictional effects. It has the additional advantage of using easily comprehensible parameters, and seems to give realistic behaviour.

CHAPTER 8:

The Transfer System

8.1   Introduction

The transfer system, or bypass system, is that part of the engine which transfers the fuel and air mixture from the crankcase to the cylinder. Basically this requires transfer ports to admit the gas to the cylinder and transfer passages leading from the crankcase up to those ports (Figure 8.1.1). The passages are characterised by their number, length, cross-sectional area and shape. The ports are characterised by number, timing (angular duration), maximum area, angle-area, shape, and direction of entry to the cylinder. Figure 8.1.2 summarises the main transfer port configurations.

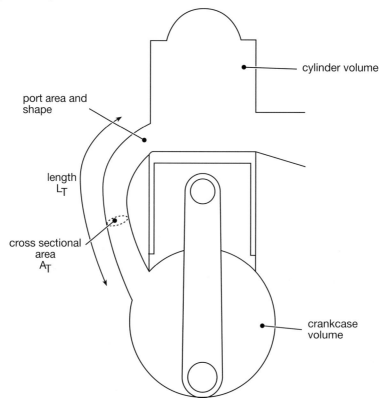

Figure 8.1.1. Essential parts of the transfer system.

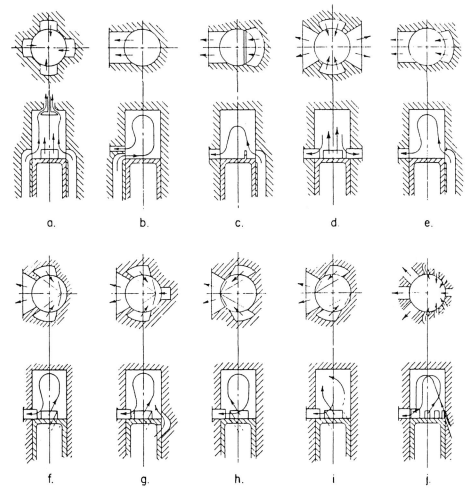

Figure 8.1.2. The main types of transfer porting used with crankcase scavenging, as summarised by G. Lee. (The term Curtis porting often refers to a full ring of transfer porting for axial scavenging, with some tangential entry velocity. Laminar porting (e) is a misnomer, really being Coanda effect, and not laminar flow.)

As with the inlet system, the gas in the transfer passage has inertia. Combined with the compressive gas stiffness in the crankcase and cylinder, this has a natural frequency and resonant effects. The entry and exit of the passages, with their length, cross-sectional area and shape give resistance to the flow, including the effect of partial opening due to the piston position.

The crankcase inlet port closes as the piston descends, at around 30° to 80° atdc according to the particular engine, sealing the crankcase. Further descent of the piston increases the pressure in the crankcase. The exhaust opens at 80° to 120° atdc, followed some time later by opening of the transfer, usually at about 115° atdc (corresponding to transfer duration 130°). Between exhaust opening and transfer opening, called the blowdown period, the cylinder pressure falls rapidly. However, the transfers will normally start to open when there is still a higher pressure in the cylinder than in the crankcase, because although

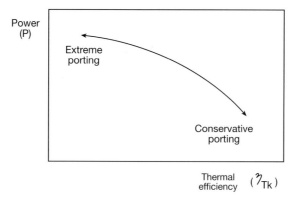

Figure 8.1.3. Trend of power versus thermal efficiency, varying according to port size and timings. High power at high engine speed requires extreme porting which causes poor fuel consumption, even relative to the power.

this gives some initial reverse flow it allows a larger transfer port area and later transfer closing. As the transfer opens more, the forward transfer flow begins. The fresh gas entering the cylinder forces the old gas out. This is cylinder scavenging, on which transfer port size and shape have an important influence.

Transfer systems fall into two categories:

1. Axial scavenge
2. Reverse flow scavenge

For axial scavenging, the transfer gas enters at one end of the cylinder and leaves at the other, so valves are required at both ends. In reverse-flow scavenge, the ports are all at one end, with the fresh gas going up the cylinder in one area and then coming back down again elsewhere. This is the usual system for competition two strokes.

Reverse flow scavenge further divides into:

1. Peripheral scavenge
2. Cross-flow scavenge
3. Schnürle scavenge

which may be further subdivided.

For ultimate power output the modern Schnürle system with resonant exhaust dominates, but competition classes don't always allow such configurations, and anyway maximum power is not always the goal. Controllability, fuel efficiency, certain running characteristics, or high torque at lower speed may predominate, especially in *Formule Libre* or where the allowable engine swept volume is large enough for ultimate specific output not to be useful (Figure 8.1.3). For such applications, other portings may be adequate or preferred.

8.2 Axial Porting

Porting for axial scavenging is more complex than reverse flow. Nowadays it is mainly applied to very large marine engines. The ultimate in axial-flow scavenging is perhaps the opposed-piston engine (Figures 8.2.1. and 8.2.2), with fully piston-controlled ports. At one end there is a circumferential band of transfer ports, and exhaust ports at the other. With no cylinder heads thermal losses are low and thermal efficiency high. However, the pair of widely separated crankshafts, geared or linked together, is not very convenient. This

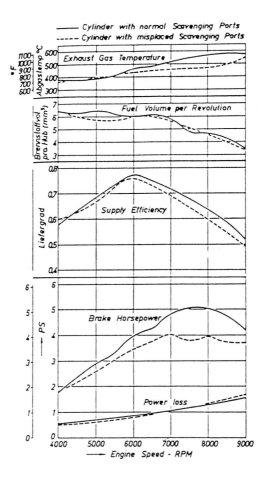

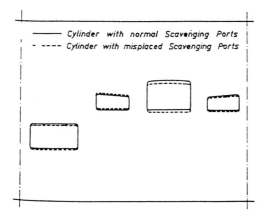

Figure 8.1.4. The effect of inaccurate manufacture of the ports, as investigated by C. Waker, 1966. (SAE 660 009).

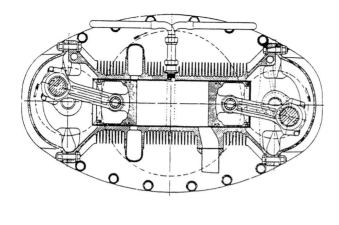

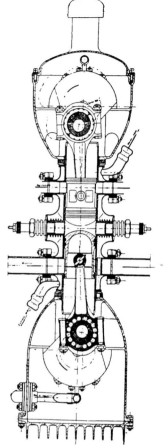

Above: Figure 8.2.1.
Opposed-piston axially scavenged layout,
with crankshafts synchronised by gearing.
(McCulloch).

Right: Figure 8.2.2.
Opposed-piston Fiat racing engine of 1927.

configuration was extended to make the compact Deltic locomotive diesel, with three crankshafts and three cylinders forming a triangle. See also the DKW opposed engine, Chapter 1, Figure 2.3.10.

By folding the cylinder at the centre, the two shafts may be brought more conveniently close, or even into one crankshaft, although at the cost of introducing a cylinder head. The axially-scavenged folded cylinder formed the basis of many successful racing motorcycles of the 1930s.

Alternatively, axial scavenging is possible in a conventional cylinder by having some valves in the cylinder head. Figure 8.2.3 shows the two main options: exhaust ports in the head, giving 'upward' scavenge, or in the cylinder, giving 'downward' scavenge. The head valves are shown as poppets, but other forms are possible, including sleeve valves and rotary valves of various kinds. Head transfer does not lend itself to crankcase scavenging because the transfer passage becomes very long, but it can be done (Figure 8.2.4). The head exhaust system offers good potential power because the port areas can be so large, much larger than for a four-stroke of similar bore. However, the fact that the two-stroke fires on every cycle causes worse thermal problems in the head than with the alternate firing four-stroke. Exhaust poppets would have a difficult job in a high specific power engine. Also, overhead valves are normally camshaft-driven, thus losing the simplicity of the crankcase-scavenged two-stroke.

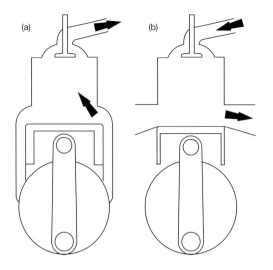

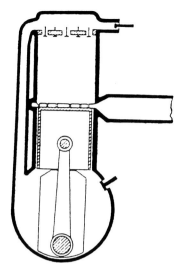

Figure 8.2.3. Axial scavenge with head valves.
a. Upward scavenge (head exhaust)
b. Downward scavenge (head transfer)

Figure 8.2.4. The Kylen two-stroke engine had axial scavenge with transfer through valves in the head. The valves were simply spring loaded, with no valve gear. Obviously this was only a low-speed engine

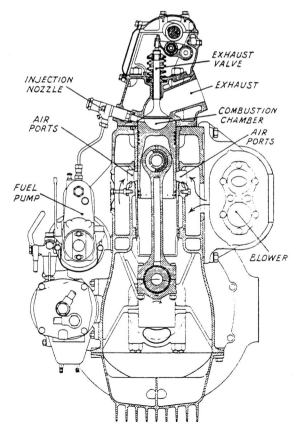

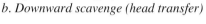

INJECTION
NOZZLE

EXHAUST
VALVE

EXHAUST

AIR
PORTS

COMBUSTION
CHAMBER

AIR
PORTS

FUEL
PUMP

BLOWER

Left: Figure 8.2.5.
Two-stroke car engine with head exhaust valve and scavenge blower, circa 1920. (Foden).

Opposite top left: Figure 8.2.6.
Schliha porting concept.

Opposite top right: Figure 8.2.8.
Ivanko porting.

Opposite bottom: Figure 8.2.7.
Schliha twin-cylinder car engine from circa 1930.

159

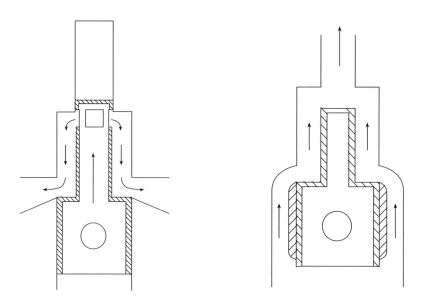

Peripheral (radial) transfer entry for axial scavenge forms a central column of gas and leaves the periphery unscavenged. A better arrangement is semi-tangential entry, called Curtis scavenging.

One method of achieving axial scavenge without the complexity of head poppet valves is Schliha porting (Figure 8.2.6). The inlet is controlled by the sliding tube valve, and part of the piston, with exhaust ports in the cylinder wall. This configuration has been built in various sizes. Transfer occurs out of the spigot on the piston, the fresh gas pushing the old gas down towards the exhaust ports in the cylinder wall. A disadvantage is the overall height of the engine.

A simpler system is Ivanko porting with the exhaust in the head controlled by a piston spigot (Figure 8.2.8). The power potential is good because of the large transfer port area that is possible. The swept volume should, perhaps, be based only on the annular part of the piston forming the actual combustion chamber.

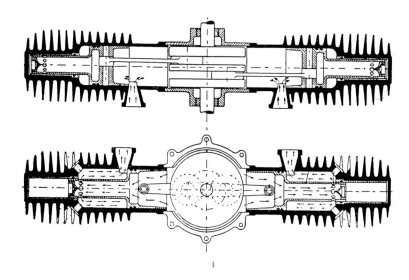

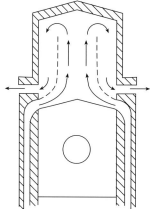

Figure 8.3.1. Scavenging of banded peripheral ports.

8.3 Peripheral Ports

Peripheral ports for reverse-flow scavenging were once favoured. They come in two forms – Banded and Alternating.

With banded or tiered ports, each type of port forms a more-or-less continuous band around the circumference. The transfer must therefore be entirely below the exhaust ports (Figure 8.3.1).

For banded ports, the transfer streams enter radially at a low angle. They then meet in the centre of the piston and rise up the centre of the bore like a fountain. The stream then spreads at the head, and comes down the bore periphery, as in Figure 8.3.1. The piston crown may be flat, curved or conical. Axial symmetry is maintained, which keeps thermal expansion as uniform as possible. Piston and cylinder remain truly circular.

Banded peripheral ports may be made by drilling, giving about 20 holes for each type of port, or by milling, slotting or broaching, giving typically three of four transfers and an equal number of exhaust ports.

For drilled ports, there are simply two rows of holes, with lateral spacing of at least $D/4$ for cylinder strength. Vertically spacing between the ports reduces mixing and entrainment of the transfer into the oppositely moving exhaust. Hence the vertical space below the exhaust upper edge, limited by exhaust timing, must be distributed between the exhaust band, the clearance, and the transfer band, e.g. holes of diameter 12% of the bore and 0.5 D vertical clearance, (6mm holes on a 50mm bore). The exhaust timing edge is at 30% of the stroke giving an exhaust timing of about 149°, and a transfer timing of about 93°. This highlights the problem of banded peripheral ports – short transfer timing. This is partly solved by excessive exhaust timing or by reducing separation between the exhaust and transfer, with consequent loss of fresh gas into the exhaust.

In compensation, a good total port width is possible because the full circumference can be used. The clearance between drilled holes should be at least one radius. With a hole diameter of 12% of the bore, the cylinder circumference is 26.2 hole diameters, so about 18 holes can be used. On a 50mm bore and stroke engine, the hole size could be around 6 mm diameter. The port areas are then 5.1 cm^2, with normalised area 26% and specific area 51 cm^2/litre. (5.1 mm^2/ cm^3).

With milled or sawn peripheral ports, there are usually four of each port. These may be stacked vertically, above each other, or offset. The latter minimises the interference between transfer and exhaust streams, but is structurally weaker. The port depths and spacing can be as drilled ports, i.e. port depth *h* can be about 12% of the bore. The four port circumferential widths can each be up to 20% of the circumference, or 60% of the bore. Each port would then be 6mm deep by 30mm wide, with an effective area of 1.80 cm², giving a total transfer area of 7.2 cm², and the same for the exhaust. The port normalised maximum area is then about 37%, and specific area 72 cm²/litre. This improvement over the drilled-holes is because the rectangular port provides more area than the circular one. For banded ports the areas are adequate. However, the short timing of transfer porting and its resulting poor angle-area are a limitation. Favouring the transfer depth at the expense of the exhaust depth sometimes helps.

The transfer passage for the peripheral band system is usually just an annular space around the lower cylinder. The cross-sectional area of a full annulus is

$$A = \frac{\pi}{4}\left(D_o^{\,2} - D_i^{\,2}\right)$$
$$\approx \pi D t$$

where *t* is the annular thickness, for which around 5% or 6% of the bore is usually adequate. This gives a normalised transfer cross-sectional area of 25% to 30%. With a full annulus, liner location must be provided elsewhere. In some cases, the full annulus is not used, but only passages to the individual ports. This design of porting is cheap to manufacture.

To reduce mixing of fresh transfer gas with the exhaust, and losses directly into the exhaust port, the odd configuration of Figure 8.3.2. was once proposed, with a similar scavenge pattern.

To overcome the problem of short transfer timing of banded ports, one must move to a system where the transfer and exhaust occupy different circumferential parts of the cylinder, so that the transfer timing can be longer. This can be done with peripheral porting by alternating the ports. The transfer ports can then be inclined quite steeply upwards (Figure 8.3.3). The scavenge pattern will then be entirely different from that of the banded

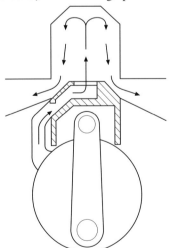

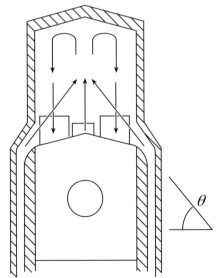

Figure 8.3.2. Fountain scavenge from the piston centre (after Söhnlein) intended to reduce fuel mixture loss to the exhaust flow. However, combustion chamber shape is a major problem.

Figure 8.3.3. Scavenging of overlapped peripheral ports. The angle is typically 50 degrees.

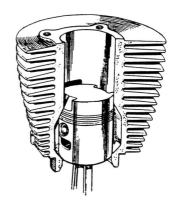

Figure 8.3.4. Early Villiers engine with peripheral porting, using two opposed exhaust ports with a pair of transfers between each. The transfers are inclined steeply upwards, and further guided up by the channels in the piston. The channels require the rings to be rather low, and also spoil the combustion chamber shape.

system. The transfer streams should meet near the top centre and puddle there, whilst the exhaust flows down between the transfer streams.

The exhaust ports must now be narrower to allow room for the transfers in between, and the clearance between the streams now requires circumferential space between the two types of port. Each exhaust port can subtend up to about 45° viewed axially. They do not need to be open right down to bdc. The actual normalised area may be 25%. The transfer ports are typically much narrower, each subtending about 25°, but are much deeper, running down to bdc. The transfer top edge allows some blowdown according to intended operating speed. The developed normalised maximum transfer port area is about 25%, but, because of the steep inclination angle, the effective normalised flow area is reduced by a cos θ factor to give a normalised flow area of about 15%. Although the transfer flow area is not improved over banded ports, the longer timing may give a better angle-area. Also the exhaust timing can be shorter, which suits lower speed engines with this type of porting. The overall result is improved performance (perhaps 10% more power), but more significantly fuel efficiency benefits because less of the fresh transfer mixture disappears with the exhaust.

8.4 Cross Flow

From the peripheral design with two transfers and two exhausts, a further reduction leads to only one transfer and one exhaust, placed on opposite sides of the cylinder. This is the cross-flow system. To prevent the piston rings from expanding into the ports several vertical port bridges are required, so each of the ports is subdivided into three to five sections. Nevertheless, a single transfer passage is normally used to feed all of the ports (Figure 8.4.1).

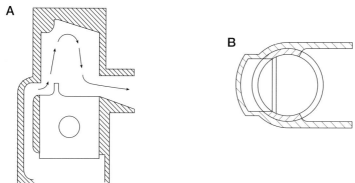

Figure 8.4.1. Schematic of cross-flow system (a) vertical section (b) horizontal section.

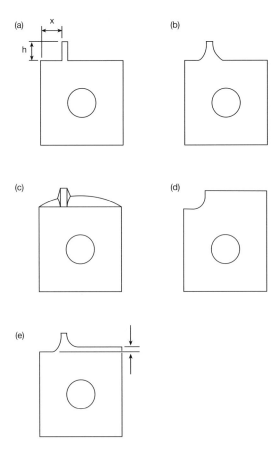

Figure 8.4.2. Baffled piston configurations (a) plain baffle, (b) filleted baffle, (c) crowned piston with filleted baffle, (d) stepped piston, (e) unequal levels.

Abandoning axial symmetry has its consequences. The transfer stream must now be prevented from exiting directly into the exhaust port. This is done by the baffle or step on the piston. This baffle has a considerable influence on the shape of the combustion chamber, and increases cooling of the combusted gas and heating of the piston and head. However, it can help with vaporisation of the fuel. The piston crown shape has had many variations.

Ideally, the transfer stream is deflected to a near vertical scavenging motion pushing up the transfer side of the cylinder and back down the other side. This gives uneven internal cooling. The quality of scavenging is strongly affected by the piston crown and baffle design. Figure 8.4.2 shows several types of piston and baffle. For the plain baffle, the baffle is typically 25% of the diameter from the transfer side and about 20% of the diameter in height ($x = 0.25 B$, $h = 0.20 B$). The normalised piston area on the transfer side of the baffle is then about 20%.

The best figures depend of course on the port sizes and shapes. A low baffle allows the transfer stream to cross the cylinder more, and encourages four-stroking (alternate firing). Some consider filleting of the baffle advantageous as it reduces the upper surface area of the piston, and possibly improves the transfer flow. An adverse side effect is that it can make it more difficult to fit the piston rings. The basic piston crown itself need not be flat. A stepped piston, as in Figure 8.4.2(d), gives the baffle effect with some possible advantages in combustion chamber shape. Mills in England patented such a layout in about 1950, claiming improved fuel atomisation.

For cross-flow scavenge and baffled pistons, the transfer passage may run down below the normal piston skirt, as in Figure 8.4.1(a), or be shortened and fed by an area from a notched skirt, especially where the alignment places the transfer passage over the shaft. Shortest of all, the passage may be fed from holes in the piston wall (skirt). This gives minimum passage length and volume, with the best crankcase compression, as well as cooling the piston and little end.

Figure 8.4.1(b) shows how compact the cross-flow system is in a direction transverse to the porting. This makes it especially suitable for multi-cylinder engines, where compactness is vital. It is also favoured for marine outboards.

For cross flow, the exhaust ports may subtend up to 180° peripherally but 150° is more usual. The transfer for a normal baffle position subtends 120°. For the example engine, the actual widths are 48mm and 43mm less any ring bridges. The flow is nominally radial, but there are losses due to the bridges, and to flow redirection of the baffle. The transfer passage may also limit the flow at the outer edges of the port. The timing is typically 140° exhaust, 120° transfer (possibly rising to 155° exhaust, 130° transfer or more, for maximum power). At 155°/130° timing the exhaust height is therefore about 0.324 S, and the transfer is 0.231 S. The maximum effective port area for the exhaust is then about 6.5 cm² and 4.3 cm² for the transfer. The normalised exhaust area is 33%, and the transfer about 22%. The baffle may however cause further restriction, as the normalised area on the transfer side of the baffle is only around 20%, and the flow shape is poor, with directional changes.

The basic cross-flow system has been improved by adding small supplementary ports to direct mixture from alongside the exhaust towards the baffle (Figure 8.4.3). The best flow direction is obtained when each supplementary port is in two thin vertical slits, a system patented by Perry in about 1975. These can be fed from the top of the existing transfer passage, rather than from separate vertical passages. These additional ports give a little more torque and power, improve piston cooling and possibly improve fuel efficiency. The result is nearly a Schnürle system but with small main transfers and a very large boost port, retaining the baffle.

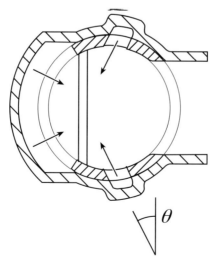

Figure 8.4.3. Supplementary transfer ports for a baffled piston (Perry ports).

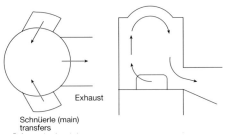

Figure 8.5.1. Basic concept of Schnürle porting.

8.5 Schnürle Ports

Where ultimate specific power output is required, there seems to be no substitute for ports based on the principle patented by Ing. Dr. E. Schnürle in 1925. He was actually designing for larger diesels, but the racing fraternity adopted his ideas, hence the DKW 125 cm^3 single cylinder racer designed by Zoller in the 1930s.

Schnürle wanted to use a flat-topped piston, avoiding the existing complex head shape and baffled piston crown, thus reducing thermal distortion and consequent seizure at high power. His idea was to have one exhaust port flanked by a pair of transfer ports directing the transfer gas away from the exhaust port (Figure 8.5.1). The transfer streams meet near to the far wall, where they turn up and loop back, over the top, and down on the exhaust side. This

Figure 8.5.2.
Diagrams of Schnürle's original German patents, 511102 of 1924, left, 520834 of 1925, right. The earlier version has the transfer stream entering at a steep upward angle. In the later version the entry is horizontal.

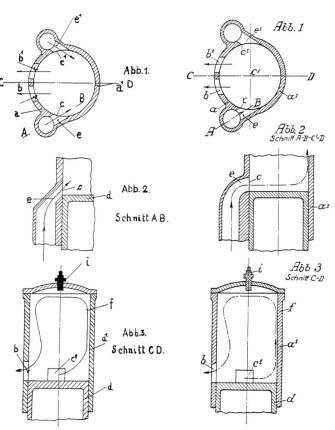

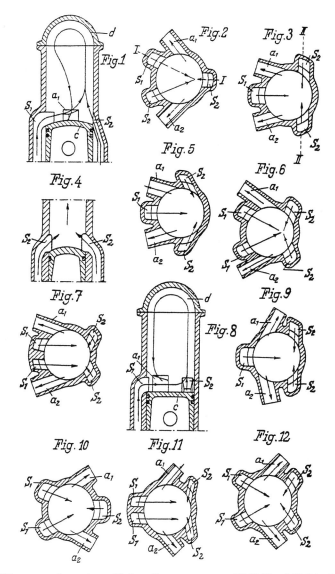

Figure 8.5.3. Diagrams from Auto Union German patent 716989 of 1935, showing porting concepts by Venediger. In contrast to the Schnürle patents, there are two exhaust ports, and several transfers and boost ports. These are mainly of historical interest and did not lead to significant products.

is why it is called loop scavenging. Once the streams join, the subsequent scavenging pattern is similar to a cross flow. Because the streams come from the exhaust side, their momentum prevents any major reversal of flow directly into the exhaust, so the piston can have a generally flat surface. Correct functioning requires careful choice of the flow directions. The power-producing ability of this porting system results from its large transfer port areas, coupled with an efficient combustion chamber shape because of the baffle-less flat piston. Relatively uniform piston temperatures minimise distortion.

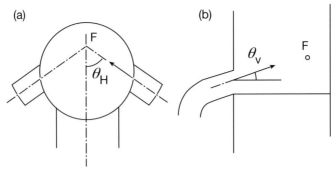

Figure 8.5.4. Basic Schnürle transfer flow-direction geometry
(a) 'Feed-point' and horizontal angle.   (b) Vertical angle.

Figure 8.5.4 defines the geometry of Schnürle transfer ports, comprising a horizontal angle θ_H from the line of symmetry, a focal point F, and a vertical angle θ_V. The gas stream does not actually emerge exactly according to the passage and port alignment. The flow angles, especially the vertical angle, vary with port opening. For a barely open port the stream initially emerges at about 50° to the horizontal; when the port is fully open it will emerge at some angle influenced by the port, according to the length of passage used to guide the flow. Similarly for the horizontal angle; when the port is barely open, the passage itself can exert little effect and the gas emerges radially. However, most of the mass flow occurs with the port fully or nearly fully open. This is the condition to be considered for design purposes. The horizontal angle influences the best vertical angle. For small θ_H, say 45°, the vertical angle θ_V must be small, 10° or less, otherwise the streams will hit the far wall high up, spreading sideways and remaining too close to the wall to give good displacement of the old gas.

Passages with a wide horizontal angle, say 70°, produce gas streams that meet over the piston before hitting the wall. They then spread forward, upwards and backwards in a central sheet, some probably going straight into the exhaust. To discourage this, a large θ_H needs a large θ_V to push the new gas up into the cylinder, avoiding the exhaust port.

A good compromise is a horizontal angle of 55° to 60°, with a vertical angle of about 15° for the port top edge. This behaves well in all circumstances. However, for the best performance in individual applications, these angles benefit from detailed optimisation. Larger θ_H allows a larger effective flow area for the port, possibly giving better power, but with lower trapping efficiency and worse fuel efficiency. For high thermal efficiency, θ_H should be smaller, pointing the streams further from the exhaust. The clearance between exhaust and transfer edges (the pillar width) has a similar effect. A narrow pillar, say 8% of the bore, allows a wide port with maximum power but greater entrainment fuel loss, whilst a wide pillar, say 16% of the bore, gives less power but better fuel efficiency. A classification of dimensions may therefore be as follows.

Horizontal angle from line of symmetry:		Vertical angle of top of main port:		Exhaust to transfer pillar width (% of bore)	
50°	Very small	0	Very small	6%	Very small
55°	Small	5°	Small	9%	Small
60°	Medium	10°	Medium	12%	Medium
65°	Large	15°	Large	15%	Large
70°	Very large	20°	Very large	18%	Very large

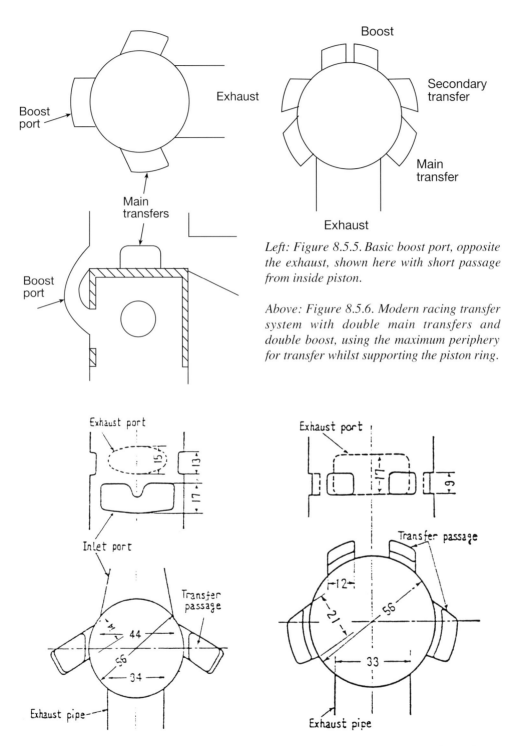

Left: Figure 8.5.5. Basic boost port, opposite the exhaust, shown here with short passage from inside piston.

Above: Figure 8.5.6. Modern racing transfer system with double main transfers and double boost, using the maximum periphery for transfer whilst supporting the piston ring.

Figure 8.5.7. Some example transfer sections (Ohigashi S, Hamamoto Y and Tanabe S, B.J.S.M.E., V14, N71, 1971).

169

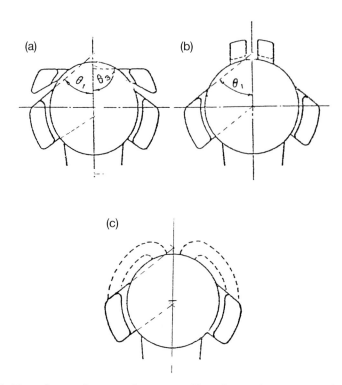

Figure 8.5.8. Transfer sections used on some Yamaha racing motorcycles (Naitoh and Nomura, 1971, SAE 710084).
(a) With supplementary transfers leaving space for a piston-controlled inlet.
(b) With twin boost ports, for rotary disc induction.
(c) Boost fed from main transfer passages, allowing piston inlet.

The vertical angle of the port also affects the power band. A small vertical angle tends to give higher peak power but a narrower power band. For maximum performance this should be optimised to within 1° or 2°.

By the mid 1950s, Schnürle porting for racing motorcycles was quite well understood, and attention turned to using the area of metal opposite the exhaust port for extra ports to increase the power. Further down the cylinder, this space was conveniently used for piston-controlled induction, but for rotary-valved engines this whole side of the cylinder remained unused. The first such extra port, or so-called 'boost port', was probably due to Kaaden, for MZ, in 1957 to 1959. This was a single port directly opposite the exhaust (Figure 8.5.5) fed from a short passage drawing mixture from inside the piston, improving little end cooling. The vertical angle of the top edge of this boost was 50° to 60° from the horizontal, to avoid disrupting the main transfer pattern. The piston port at passage entry should be deeper than the port itself to keep it fully open over the full duration of the port. By the mid 1960s most rotary-induction racing engines had at least one boost port. Then the Japanese picked up the Eastern European ideas and the number of ports proliferated. By the early 1970s there were many systems. The legacy has been the single or double boost port, effectively just a wide boost with a bridge, and secondary transfer ports (Figure 8.5.6).

The main variations shown in the accompanying illustrations are (a) boost, (b) double boost, (c) double boost with spreading passages to allow for piston induction, (d) secondary

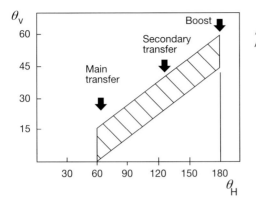

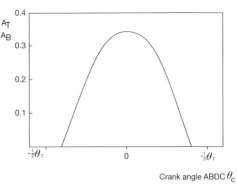

Figure 8.5.9. Trend of port angle with horizontal angle.

Figure 8.5.10. Flow area A(θ) for Schnürle systems (example).

transfers. Without a baffle on the piston, it is not possible to use a small vertical angle for the boost ports. The best vertical angle of a port is related to the horizontal angle of the individual port according to the trend of Figure 8.5.9.

Because of the need for a steep vertical angle on the boost ports, and because the secondary transfers need a more vertical angle than the mains and call for somewhat narrower main transfers, the effective flow area is not greatly increased by the extra ports. For low-speed engines they may not help at all. However for high-speed maximum-power engines they can certainly give some extra performance.

With a tuned exhaust pipe, the top edge of the exhaust port is very high, up to around half of the stroke. This gives a large port area even with a modest width. With untuned silencers, the exhaust timing is from 125° to 165° according to application. Slightly greater width may be advantageous. Plain transfers can have an effective flow width of about 0.45 bore each for a total normalised width of 0.90. Allowing for the effect of the required vertical angle on flow area, a full multiport system may reach a total normalised flow width of around 1.30, better than other systems. A graph of $A(\theta)$ is given in Figure 8.5.10.

Table 8.5.1 classifies the effective flow area of the transfer ports, normalised against bore area.

Table 8.5.1 Classification of transfer port areas

	H/B	W_{ET}/B	A_{ET}/A_B
Very small	0.14	0.5	0.09
Small	0.17	0.7	0.15
Medium	0.20	0.9	0.23
Large	0.23	1.1	0.32
Very large	0.26	1.3	0.43

The normalised port heights correspond to the transfer timing classification. Note the considerable variation in the port area. This is because both height and width may vary. Naturally, the associated passage cross-sectioned areas should also vary. For a racing engine, the passage shape and area are determined by power considerations, but for multi-cylinder engines, compactness may dominate. Figures 8.5.11 and 12 show two extremes of passages in axial view, the first for a multi-cylinder marine outboard, the second a 50 cm^3 motorcycle engine.

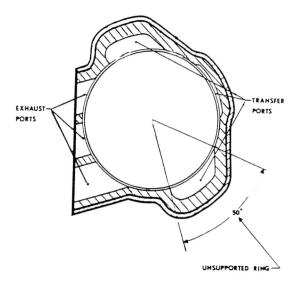

Figure 8.5.11. *Extremes of transfer passage cross-sectional shape. The label 'transfer ports' really refers to the transfer passage cross-section. Marine engine. (Kueny & Boerma, SAE 710580, 1971).*

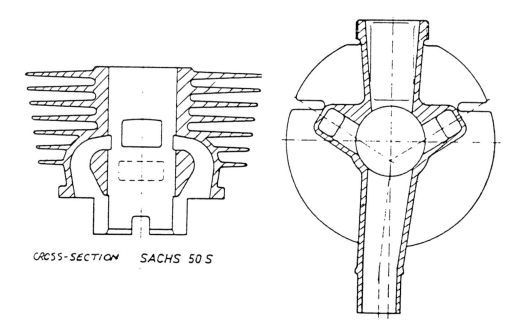

Figure 8.5.12. *Extremes of transfer passage cross-sectional shape. Sachs 50S motorcycle engine. (Waker, SAE 660009, 1966).*

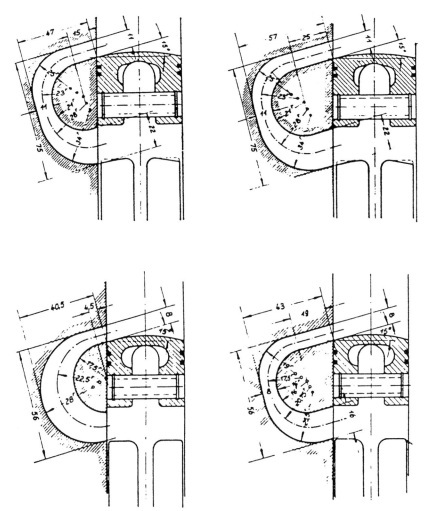

Figure 8.5.13. E. Ansorg investigated many transfer passage shapes, including these examples (Motor-Rundschau, 17/1966). One aim was to lengthen the passage to obtain better gas inertia properties, reducing the natural frequency.

For convenience of construction, the passage is sometimes cut right through from the cylinder inner wall, leaving no metal at all between the piston and the passage. This aspect of the passage shape may be characterised by the normalised maximum distance from the piston to the passage inside wall, on the passage centre plane, with values:

0% very small   5% small   10% medium   20% large   50% very large

Entry to the transfer passages can be from below the liner, partially notched into the lower edge of the liner, or from ports in the piston walls. The choice usually depends on the exhaust port position relative to the crankshaft. If the transfer passage entry is over the crank webs either the piston skirt and liner must be considerably notched, or a very long con-rod must be used. The former is preferred. The curvature of the passage has been found to affect the power curve, with a smooth passage curvature giving no more peak power, but more power away from the peaking speed.

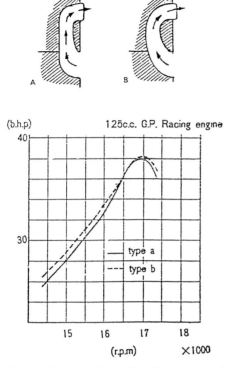

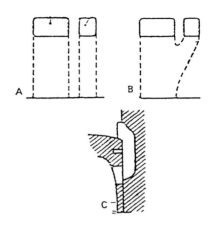

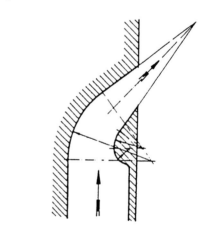

Above: Figure 8.5.15. Layout of transfer passages.
(a) Supplementary transfers
(b) Supplementary transfers fed from main passage
(c) Boost section
(Naitoh and Nomura, SAE 710084, 1971).

Above: Figure 8.5.14. The effect of transfer passage shape as found by Naitoh and Nomura, SAE 710084, 1971.

Right: Figure 8.5.16. Passage profile proposed by A.Jante (SAE 680468, 1968) intended to discourage flow separation at the inner surface.

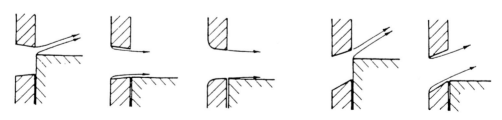

Figure 8.5.17. Gas flow pattern from conventional transfer ports, with various shapes and various piston positions. (Annand W.J.D. and Roe G.E., Gas Flow in the Internal Combustion Engine, Haessler, 1974.)

174

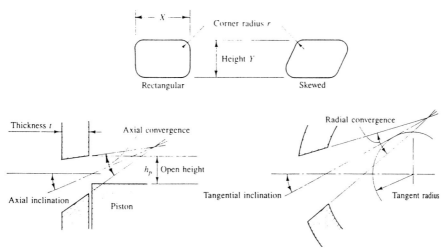

Figure 8.5.18. Transfer port geometry definitions (after Annand and Roe, 1974).

8.6 Resistance

The resistance of the transfer passages and ports can be measured in a flow rig for various degrees of port opening, or it can be analysed theoretically to show the relative importance of the various factors. From the point of view of power, it is better to minimise the resistance, consistent with timing and port size in relation to fuel efficiency, broad power band, etc.

The length and cross-sectional area of the transfer passage must be related to the port area to suit the intended use of the engine – high speed or low speed operation. The normalised total transfer passage cross-sectional area (area, including boost, divided by bore area), range from 6% minimum to as much as 36%, with 18% as an average figure.

For low speed operation, a passage area of 10% to 15% is generally best. The larger values are for very high-speed engines only.

A larger cross-sectional area reduces the passage frictional losses because the gas speed is lower. However, there is little advantage in making the passages disproportionate to the port area. Over-large passages cause problems at lower speed or part-throttle. They also increase the effective crankcase volume at tdc for the inlet process. The transfer passage cross-sectional area is therefore important for optimisation.

For comparative steady-state analysis it is convenient to work with an air volumetric flow rate of about $N_s V_s$, as for the inlet system, which is about 20 litre/s for the example engine.

For a given steady mass flow rate of air or fuel/air mixture, the steady-state transfer pressure losses (Figure 8.6.1) are the sum of

1. Entry loss
2. Pipe friction
3. Bends
4. Passage section changes
5. Port area change
6. Exit energy

Because the piston itself acts as the transfer valve, when the port is barely open the resistance depends almost entirely on the exit area and local shape. Nearly all the pressure

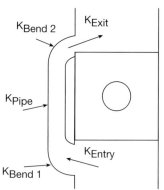

Figure 8.6.1. Transfer flow resistance pressure losses.

goes to produce exit kinetic energy with a high exit speed. However, when the port is fully or nearly fully open all the other factors come into play.

The basic pipe friction can be estimated from the equivalent diameter and length, considering the Reynolds number and roughness according to the Moody equation, as described for the inlet. A multiplicity of passages has more resistance than a single passage of the same cross-sectional area. Sandcast passages have significant roughness.

The entry loss is minimised by having an inlet somewhat larger than the general passage area, with rounded entry edges.

Passage bend loss is less for a single smooth 180° curve than for two sharper 90° bends. However, this aspect of design may be governed by the practicalities of construction and the thickness of the cylinder liner walls. Eliminating the first bend by an L-shaped passage as in Figure 8.6.2(c) may help, but the sharp radius of the re-entrant top edge of the entry is a disadvantage. This may be acceptable if blended to the piston gudgeon pin (wrist pin) boss at bdc.

Increase of the cross-sectional area along the flow direction makes the boundary layer operate against an adverse static pressure gradient. Flow separation from the walls may then occur, especially on the inside of a bend. A slightly contracting area prevents such separation. An expanding area is better avoided. An entry area of 20% to 50% more than the port maximum flow area with a smoothly reducing cross-section is good.

For a uniform-section passage the total loss coefficient may be estimated along the lines of Table 8.6.1. Usually the cross-sectional areas are different, so the K values cannot simply be added. Pressure loss coefficients can only be summed if they are based on the same flow velocity, or the same cross-sectional area. This is rarely the case. It is the actual pressure losses that must be added. This total pressure loss can then be expressed as a loss coefficient

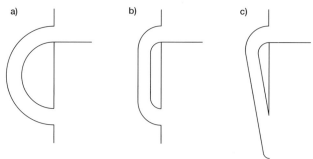

Figure 8.6.2. Practical transfer passage bends.

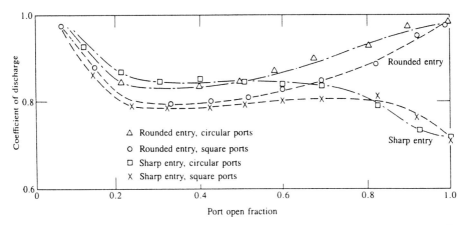

Figure 8.6.3. Experimentally observed steady-state transfer discharge coefficients (from Wallace, Proc. I. Mech. E., V182, Pt 3D, pp134–144, 1967).

on some particular speed or area, such as the exit area, or some reference area. Figure 8.6.3 gives some results for experimental discharge coefficients.

Table 8.6.1. Example transfer passage pressure loss coefficients K

Feature	K value
Entry	0.5
Bends	1.6
Pipe (L/D ~ 5)	0.4
Exit	1.0

The expected mean flow velocity is given by Bernoulli's equation applied from the crankcase through to the cylinder. The speed U_1 in the case is negligible, so

$$P_1 - P_2 = \tfrac{1}{2}\rho U_2^2 K$$

where the K factor is the value relating the pressure losses to the speed U_2. The flow speed is then given by

$$U_2 = \left[\frac{2(P_1 - P_2)}{\rho K}\right]^{1/2}$$

For gas density 1.2 kg/m³ and an average pressure difference 30 kPa (0.3 atmospheres), with $K = 3.5$, the resulting air speed is 120 m/s. As this is around Mach 0.35, compressible gas dynamics are needed for accurate results. Considerable gas speeds do occur.

With a maximum normalised transfer passage/port area of 30%, on the example engine this is 5.89 cm² and the volumetric flow rate at the calculated velocity is

$$\dot{Q} = UA$$
$$= 0.0789 \text{ m}^3\text{/s}$$
$$\approx 79 \text{ litre/s}$$

The swept volume of 100 cm³ could then be transferred at this rate in 1.27 milliseconds. Considering a realistic transfer angular duration of about 120° corresponding to the 1.27 ms, the time for one whole revolution will be 3.8 ms, allowing good breathing up to 260 rev/s or 15,800 rev/min. This is well in excess of potential running speed, possibly because neither the exhaust port resistance nor the inertia of the transfer gas have been considered. However, the figures are in a moderately realistic range. A more detailed study would consider the angle-area integral of the port, as the above basic calculation treats the port as fully open throughout.

Because K is not a small value, for a low resistance of the complete transfer system the passage cross-sectional area should exceed the port exit area.

8.7 Resonance

The action of the gases in the transfer passages is subject to more complex dynamics than is indicated by simple steady flow resistance. Because of the high frequency of operation the inertia of the gas must be considered. The transfer action therefore takes some time to build up speed, and may be subject to resonance. Because the passages are relatively short the resonance is of the Helmholtz type, rather than acoustic where a pressure wave moves along the system.

Figure 8.7.1 shows the solid dynamic analogue of the mass of transfer gas suspended on two springs, and also having a quadratic resistance from gas friction, as seen in the previous section.

For more than one transfer passage, the passages may be considered equivalent to one passage of the total cross-sectional area, A_T, and mean length L_T. The mass of gas is then

$$m = \rho A_T L_T$$

The piston is at or around bottom dead centre, so the crankcase bdc volume must be used for the first stiffness, excluding the transfer volume. The effective crankcase gas stiffness (as developed in Chapter 7) is

$$k_1 = \frac{\gamma P_0 A_T^2}{V_{CB}}$$

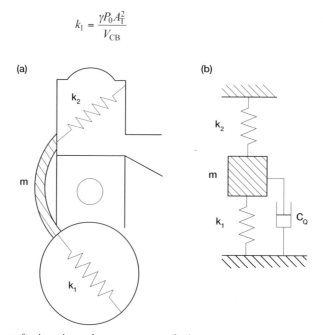

Figure 8.7.1. Transfer inertia and resonance analysis.

The stiffness due to the cylinder gas is

$$k_2 = \frac{\gamma P_0 A_T^2}{V_{CyB}}$$

where V_{CyB} is the bdc volume of the cylinder, slightly more than the swept volume.

Our example engine has a transfer passage length $L_T = 1.4\ S = 70$ mm and a normalised transfer passage cross-section area of about 0.30, with $A_T = 6$ cm^2 in total. The transfer volume is then $V_T = 42$ cm^3 (0.42 V_S), and the mass of air in the passages is 0.051 g. A pressure difference of 30 kPa on an area of 6 cm^2 gives a force of 18 N. The resulting gas acceleration would be 350 km/s^2 (36,000 g). Compared with the resistive speed calculated as 134 m/s, at this acceleration it would take 0.38 ms to reach that speed, which is 27° of crank motion. This is significant in relation to the resistive transfer period of 1.27 ms. This confirms that gas inertia does need to be considered.

Unfortunately, the actual transfer dynamic analysis is not easy to perform to worthwhile accuracy, because the cylinder gas exits to the exhaust system, and not to a constant pressure. Hence the cylinder pressure does not depend solely on the transferred quantity of gas, so the cylinder gas does not really have a predictable effective stiffness. About all that can be done is to assume a constant pressure in the cylinder, and that the exhaust system does its job properly.

Then the resonance equation is similar to the inlet and, with a transfer natural frequency

$$f_{NT} = \frac{C}{2\pi} \sqrt{\frac{A_T}{V_{CB} L_T}}$$

For the example engine the transfer natural frequency is $f_{NT} = 350$ Hz, indicating that resonance effects may be important. In fact, because the transfer passages are short, and their area largely dictated by other factors, for production engines the transfer natural frequency is high relative to transfer period and the engine speed. However, for racing engines it may be possible to tune the transfers to a useful half oscillation at peak speed, and enhance the power. Because the transfer resonance of practical transfer passages tends to be too fast, it may help to make them longer. It also means that excessive cross-sectional area is disadvantageous. Hence the passage area is a compromise between low losses and best gas inertia.

Ideally, detailed analysis of this factor should be achieved by numerical time-stepping simulation of the whole engine, but at present this is beyond the private tuner or developer.

CHAPTER 9:

Scavenging

9.1 Introduction

Scavenging is the removal of old exhaust gas from the cylinder.

The transfer system should maximise the gas flow from the crankcase to the cylinder, filling the cylinder, but without the new gas escaping from the exhaust port. For the new gas to displace the old gas, and not merely mix with it, the streams of transfer gas must be carefully directed and shaped. Hence the shape of the transfer passages and ports is important.

For a cross-scavenged engine, the position, height and shape of the piston crown and baffle are critical. How the transfer streams behave is investigated by watching the gas flow and dynamic pressures with the cylinder head removed. These give what are called Jante (pronounced yanter) pressure patterns, which indicate how to improve the port shapes.

The head shape influences the way the transfer streams reverse at the top of the cylinder. The transfer streams partially mix with the old gas, giving rise to alternative scavenge models based on displacement or mixing. With a tuned exhaust, some fresh gas is deliberately drawn out into the exhaust header, and then forced back into the cylinder just before exhaust closure. When the cylinder is finally closed, the trapped gas will contain pockets of old gas and pockets of pure fresh gas with all gradations of mixes. These are likely to affect ignition and subsequent combustion. Also the gas is moving when trapped, and will continue to move and mix during compression, combustion and the power-stroke.

All these factors need to be considered in analysing the scavenge process.

9.2 Jante Patterns

For correctly designed transfer ports, the scavenge gas passes up the scavenge side of the cylinder, as shown in Figures 9.2.1 for a cross-flow engine and in Figure 9.2.2 for Schnürle ports. By removing the cylinder head and then pressurising the case, the flow emerging from the top of the cylinder can be studied. This is sometimes done by a comb of Pitot tubes for measuring the dynamic pressure, from which the velocity distribution may be deduced. Figure 9.2.3 shows a Pitot comb with its array of manometers over a simulated engine cylinder. The resulting velocity patterns, (Figure 9.2.4) are named after Alfred Jante, who first performed such tests. Comparison of cylinder designs that perform well with those that

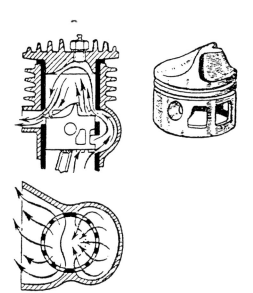

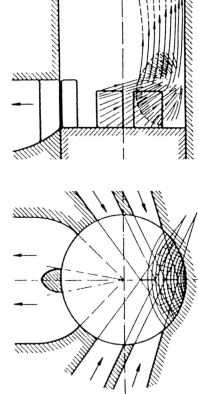

Figure 9.2.1. Czechoslovakian Sladky engine of 1955 with baffled two-ring piston, showing pattern of cross-flow scavenging. Note the short transfer passage, with the gas fed into the passage from large holes in the piston skirt and from just below the piston.

Figure 9.2.2. Schnürle scavenging, also with a rising column of gas on the transfer side of the cylinder (Jante, 1968, SAE 680468). Without a cylinder head, the velocity distribution of the rising air can be investigated by Pitot tube. With the head on, the gas reverses and comes back down on the exhaust side.

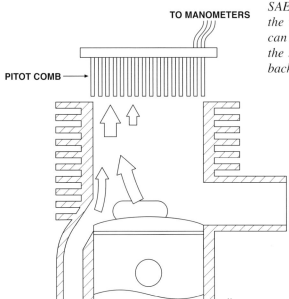

TO MANOMETERS

PITOT COMB →

Figure 9.2.3. Investigation of scavenge flow by comb of Pitot tubes.

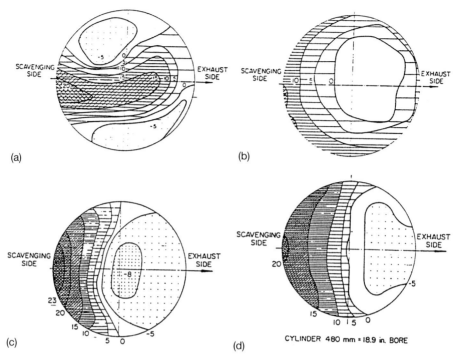

Figure 9.2.4. Jante patterns of scavenging flow (Jante, 1968, SAE 680468, reviewed in Shaeffer 1970): (a) tongue pattern (bad), (b) wall pattern (bad), (c) and (d) good.

perform poorly has shown good and bad patterns. Figure 9.2.4 shows (a) a tongue pattern, (b) a poor wall pattern, (c) and (d) being good patterns in which the rising flow is intermediate between (a) and (b).

Another poor pattern is where the displacement shape is satisfactory but displaced round the cylinder, perhaps by 10° or 20°.

In Figure 9.2.4 (a) there are actually negative velocities where the tongue is creating a circulating flow at its sides. Figure 9.2.5 shows how the tongue pattern and wall pattern arise from incorrectly aligned ports.

Figure 9.2.4 (c) actually shows a dynamic pattern obtained by motoring the engine, whereas (d) was obtained by steady flow with a pressurised crankcase. The steady flow test

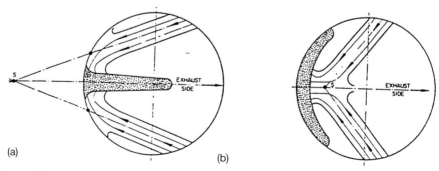

Figure 9.2.5. Misalignment of transfer ports resulting in (a) tongue and (b) wall scavenge patterns. (Jante, 1968, SAE 680468, reviewed in Shaeffer, 1970.)

may actually be more difficult as the flow is sometimes prone to lateral instability when the ports are fully open. This may not appear with partially open ports or in motored testing because the unstable period is too short for the problem to develop.

One must recognise the distinction between the oscillatory flow of a motored test and steady flow. The distance that the gas emerges from the transfer ports in a real engine for one scavenge period (distance X) is two or three times the diameter of the cylinder. The average efflux velocity is U, and the time of efflux is

$$t = \frac{X}{U}$$

For a moving engine, this depends on the engine speed. At high speeds, in general t is less, so X is smaller, giving incomplete scavenge. Therefore, in a motored scavenge test the speed of motoring (N_S in rev/s or N_M in rev/min) can be important. At very high speed the ports will already be closing when the pulse of gas first reaches the head or test comb.

In terms of dimensional analysis, the flow pattern depends on what is called the Strouhal number of the test, which is defined as

$$N_{Str} = \frac{N_S B}{U}$$

where N_S is the motoring speed in rev/s, B is the bore and U is the average efflux velocity from the ports. The Strouhal number is zero for a steady flow test. The motoring test is best done at running speed. If this is impractical, the steady flow test can still be of value.

9.3 Scavenging Models

Ideally, the fresh gas entering the cylinder simply drives the old gas before it, without mixing, until the cylinder is full of the fresh gas and no old gas remains. If the exhaust port could then be closed at the right moment this would give excellent torque and fuel economy. This ideal is called 'perfect displacement scavenging', usually shortened to displacement scavenging.

This ideal model is not achieved in reality. Some turbulence and mixing of old and new gas always occurs, and some fresh gas always escapes. In general, every degree of mixing occurs, though it sometimes helps to think in terms of pure new gas, mixed gas, and old gas (Figure 9.3.1), for various degrees of scavenge. Even after the exhaust port has closed there can be pockets of old gas in the cylinder. The mixing occurs at the turbulent interface between the incoming jet of fresh gas and the old combusted gas. At (b), even though scavenge is incomplete, the new gas is about to start escaping.

The transfer jets are actually turbulent free jets, and likely to mix substantially with the old gas. As explained in the Fluids chapter, the boundary of a free jet expands at a total included angle of about 15°. The gas exterior to the jet is drawn in radially and then retained and becomes part of the jet itself, diluting the gas of the original jet. The core of pure gas reduces in size to zero over a length equal to a few inlet diameters.

Well away from the source, the overall jet diameter is proportional to distance X from the source. The jet cross-sectional area is proportional to X^2, local velocity to $1/X$ and the total jet mass flow rate to X, the momentum flux mU being constant. The mass flow rate increases with X, because of entrainment of extra gas, so the average purity of the source gas is proportional to $1/X$. Of course the purity is not uniform across the section, being highest at the centre and reducing to zero at the edges. In an engine, a typical equivalent port diameter is about 20% of the bore, and the total travel needed for scavenging is $2B$ or more, so the jet

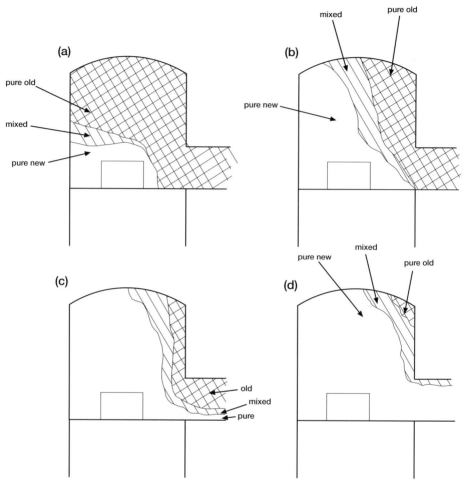

Figure 9.3.1. Partially scavenged cylinder containing some pure fresh gas, some old exhaust gas, and some mixed gas. Alternatively old gas may be left in the centre, with the new gas passing around it, depending on the porting arrangement.

length is likely to be about ten times its initial diameter, giving scope for considerable mixing.

When a jet is near a solid surface, such as an engine cylinder, the situation is different, because old gas cannot be entrained at the metal surface. Therefore turbulent mixing and jet area expansion cannot occur at the solid side. If the jet is near to a metal surface then entrainment of existing gas from between the jet and the solid surface draws the jet down onto the surface. Jets inside a cylinder therefore tend to attach to the metal. A jet will try to follow around the outside of a curved surface. This is called Coanda effect. How much the jet deflects before it separates from a surface depends upon a balance between the build up of the boundary layer of low speed gas from friction, and the entrainment effect speeding it up again.

A jet directed down onto a solid surface spreads in a thin layer, which is bad for displacing the old gas. It increases the surface area of the jet and hence the turbulent mixing. Similarly, a non-circular jet, especially a wide flattened one, will mix more quickly.

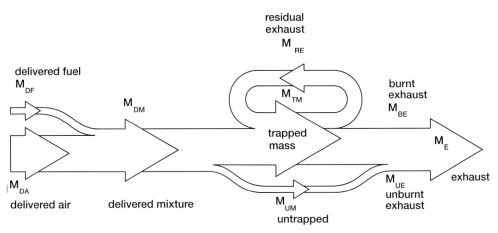

Figure 9.3.2   Mass flows during scavenging.

With well-designed Schnürle ports, the jets meet and rise up the cylinder, giving a suitable Jante test pattern. Inevitably, there will be some mixing on the exposed surface across the centre of the bore (Figure 9.3.1), and similarly for a baffled cross-flow engine. Banded peripheral ports will have mixing above the incoming jets, and around the rising central integrated jet fountain

An alternative scavenging model developed in light of the above is called the perfect mixing model. Again, this is an extreme case, not met in practice. In this model as soon as any fresh gas enters the cylinder, it instantly mixes perfectly with all existing gas. Therefore the gas in this model is always uniform, with no regions of greater purity of new or old gas.

The perfect displacement model and the perfect mixing model of scavenging are two idealised extremes, originally introduced by Hopkinson for large marine diesels. Real engines behave between these two extremes.

The actual cylinder contents vary up to when the piston closes the exhaust port. Neglecting leakage, this trapping or captive point determines the mass and character of gas available for combustion.

Figure 9.3.2 shows the mass flows through the engine, per cycle.

The basic types of material involved are:

1. Air
2. Fuel
3. Mixture (of fuel and air)
4. Exhaust (burned gas)

At any instant during the scavenge process, the masses of each of these materials in the cylinder are m_A, m_F, m_M and m_E respectively, where

$$m_M = m_A + m_F$$

Note that the term 'mixture' refers to mixed air and fuel, rather than to mixed air, fuel and exhaust.

The mass of air and fuel brought through the inlet system into the crankcase equals the mass transferred from the case to the cylinder, over one cycle, because for steady operation the mass in the crankcase is constant across whole cycles.

The masses are classified not just by the type of material (A, F, M, E) but also by the process which it undergoes (Figure 9.3.2). Hence there are:

1. Delivered mass (D)
2. Trapped mass (T)
3. Untrapped mass (U)
4. Residual exhaust mass (RE)
5. Burned exhaust mass (BE)
6. Unburned exhaust mass (UE)
7. Exhaust mass (E)

The delivered mass (per cycle) is the mass taken through the inlet system. It is equal to that transferred from the crankcase to the cylinder. The trapped mass is that actually held in the cylinder when the exhaust port closes. The untrapped mass is the part of the delivered mass that passes right through the cylinder during scavenging and is left outside the cylinder with the burned exhaust. The recycled mass is the mass of exhaust fumes retained in the cylinder, as in an unscavenged pocket or by mixing with incoming gas, or which makes a temporary escape to the exhaust, only to be forced back into the cylinder.

The exhaust mass is simply the mass left outside the cylinder, and by conservation of mass must be equal to the delivered mass. The exhaust partially comprises burned gas, and partially the unburned, untrapped mixture.

Using r_{FA}, the fuel/air mass ratio defined by

$$r_{FA} = \frac{m_F}{m_A}$$

and combining the above mass specifications gives the following detailed masses:

1. m_{DA}, delivered air
2. m_{DF}, delivered fuel
3. m_{DM}, delivered mixture
   $$m_{DM} = m_{DA} + m_{DF} = m_{DA}(1 + r_{FA})$$
4. m_{TA}, trapped air
5. m_{TF}, trapped fuel
6. m_{TM}, trapped mixture
   $$m_{TM} = m_{TA} + m_{TF} = m_{TA}(1 + r_{FA})$$
7. m_{RE}, residual exhaust
8. m_T, trapped mass
   $$m_T = m_{TM} + m_{RE}$$
9. m_{UA}, untrapped air
10. m_{UF}, untrapped fuel
11. m_{UM}, untrapped mixture
    $$m_{UM} = m_{UA} + m_{UF} = m_{UA}(1 + r_{FA})$$
12. m_{BE}, burned exhaust
13. m_{UE}, unburned exhaust
14. m_E, exhaust mass
    $$m_E = m_{BE} + m_{UE}$$

In the following explanation of the above terms, it is useful to refer to Figure 9.3.2. The unburned exhaust mass equals the untrapped mixture mass, as these are the same thing:

$$m_{UE} = m_{UM} = m_{UA} + m_{UF}$$

The burned exhaust mass equals the trapped mass minus the residual exhaust that does not escape from the cylinder:

$$m_{BE} = m_T - m_{RE}$$

From Figure 9.3.2, the burned exhaust mass also equals the delivered mixture mass minus the untrapped mixture.

$$m_{BE} = m_{DM} - m_{UM}$$

The fuel/air ratio in the equations for the delivered, trapped and untrapped mixture masses above has been taken as constant. In principle this may be variable: the untrapped mixture may be richer or leaner than the trapped mixture. Obviously this could be so for an engine with direct fuel injection, but for a normal two-stroke with carburettor or low-pressure fuel injection to the inlet pipe, the constant ratio approximation should be acceptable. This is an important issue for fuel efficiency and emissions. The ratio is not constant for an engine with air scavenging and timed fuel injection through, for example, the transfer port.

From the above, certain non-dimensional ratios may be formed, to indicate the behaviour of the engine. The masses used per cycle above may be compared with each other, or with a reference mass m_{ref}. This reference mass is taken as the ambient air density ρ_{AA} multiplied by a reference volume. In studying the engine behaviour it may be best to take the reference volume as the trapped swept volume, or perhaps as the trapped capacity, i.e. the trapped swept volume plus the combustion volume. However, it is easier to use the total swept volume V_S, so

$$m_{ref} = \rho_{AA} V_S$$

For the example engine this is:

$$m_{ref} = 1.225 \, \text{kg/m}^3 \times 98.2 \times 10^{-6} \, \text{m}^3 = 0.120 \, \text{g}$$

The volume of air at atmospheric pressure consumed by the engine in one revolution, compared with the reference volume, is the air delivery ratio, or just delivery ratio (η_D):

$$\eta_D = \frac{V_{DA}}{V_{ref}}$$

In volumetric comparisons the air volume is always considered to be at reference pressure, so the volumetric ratios are equal to the corresponding mass ratios.

Delivery ratio should not be called volumetric efficiency. The correct definition of volumetric efficiency excludes the air passing untrapped through the cylinder. Hence the volumetric efficiency (η_V) is

$$\eta_V = \frac{m_{TA}}{m_{ref}} = \eta_{TA} \eta_D$$

where η_{TA} is the air trapping efficiency. The volumetric efficiency is lower than the delivery ratio because of imperfect trapping. The air trapping efficiency is normally taken as equal to a general trapping efficiency applicable to the mixture of air and fuel. Charging efficiency usually relates to masses, whereas volumetric efficiency relates to volumes.

As much of the fuel will probably vaporise, the mixture delivery ratio is relevant. This is

$$\eta_{DM} = \frac{m_{DM}}{m_{ref}}$$

The air trapping efficiency is the trapped air as a fraction of the delivered air:

$$\eta_{TA} = \frac{m_{TA}}{m_{DA}}$$

and the mixture trapping efficiency is

$$\eta_{TM} = \frac{m_{TM}}{m_{DM}}$$

For a uniform distribution of fuel in the air, the mixture trapping efficiency is equal to the air trapping efficiency. Therefore both of these can be represented simply by η_T, and simply called the trapping efficiency.

Hence the mass of trapped air is

$$m_{TA} = \eta_T \, m_{DA}$$
$$= \eta_T \, \eta_D \, m_{ref}$$
$$= \eta_V \, m_{ref}$$

The air scavenging efficiency is defined as the delivered air mass divided by the total mass trapped in the cylinder:

$$\eta_{SCA} = \frac{m_{DA}}{m_{TT}}$$

The mixture scavenging efficiency is

$$\eta_{SCM} = \frac{m_{DM}}{m_{TT}}$$

To some extent these indicate how well the porting, for a given engine speed, will drive the old gases from the cylinder. Hence the use of mixture scavenging efficiency is probably more appropriate. At low speed the scavenging efficiency may be well over 1.0, indicating excess mixture supply, good for driving out old gas, but inefficient in terms of fuel wastage for a carburetted engine.

The purity of the (trapped) air is defined as

$$\eta_{PA} = \frac{m_{TA}}{m_T}$$

which relates the trapped air mass to the trapped total mass. More significant physically is the mixture purity value

$$\eta_{PM} = \frac{m_{TM}}{m_T}$$

as a perfect filling of fresh mixture gives a value of 1.0 to η_{PM}, but significantly less for η_{PA} because of the fuel mass.

The mixture charging efficiency is

$$\eta_{ChM} = \frac{m_{TM}}{m_{ref}}$$

Some of the above are more appropriate to use with large two-stroke diesels, which are scavenged by air rather than by mixture.

The main parameters of interest to a competition two-stroke are:

1. air delivery ratio, η_{DA}
2. mixture delivery ratio, η_{DM}
3. trapping efficiency, η_T
4. air volumetric efficiency, η_V
5. mixture charging efficiency, η_{ChM}
6. trapped mixture purity, η_{PM}

These are all of interest with regard to torque and power. The third is of special interest with regard to fuel efficiency.

In particular, the trapped air mass is

$$m_{TA} = \eta_T \eta_D \, m_{ref}$$
$$= \eta_V \, m_{ref}$$

where η_V is the air volumetric efficiency, i.e.

$$\eta_V = \eta_T \eta_D$$

Figure 9.3.3 shows the variation of delivery ratio, trapping efficiency and volumetric efficiency for perfect displacement scavenging. This is based on unlimited supply of air. The delivery ratio does not really rise exactly linearly with time or crank angle. For this scavenge model, the trapping efficiency is 1.0 (100%) until the cylinder is full of fresh mixture, with no escape of mixture up to that point. Once the cylinder is full, any further delivery simply results in an equal mass of mixture being lost through the exhaust. The volumetric efficiency therefore remains at 1.0. Increasing losses cause a drop in the trapping efficiency, which is inversely proportional to the delivered mass. The engine torque basically depends on the volumetric efficiency. Low engine speeds occur to the right of the diagram (long time to allow scavenging) whilst high speeds occur at the left, where volumetric efficiency falls due to lack of time. The fuel efficiency of the engine depends on the trapping efficiency η_T. At higher speed this is good. At low speed there is overcomplete scavenge with losses from the exhaust port.

Figure 9.3.4 shows the corresponding diagram for the idealised model of perfect-mixing scavenging. The trapping efficiency is initially 1.0, but as the amount of delivered air builds

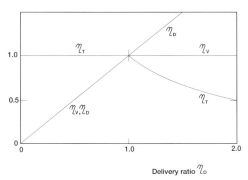

Figure 9.3.3   Delivery ratio η_D, trapping efficiency η_T and volumetric efficiency η_V versus delivery ratio for idealised perfect-displacement scavenging.

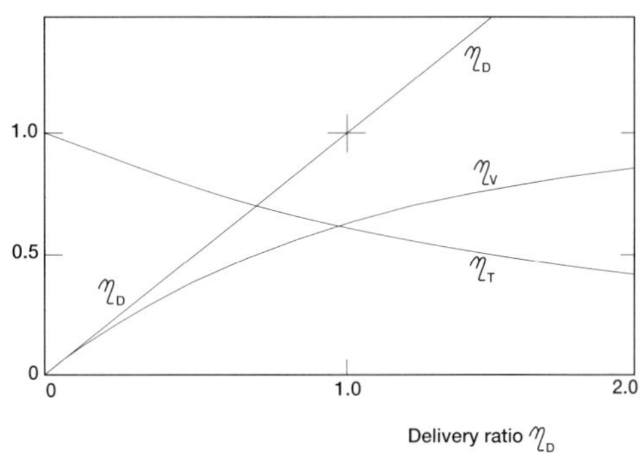

Figure 9.3.4   Delivery ratio η_D, trapping efficiency η_T and volumetric η_V versus delivery ratio efficiency for idealised perfect-mixing scavenging.

up the trapping efficiency steadily falls, whilst the volumetric efficiency rises. The equations are:

$$\eta_V = 1 - e^{-m_D/m_{D2}}$$

$$\eta_T = \frac{\eta_V}{\eta_D}$$

Figure 9.3.5. compares the volumetric efficiency curves for the two theoretical types of scavenging, whilst Figure 9.3.6. compares the trapping efficiency.

Real scavenge behaviour, requiring special rigs and instrumentation to measure, is conveniently illustrated on graphs which include the ideal models for comparison. In practice, engines generally behave between the two model extremes, with a combination of displacement and mixing. Even though some mixing starts immediately, this is not perfect mixing, and does not necessarily lead to immediate loss of fuel/air mixture. Most real engines at first tend to approximate pure displacement, followed by increased mixing behaviour later in the scavenge process.

Bigger ports increase delivery ratio, with improved volumetric efficiency and purity, but decreased trapping ratio, generally resulting in better power at the cost of fuel efficiency.

With longer exhaust timing, allowing bigger ports, the trapped capacity (trapped swept volume plus combustion volume) is smaller. The effective engine volume is therefore smaller with less torque produced. Because scavenging can occur more quickly, the power can increase. This is limited by two factors. Other resistances in series (e.g. the inlet system) put an upper limit on the useful cylinder port sizes. Also, large ports allow poorer trapping with more mixture escaping. Therefore, the optimum cylinder port size and the timing for maximum power depend on the inlet system, and, of course, on the exhaust.

The gas finally trapped in the cylinder is by no means uniform. There may be pockets of almost pure fresh mixture and other pockets of old gas, with a complex distribution of mixing. The old hot low-density gas results in wide variations of local temperature and density.

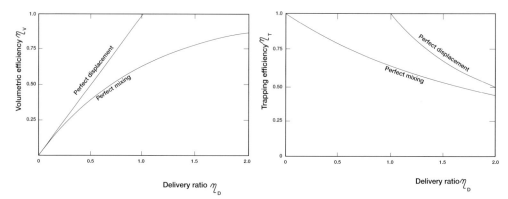

Figure 9.3.5. Volumetric efficiency compared for the two theoretically idealised types of scavenge.

Figure 9.3.6. Trapping efficiency compared for the two theoretically idealised types of scavenge.

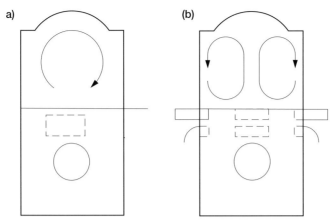

Figure 9.4.1. Tumbling motion of trapped gas, at port closure;
(a) Cross flow or Schnürle, (b) Peripheral ports (vortex ring seen in section).

Swirl and Tumble
Swirl is motion of the trapped gas around the cylinder axis. It is important for four-stroke engines, but for crankcase-scavenged two-strokes it should be small, because the flow is normally symmetrical about the central plane. However, flow asymmetries may occur.

Tumble is motion of the trapped gas about a transverse axis, Figure 9.4.1. This can be considerable for a cross-flow or Schnürle scavenge engine. On the other hand, for peripheral ports with low horizontal entry, the overall tumble is technically zero, but there maybe counter-rotating cells with local tumble motion, or an axisymmetrical vortex ring as in Figure 9.4.1(b).

For Schnürle ports, the tumble motion is about 360° during the transfer period. Friction causes the tumble motion to reduce with time. However, the compression process greatly reduces the relevant moment of inertia of the gas about its axis of rotation. This tends to speed up the rate of tumble. Tumble motion during the compression stroke improves the mixing and prepares the gas for combustion. It also has considerable effect on the combustion process itself.

CHAPTER 10

The Exhaust System

10.1 Introduction

In the early days of engines, the exhaust was simply there to allow the used gas out of the cylinder. Today the exhaust system of a racing engine is a vital part of the design. The divergent-convergent exhaust system can more than double the power output of the engine.

The complete exhaust system can be considered in three parts

1. The exhaust port
2. The exhaust passage
3. The exterior system

This is a convenient division because the port may be in a cylinder liner, the passage is in the cylinder or crankcase casting, and the exterior system is the removable part.

The exterior system takes one of many possible forms, according to the type of engine. The main possibilities are:

1. Open exhaust
2. Expansion box muffler
3. Minipipe
4. Megaphone
5. Divergent-convergent tuned pipe
6. Magic muffler
7. Modified di-con tuned pipe

The choice of exhaust system depends very much upon the application.

The various systems have considerably different effects on the torque and power curves. Other issues involved in the selection include noise, fuel consumption, weight and packaging, the last of these tending to be more problematic for multi-cylinder engines.

The terms quarter-wave, half-wave and full-wave are sometimes used to describe certain exhaust systems. Quarter-wave means mini-pipes and short megaphones; half-wave (perhaps illogically) means mid-length megaphone; full-wave means complete resonant exhausts. These terms refer, of course, to the passage of pressure waves along the system.

10.2 The Exhaust Port

In the case of peripheral ports, there may be several equal-sized exhaust ports. For baffled cross-flow engines, there are likely to be four exhausts and four transfers, with vertical bars providing support for the rings. For Schnürle transfer there is often only one exhaust port.

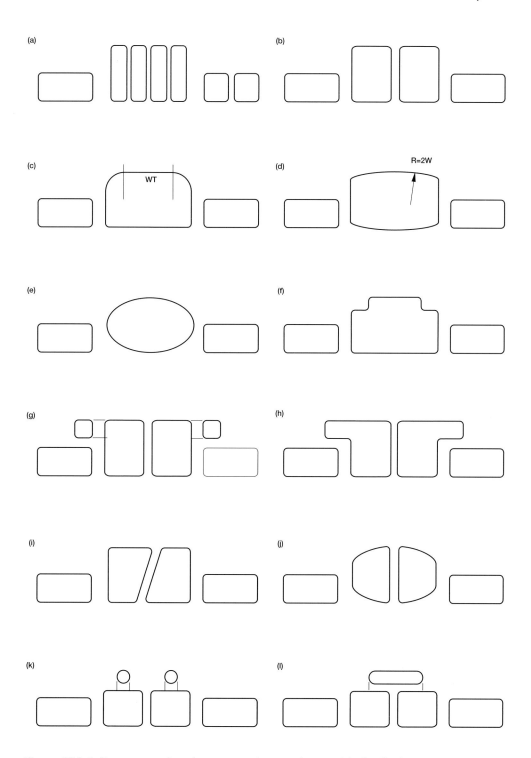

Figure 10.2.1. Some example exhaust port shapes, shown with the flanking main transfers, as a cylinder development.

Figure 10.2.1 shows some of the shapes that have been used. Individual port widths should normally be kept below about 60% of the bore, maximum 70%, to prevent ring problems. Up to 80% may be possible for short life with special design. The latter figure is only possible with rounded port corners and careful detail shaping of the upper and lower edges to ease the ring back into its groove. In practice, therefore, it is common to have a single bridge in the centre of the exhaust port. This disrupts the flow, which is clearly disadvantageous where absolute maximum power is required. A bridge is also subject to extreme heating and can cause problems with distortion. Hence the bridge itself may need relieving by up to 0.10 mm, in a smooth progression.

In Figure 10.2.1, (a) shows a typical safe multi-bridged port, which is easy on the rings where maximum power is not essential. Part (b) shows a single bridge. Part (c) shows a single bridgeless port. In this case the straight top edge should not exceed about 30% of the bore regardless of the total port width, for the sake of the ring. The bottom edge also benefits from shaping. A wider port is possible with the arched port as in (d) where the top and bottom edges typically have a radius of about 1.2 to 1.3 times the bore. The bottom edge of the port also needs consideration, because the rings normally ride over this edge near to bottom dead centre. This could be avoided by lengthening the port, but this causes other problems. Modern developments favour the elliptical port as in (e), which can be the widest and transforms efficiently into a circular passage. Design (f) is worth considering where the timing is to be lengthened, raising only the centre portion. The intrusions can then be chamfered to guide the rings very effectively.

When a resonant exhaust is used, the exhaust port is normally much deeper than the transfer ports. It is then possible to add supplementary exhaust ports above the transfers, as in (g). The supplementary passages may be opened or closed according to engine speed. These can also be integrated with the main ports as in (h). A variation on this is to have the exhaust wider at the top than at the bottom, with angled sides, and transfers with a matching angle.

As an alternative to type (b) the bridge can be angled as in (i), with the intention of spreading the wear of the ring due to bridge distortion and poor lubrication at high temperature. Careful relieving of the bridge seems a better solution.

A basically elliptical port can be widened if a bar is used as in (j). Separate additional ports above the main port are sometimes used, as in (k) and (l). Again, such separate passages may be controllable.

Exhaust timing figures and areas have already been mentioned. Raising the top of the exhaust port is a common timing modification, but can easily be overdone. When a resonant exhaust is used, the effectiveness of the exhaust in boosting the output is dependent on a strong exhaust pulse, so long timing then gives high peak power but a very narrow power band. The port is then very high, about half of the stroke, so its area is great and the integrated angle-area is large. The desired timing is easily met, being governed mainly by the intensity of the exhaust pulse required rather than by the angle-area requirements.

Because of the great effect of the exhaust system, variable effective exhaust port height (timing) is a desirable feature. Some ways in which this has been achieved are shown in Figure 10.2.2 onwards. Shorter effective exhaust timing moves the exhaust resonance to lower rpm, as does effectively lengthening the exhaust passage, and spreading and delaying the pulse with a side chamber.

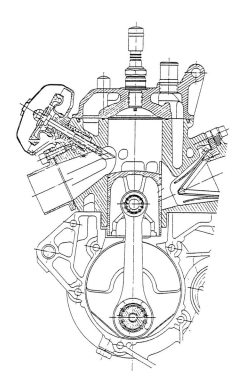

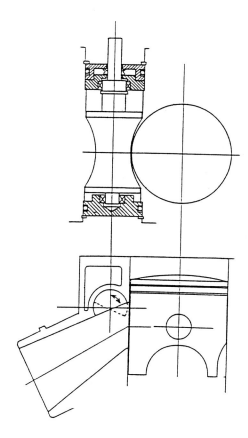

Figure 10.2.2. The Rotax variable exhaust port has a spade on a plunger, activated by gas pressure at the outer side of the spade. The spade is clear of the piston, but the timing is effectively variable. The exhaust passage has a roughly 25° downdraft angle.

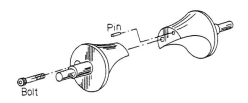

Figure 10.2.3. The Yamaha variable exhaust port (YPVS - Yamaha power valve system) has a rotatable barrel, profiled to match the cylinder shape, giving effectively variable timing. The exhaust passage downdraft angle is 30°.

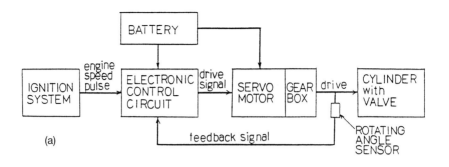

(a)

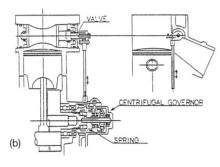

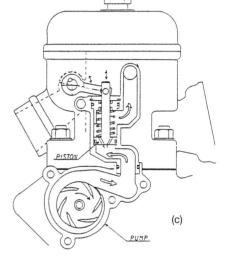

(b)

Figure 10.2.4.
The Yamaha variable exhaust has been
used with several types of actuators and
sensors
(a)   electrical
(b)   mechanical centrifugal
(c)   hydraulic

(c)

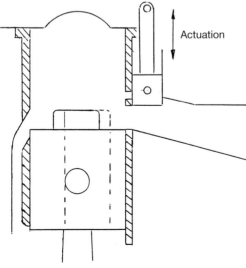

Actuation

Figure 10.2.5. The Jawa type variable
exhaust port has a direct-acting
plunger valve. Various types of
actuation are possible. The plunger
opens or obstructs one or two
supplementary exhaust ports above
the main port, giving variable timing,
e.g., exhaust ports as Figure 10.2.1.
(k) or (l).

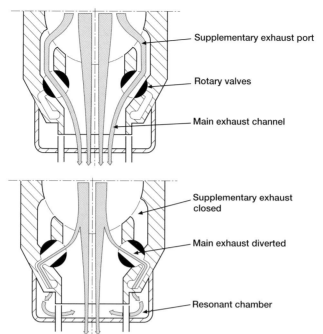

Supplementary exhaust port

Rotary valves

Main exhaust channel

Supplementary exhaust closed

Main exhaust diverted

Resonant chamber

Figure 10.2.6. The Kawasaki KIPS type variable exhaust port clears or obstructs supplementary exhaust ports alongside the main port, e.g., Figure 10.2.1.(g). The supplementary ports may be of different timing to the main port. In the obstructed (low speed) setting the main exhaust port is also connected to a side chamber, possibly resonant. This spreads the pulse and delays it, improving low speed behaviour.

Figure 10.2.7. The Suzuki type variable exhaust does not alter the effective timing of the liner. A rotatable barrel opens the passage to a side chamber for low speed, spreading and delaying the exhaust pulse.

Figure 10.2.8. The Honda type variable exhaust is similar in principle to the Suzuki type, but with a poppet-valve type of actuator. The Honda implementation uses three dimensions to improve the layout.

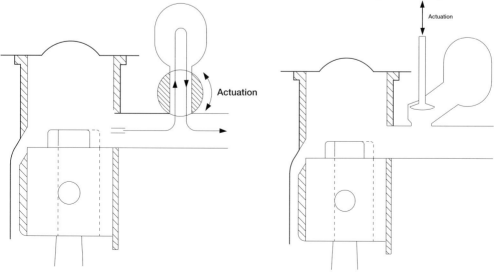

Actuation

Actuation

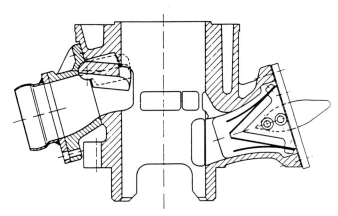

Figure 10.2.9. The KTM motocross variable exhaust alters the effective timing with a rotating flap shaped to fit close to the piston. 15° downdraft angle.

10.3 The Exhaust Passage

The exhaust passage joins the exhaust port to the exterior connection point, or occasionally direct to the atmosphere. For an open exhaust, or for a simple silencer, the flow is unidirectional. Some tuned exhausts incorporate reversed flow.

For plain expansion silencers (mufflers) the exhaust passage design is not critical, provided that excessive resistance is avoided. This means aiming for a passage cross-sectional area somewhat greater than that of the port itself. Preferably the cross-section is circular to minimise heat transfer into the metal, to reduce cooling and distortion problems.

The situation is different with tuned exhausts. The passage must be designed for efficient gas flow to create the strongest pulse for a given exhaust timing, and so that the reverse flow can push the surplus fresh mixture back into the cylinder. Heat transfer and distortion must be minimised, because with a tuned exhaust the running temperature is higher. Cooling of the gas will reduce the intensity of the exhaust pulse.

The detachable exhaust itself is normally of circular section, so the passage must transform from the exhaust port shape to a circular shape of a suitable diameter in the smoothest way possible. The normalised exhaust port area (port area/bore area) with a tuned pipe may be near to 50%. The exhaust header inner diameter will usually be of similar area, with a normalised diameter of around 70%. For example, the exhaust port may be 25 mm high and 40 mm wide, transforming to a circle of diameter 37 mm. Hence the depth needs to increase whilst the width reduces, in a progressive way.

The length of the crankcase exhaust passage is typically about equal to the bore, but varies widely. It is usually only within the engine modifier's scope to smooth out the passage, although with alloy welding facilities it may be possible to alter the outlet size.

The passage is usually located somewhat below the mean level of the exhaust port, and this will especially apply where the port upper edge has been raised for longer timing. This lower position is advantageous because of the flow characteristics of the blowdown, which are helped by the downward inclination. Ideally the whole exhaust is straight but angled down from the cylinder, but this is not normally practical for installation reasons.

10.4 Blowdown

Blowdown is the process by which the cylinder pressure is reduced before the transfer process begins. Where a normal expansion silencer is used, the blowdown angle (the crankshaft rotation from exhaust opening to transfer opening) will be typically around ten degrees, which is sufficient. For a given transfer timing, increasing the blowdown angle θ_B necessarily increases the exhaust timing, because

$$\theta_E = \theta_T + 2\theta_B$$

and the long exhaust timing means a shorter useful power stroke. This means poorer torque, worse fuel consumption, and more noise. Therefore a moderate blowdown angle is better on normal engines.

In the case of tuned exhausts, the blowdown angle is simply the result of the predetermined exhaust and transfer timings. The exhaust is governed basically by the required pulse strength. The transfer timing is a compromise around the period to achieve gas transfer with a 'blow-up' period available for the exhaust supercharge effect. With such exhausts, the blowdown can occur relatively easily in the long blowdown period, because of the high cylinder pressure at exhaust opening.

During the power stroke, some combustion continues, but the main action is that the gas does work on the piston, with the temperature and pressure falling. The piston then exposes the top of the exhaust port, the width depending on the port shape. The pressure in the cylinder is far higher than that in the exhaust passage, so there is a very strong flow of gas out into the passage. This initial blast makes an exit from the top of the exhaust port at an angle of about 40 degrees from the horizontal, as shown in Figure 10.4.1. This angle is the result of the detailed geometry of the top edge of the piston and the top edge of the exhaust port. A rounded piston edge will have a near vertical initial flow.

The initial blast from the cylinder is obviously in a thin sheet governed by the shape of the open port. For example, the port width may be 30 mm whilst the depth open may be only about 0.4 mm per degree since exhaust opening. Inevitably there is a great deal of turbulence and mixing of old and new exhaust gas. The actual efflux velocity is governed by the equations of compressible gas dynamics. The ratio of pressures cylinder/passage exceeds that necessary to give the limiting choked flow at Mach 1 sonic velocity. Because of the high exhaust gas temperature, the relevant sonic velocity is well above the usual velocity of sound in air, which is normally about 340 m/s or 760 mph. However, the turbulent mixing quickly reduces the velocity of the gas jet.

In a relatively short time, requiring only about ten degrees of crank motion, much of the mass of gas that was in the cylinder has passed out into the exhaust passage and exhaust

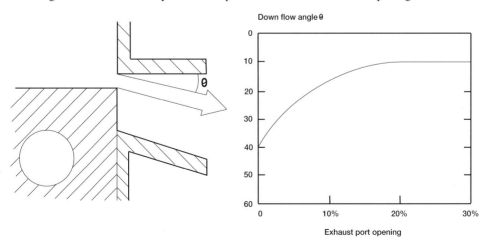

Figure 10.4.1. Blowdown jet flow direction (after Jante, 1968, SAE 680468).

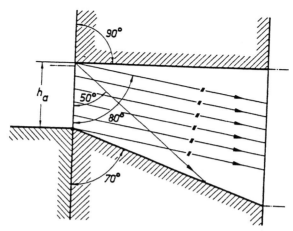

Figure 10.4.2. Gas flow with fully open port into suggested exhaust passage. (Jante, 1968, SAE 680468). Note that the steep initial, very hot, blowdown strikes the bottom of the passage, causing severe heating.

header pipe, but the gas loses most of its extreme velocity, resulting in a region of high pressure in the exhaust passage. This pressure pulse then moves out into the exhaust system, at a high velocity of about 500 m/s leaving behind the mass of new exhaust gas in the header pipe.

Initially the opening exhaust port gives an increasing blowdown mass flow rate. However, in due course the pressure in the cylinder falls enough for the blowdown flow to cease being choked at Mach 1. The blowdown velocity continues to fall and generally the blowdown mass flow rate reduces. About ten degrees after exhaust opening, the primary blowdown process is over. The residual exhaust gas in the cylinder continues to flow out at declining pressure, until the transfer ports open, from which point the transfer process will expel most of the remaining exhaust gas.

During this scavenge process, more old exhaust gas is forced out into the exhaust passage. With the large exhaust opening, the flow angle is now around 10° to 15° from the horizontal. Figure 10.4.2 shows a design scheme for the exhaust passage, indicating angles of zero and 20° from the horizontal for the top and bottom edges, with an average downdraft angle of 10°. As seen earlier, downdraft angles of 30° or even 40° may be used (e.g., the Rotax 454, Figure 2.3.5).

In practice the transfer ports may open before the cylinder pressure has fallen below that in the crankcase, and there is then some initial exhaust flow into the transfers. In normal running this is only a small effect. However, if the blowdown period is inadequate then there will be a very strong flow into the transfer passages. This can inhibit the transfer so severely that scavenging is insufficient and the engine fails to fire on the next cycle. However, this gives a low cylinder pressure so on the subsequent cycle the scavenging is correct and the engine fires. This repeats, and so the engine fires on alternate revolutions. This is called 'four-stroking' because, like a four-stroke engine, the piston makes four strokes instead of the normal two for each combustion.

Four-stroking is often caused by bad carburation. If the mixture is too rich, then the combustion rate is severely reduced. This means that the gas does less work on the piston, continuing to burn during the power stroke, and being hotter and at higher pressure when the exhaust opens, the blowdown period may then be inadequate, giving the reverse transfer

200

flow and alternate firing described. This problem can be alleviated by increasing the blowdown angle, or, of course, by improving the carburation. Four-stroking is also encouraged by any other factors that encourage high cylinder pressure at transfer opening, such as a small volume silencer, late ignition timing or low compression ratio (giving slower combustion).

10.5 Open Exhaust and Port Pressure

A two-stroke engine without an exhaust system is very noisy, worse than for a four-stroke of similar power. It is, in any case, not the most powerful arrangement, because in general for competitions a suitable exhaust system can significantly improve the torque and power.

Figure 10.5.1(a) shows the variation of pressure (P_E) just outside the exhaust port of an open-exhaust engine. The vertical graph lines indicate exhaust opening (EO), transfer opening (TO), bottom dead centre (BDC), transfer closing (TC) and exhaust closing (EC). For this simple case there is a conspicuous pressure pulse visible during the blowdown period. However, in the absence of any exhaust system this dissipates quickly. In the absence of any significant flow resistance beyond the exhaust passage in the crankcase, there is little pressure outside the exhaust port during the transfer phase.

In considering the effect of exhaust systems, or the design of such systems to improve torque or power, the effect of the exhaust as far as the engine is concerned is largely representable by the pressure produced at the exhaust port by the exhaust system. In order to improve the speed of scavenging, it is desirable to produce a negative pressure at the exhaust port for some or all of the transfer phase (TO to TC), as shown in Figure 10.5.1(b). It should be appreciated that such a pressure profile is not an unqualified improvement for the engine.

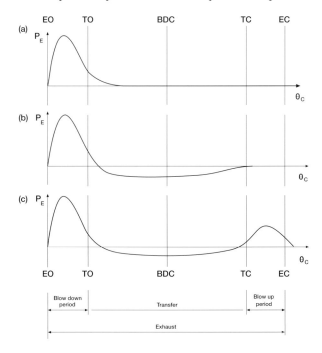

Figure 10.5.1.
(a)   *Pressure profile at the exhaust port for an open exhaust system.*
(b)   *Desirable low pressure at exhaust port during transfer (scavenge) action.*
(c)   *Addition of desirable positive pressure at exhaust port in the 'blow-up' period.*

Scavenge will occur quickly. Therefore the torque curve is shifted to higher rpm, and more power will be produced at the higher rpm. However at low rpm the engine may be worse. At a speed where the scavenging was already complete, making it faster will simply result in fresh mixture being lost out of the exhaust port, with a corresponding loss of fuel efficiency.

The exact shape of the pressure curve between TO and TC is probably not extremely critical, the results being basically dependent on the integral of the pressure against time. However, the flow velocities depend on the square root of the total driving pressure difference between the crankcase and the exhaust port, so a smooth even distribution can be expected to be a little superior in its overall effect.

The ultimate pressure distribution is that shown in Figure 10.5.1(c), where there is also a rise of pressure between TC and EC, i.e. during the blow-up period. This rise of pressure would cause gas to flow back from the exhaust passage into the cylinder. If this gas is rich in unburned mixture, rather than being just exhaust gas, then when the exhaust port closes the total trapped mass of fresh gas is greater and the torque and power will be improved. This favourable effect therefore requires that the engine rpm be low enough for the basic scavenging process to be over-complete with the low pressure during the transfer period pulling some fresh gas into the exhaust passage. In practice this so-called 'plugging pulse' in the blow-up period is achieved by the convergent cone of the divergent-convergent exhaust, for which the divergent cone provides the strong transfer suction. The exhaust system pressure pulses then become so dominant that very high rpm can be used for maximum power.

10.6 Mufflers

The term muffler, also optimistically called the 'silencer', refers to exhaust systems where the emphasis is on noise reduction rather than on performance or behavioural improvement.

The most basic form of exhaust system for a two-stroke engine is the simple expansion box without any attempt at resonant dimensions. In its simplest form this is just a single box with a tubular tailpipe, as in Figure 10.6.1. This is characterised primarily by the muffler volume V_M, and by the length L_T and diameter D_T of the tailpipe (outlet pipe). For practical values of length, the steady-state flow resistance of the tailpipe depends primarily on its inner diameter, with the length playing only a secondary role in this respect. For a given mass flow rate, the efflux velocity depends on the tailpipe flow area, and the resistant pressure drop depends on the gas speed squared, so the tailpipe resistance, giving the muffler back-pressure, is basically dependent on the inner diameter to the fourth power, so the tailpipe diameter is a critical value.

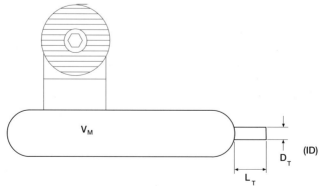

Figure 10.6.1. Basic expansion box muffler/'silencer'.

If the tailpipe is abnormally long then this will certainly increase the resistance at a given diameter. However for normal lengths, e.g. $5D_T$, this is a minor effect compared with the choice of diameter. However the shape of entry to the pipe does matter. Within the normal range of lengths, the tailpipe length increases the gas inertia in the pipe, and increases the effective resistance to very high frequencies. As a result, the length of the tailpipe affects the noise output, with a very short tailpipe giving a harsher sound, and a longer tailpipe a more mellow sound.

The blowdown process results in a sudden injection of hot gas to the muffler. The tailpipe restriction prevents this gas being immediately ejected, so there is an initial pressure rise within the muffler body. The size of this pressure rise depends on the volume of the muffler relative to the mass of gas injected, or, in a more general sense, depends on the normalised volume of the muffler V_M/V_S. To allow an effective blowdown process without high back-pressure, obviously V_M must be large enough, certainly several times the swept volume. Often, however, the muffler size or mass is a problem. The normalised volume V_M/V_S may be typically from 3 up to 10. To obtain an effective reduction of noise level, the outlet area must be sufficiently small. However this also reduces the power.

Overall, the principal muffler dimensions could be classified as follows:

Muffler volumes V_M/V_S:
3   very small
6   small
9   medium
12 large
15 very large

Tailpipe outlet: areas A_T/A_B:
0.05 very small
0.10 small
0.15 medium
0.20 large
0.25 very large

Tailpipe outlet: inner diameter D_T/B:
0.24 very small
0.32 small
0.40 medium
0.45 large
0.50 very large

The effect of the outlet area or diameter depends to some extent on the muffler volume, but the small tailpipe area (10% A_B) gives substantial noise reduction with significant performance loss (e.g. 20% power loss at higher speed) whilst the large value (20% A_B) gives only moderate noise reduction with around 10% power loss.

Figure 10.6.2 shows the variation of exhaust port pressure for a basic untuned muffler. Compared with the open exhaust (Figure 10.5.1) there is back-pressure during the transfer phase, which restricts the transfer action, which therefore takes place more slowly. Hence the torque and power are reduced at high rpm. At lower rpm the muffler may not restrict the torque, and may even give a slight improvement. Especially at low rpm, the muffler may reduce fuel consumption because it prevents overscavenging by efficient ports that are running too slowly. Of course, if it is intended to run only at low rpm, then some revision to

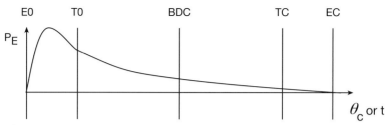

Figure 10.6.2. Exhaust port pressure profile with simple expansion muffler.

the ports may be a better solution, such as reducing the timing, which will also lengthen the power stroke.

Practical dimensions are normally such that the muffler internal pressure can fall fairly low between blowdown pulses, as may be demonstrated by analysing the muffler as a Helmholtz resonator. In principle it is possible to use the tailpipe dimensions to tune the muffler natural frequency so that there is a favourable pressure oscillation, giving suction at the exhaust port to improve the transfer and then back pressure to force fresh gas back into the cylinder, along the lines of other tuned systems.

Considering the example engine, we would require a complete pressure oscillation in the muffler in about 144° (0.4 × 360°) of crank rotation, so for the example engine the natural frequency would need to be 500 Hz, 2.5 times the engine rotational speed of 200 revs/second. The Helmholtz equation (Appendix C) for the muffler volume with its tailpipe, is

$$f_{NE} = \frac{C_E}{2\pi} \sqrt{\frac{A_T}{V_M L_T}}$$

where C_E is the effective velocity of sound for the exhaust gas, around 500 m/s. For a volume of 900 cm^3 and a tailpipe diameter of 15 mm, area 177 mm^2, the required tailpipe length is 78 mm, which is viable.

The practical difficulty of implementing such a tuned system is that, as for the resonant inlet, to obtain worthwhile pressure oscillations requires low damping, which requires a long, large diameter, tailpipe, and this is not normally acceptable because of the noise emission. However, a favourable effect may be achieved in some cases.

The Helmholtz frequency analysis assumes that the chamber is at uniform pressure. This requires that the volume not be too large, or more specifically, that the chamber is not too long, or the passage of pressure waves within the chamber becomes important, as we will see later.

A larger volume chamber allows a smaller outlet hole for a given power output, and hence less noise. Of more interest, to most users at least, a larger volume with the same outlet size will generally give more power and less noise than a smaller volume, or a slightly larger outlet with large chamber volume will give more power with the same noise level.

The pressure within the muffler chamber for a given mass of gas is reduced by cooling the gas. Similarly, the back-pressure arising from a given mass flow rate through the tailpipe is less for cooler higher-density gas. Hence, for high power and low noise with a plain muffler, the maximum muffler cooling is desirable. It helps to maximise heat transfer from the exhaust gas to the chamber wall, for example by directing the gas flow against the wall, and to maximise external cooling by having a flow of air over the outside. This may be achieved by suitable positioning, or possibly by air ducting or the use of cooling fins on the muffler body.

For a given total volume of muffler, silencing is enhanced by division into two or more chambers. The interconnections between the chambers may be by simple holes of various forms or by tubes. With suitable design, for a given noise limit the power can be improved with these more elaborate silencers. This complex area of design calls for reference to research literature.

10.7 The Minipipe

The minipipe is simply a fixed diameter and fairly short constant diameter exhaust pipe, as in Figure 10.7.1. It is capable of giving a significant power increase over open exhaust, up to about 15%, but is just as noisy, possibly even more so, and therefore its application is rather limited nowadays. Both diameter and length are quite critical.

Figure 10.7.1 shows the pressure profile at the exhaust. Compared with the open exhaust, the presence of the pipe spreads the initial pulse somewhat. This pulse then proceeds down the pipe at around 500 m/s, leaving behind the blowdown gas. There is some frictional dissipation of the pulse due to friction at the pipe walls, but this is usually a relatively limited effect due to the shortness of the total distance travelled by the pulse.

Figure 10.7.2. shows the detailed pressure wave action of a minipipe. When the pulse reaches the open end of the pipe (b) it suddenly over-expands, reflecting about 80% of its energy back into the pipe as a suction wave, Figure 10.7.2(c). This suction wave arrives back at the exhaust port (d) and enhances the scavenging process. Considering an open exhaust as a very short minipipe, it will be apparent that the reflection effectively occurs very early in that case, so the enhancement then occurs too soon, before the transfers have come into operation. Hence a basic function of the minipipe is to control the time of the returning suction pulse.

The minipipe suction pulse is then subject to an inefficient suction reflection from the cylinder (e). This inefficiency is to some extent desirable, because if the reflection were 100% then the residual effect would be zero. In fact, some of the pulse is dissipated by the exhaust port shape, some goes down the transfers (drawing transfer gas into the cylinder) and some is reflected, still as a suction wave. This weaker and spread-out suction wave passes back down the pipe, Figure 10.7.2(f). It then over-expands and so reflects fairly efficiently (80% energy) from the open end, therefore becoming a returning positive pulse, Figure 10.7.2(g). At correct engine speed/pipe length combinations this will arrive at the exhaust port as the desired, though weak, positive 'plugging pulse' in the blow-up period between TC and EC, Figure 10.7.2 (h).

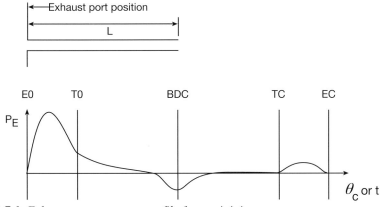

Figure 10.7.1. Exhaust port pressure profile for a minipipe.

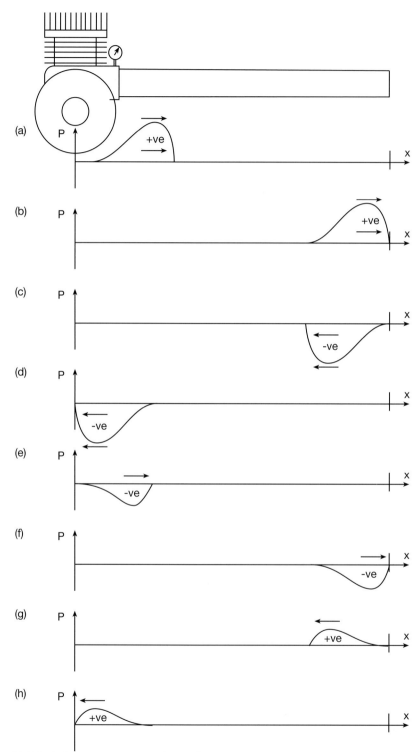

Figure 10.7.2. Pulse progression and transformation in a minipipe.

Hence the minipipe, in principle at least, can produce a desired pressure profile at the exhaust port. There are, however, some objections. It works inefficiently because of the imperfect sudden reflection conditions at the pipe open end and especially at the cylinder. The reflected suction wave is concentrated into a short duration, and is therefore used inefficiently. Also, it is extremely noisy. Because of the noise, plus the fact that the divergent-convergent exhaust performs better, it is no longer used on motorcycles or karts. However it has some merits. It is very light, and easy to use because the power band is wider than a full di-con exhaust.

The existence, or useful strength, of the plugging pulse for the minipipe may be doubted. It may be that for many engines it is insignificant. Nevertheless, it provides a convenient basis for design, as the correct length to time this pulse will place the section pulse close to bottom dead centre, which is also suitable.

For the plugging pulse, the total distance travelled is approximately $4L_E$ where L_E is the exhaust path length from the port to the outer end. The time for this to occur is

$$t_1 = \frac{4L_E}{C_E}$$

where C_E is the mean exhaust pulse velocity, around 500 m/s. Approximately, this must occur during the exhaust port open period, so

$$t_2 = \frac{\theta_E}{360 \, N_S}$$

This is by no means an exact calculation. Actually the pulse needs some extra time to enter the cylinder, and the suction pulse reflection position at the cylinder is uncertain. However it gives some indication of the required value. Setting the two times equal,

$$L_E = \frac{\theta_E C_E}{1440 \, N_S}$$

or

$$L_E = \frac{\theta_E C_E}{24 \, N_M}$$

Practical optimum values of length may be around 10% higher for the reasons given, or, arguably, a pulse speed of 10% higher is correct.

The inner diameter of the minipipe also requires experimental testing for each engine design, but will be in the range 0.60 B to 1.00 B. The optimum value is quite critical and varies with the peculiarities of the individual engine, and in particular with the exhaust timing and the quantity of gas in the exhaust blowdown pulse and its temperature. Power improvements of around 15% compared with an open exhaust are possible.

10.8 The Short Megaphone

The short megaphone is, in principle, an improved minipipe, although the supposed improvement is not always found. It is also, historically, practically and theoretically, the next step towards the full divergent-convergent tuned system. As a matter of interest, the minipipe type of system and the megaphone are also used on four-stroke engines.

Figure 10.8.1 shows how the short two-stroke megaphone is basically the same length as the minipipe, but some portion at the end is angled out in a cone. The cone half-angle θ is

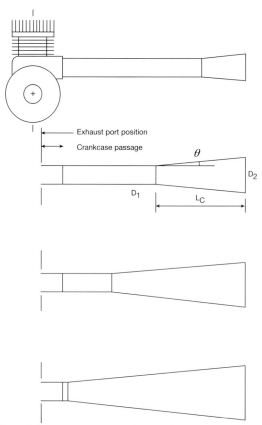

Figure 10.8.1. *Varieties of short megaphone exhaust design.*

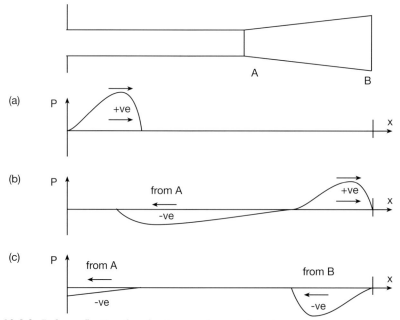

Figure 10.8.2. *Pulse reflection for short megaphone exhaust.*

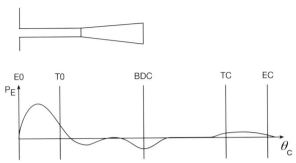

Figure 10.8.3. Exhaust port pressure profile for short megaphone exhaust.

most commonly around 4 to 7 degrees. The final diameter obviously depends upon the cone length and angle:

$$D_2 = D_1 + 2L_C \tan\theta$$

The underlying intentions evidently vary somewhat. The very short cone at the end is primarily intended to improve the efficiency of the reflection of pulses. The longer cones are intended to spread-out the reflected suction pulse to utilise it more efficiently. One undeniable effect of the cone is to improve the efficiency of sound energy production, like the horn of a musical instrument. The megaphone exhaust is exceptionally noisy.

Chapter 6 (Fluid Mechanics) discussed some issues in the reflection of pressure pulses at a conical expansion, and in particular compares the planar wave/spherical wave issue. Either way, the net effect of the cone is to reflect a spread-out suction wave from the first part of the cone (Figure 10.8.2). The reduced energy that reaches the end is then reflected as a further short suction pulse. Depending on the details of the design the pressure at the exhaust is then as shown in Figure 10.8.3, possibly also with some plugging pulse. The suction wave is more spread-out, and in principle more efficient in operation than for the basic minipipe.

Occasionally a very small-angle megaphone is seen, with a cone half-angle of about 1.5 degrees. This also appears as the front part of most modern divergent-convergent systems. The thinking here is a little different. For ideal frictionless flow, transmission of a pressure pulse along a constant diameter pipe would not give any reflection. However, the presence of entry loss and pipe friction causes a moderate positive reflection. A divergence angle of around 1.5 degrees compensates for this.

The short megaphone exhaust has an honourable place in the history of exhaust system development, but is inferior in performance to more modern systems. It is simpler, lighter, shorter and less critical in operation than many systems, with a wider power band, but the noise level is normally unacceptable, so it has effectively fallen from use.

10.9 The Long Megaphone
There is also a long version of the megaphone, as shown in Figure 10.9.1, where it may be seen that this is based on a length twice that of the normal minipipe or short megaphone, so

$$L_E = \frac{\theta_E C_E}{12\,N_M}$$

Hence this is sometimes referred to as a half-wave system, in contrast with the quarter-wave minipipe. The header pipe is about 40% of the total length,

$$L_1 = 0.4\,L_E$$

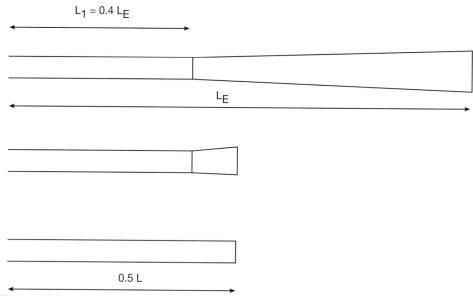

$L_1 = 0.4 L_E$

L_E

0.5 L

Figure 10.9.1. The long megaphone compared with short megaphone and minipipe.

The writer has not seen a completely convincing explanation of the design intent or operation of the long megaphone. It will be seen in Figure 10.9.1 that with $L_1 \approx 0.4L_E$ then the front end of the long megaphone agrees with the design of a short megaphone with long header pipe, with similar results for the reflection of the suction wave. The justification for extension of the megaphone to the total length is not clear. At this length it is desired to return a positive pulse to the exhaust port, but a positive return pulse from an open end requires an outgoing negative (suction) pulse. It is sometimes stated that the supposed negative wave is the result of reflection in the cone of the already once-reflected positive pulse returning as a negative wave towards the engine. In that case, there seems little justification for the total length that is used, unless rules actually demand this. An efficient megaphone will speed up scavenging, but provide no positive pulse in the blow-up period. Therefore, at normal speed it will overscavenge and waste fuel. To utilise it to best effect, it must be used at higher rpm, or with short exhaust timing, so that correct scavenging occurs.

The long megaphone has a large end diameter, is heavier and less easy to package than shorter systems, but less effective than the more modern systems. It is also probably the noisiest of all systems, very noticeably worse than a plain open exhaust, no doubt of some entertainment value in the right context, but, the long megaphone does not seem to be in current use.

10.10 The Closed Megaphone
As related in the historical introduction of Chapter 1, in the 1930s the prevalent megaphone exhaust acquired a rear blanking plate and then a convergent rear cone, which, provided that the engine was suitable, gave even better power.

Figure 10.10.1(a) shows the concept of this exhaust design with a flat or domed plate closure and tailpipe. The large rear diameter may cause packaging problems, and has little extra effect, so as an alternative the rear section may be left at constant diameter (b). This may also be compared with a conical form to the smaller diameter as in (c).

The rear closure reflects the positive pulse as a returning positive pulse with high

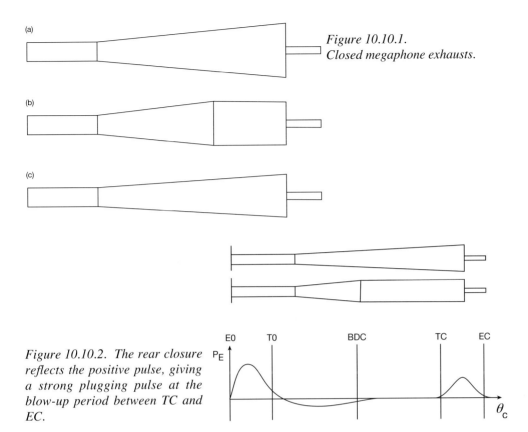

(a)

(b)

(c)

Figure 10.10.1.
Closed megaphone exhausts.

Figure 10.10.2. The rear closure reflects the positive pulse, giving a strong plugging pulse at the blow-up period between TC and EC.

efficiency, giving a strong plugging pulse at the blow-up period between TC and EC, at the correct speed, as shown in Figure 10.10.2. To do this, the exhaust system must now be approximately twice as long as for a minipipe or short megaphone. Provision must be made for the exhaust gas to leave the system in some way but the position of the exit is not critical.

The exhaust pulse must now traverse the pipe and return, a distance of $2L_E$, between exhaust opening and closure, in a time t, with

$$t = \frac{2L_E}{C_E} = \frac{\theta_E}{360\,N_S}$$

$$L_E = \frac{\theta_E C_E}{720\,N_S}$$

or

$$L_E = \frac{\theta_E C_E}{12\,N_M} \qquad (10.10.1)$$

For the example engine,

$$\theta_E = 184°$$
$$N_M = 12{,}000 \text{ rpm}$$
$$C_E = 500 \text{ m/s (estimated)}$$
$$L_E = 0.639 \text{ m} \approx 640 \text{ mm (25 inches)}$$

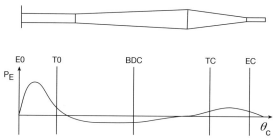

Figure 10.11.1. Exhaust port pressure profile for the double-cone exhaust system.

In practice, of course, this is only a guide length, and the exact value must be determined by testing.

Of enormous practical significance, the noise level is dramatically reduced. This is because most of the remaining positive pulse energy is reflected, and there is only a modest pulse leakage from the exit hole or tailpipe. Here at last, it seems, is the perfect exhaust system with really good power output and little noise. Almost inevitably, there is a snag. The reflection of the positive pulse from the rear plate is so fierce and so concentrated that the power band may be very narrow, although this depends very much on the exhaust timing.

10.11 The Double-Cone Tuned Exhaust

Three further developments were necessary to bring the exhaust system to ideal practical fruition. The rear plate of the closed megaphone was replaced by a cone, of modest angle, which is claimed to give a more spread-out positive pulse reflection. Also, the engine must be adjusted. The exhaust timing is lengthened giving a stronger exhaust pulse, with little change to the transfer timing. Finally, a tailpipe was added, controlling the exit resistance and, in many cases, providing a convenient mounting point. This then, as in Figure 10.11.1, is the classic double-cone exhaust system, as first used on the DKW racing motorcycles of 1952.

The basic concept of the double-cone exhaust system has not changed since then. However, it has been subject to detail development and improvement, by changes of profile. For maximum performance this general concept is without doubt the best system. The divergent-convergent exhaust has also been developed for less noise and wider power band by use of internal baffles, as discussed in the next section.

The leading dimensions of the basic double-cone system are as shown in Figure 10.11.2. Ten primary dimensions are shown, comprising six lengths, three diameters

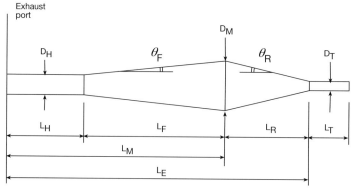

Figure 10.11.2. Leading internal dimensions of the basic double-cone exhaust system.

and two angles, although these are not all independent values. The lengths and diameters specify the angles:

$$\tan \theta_F = \frac{D_E - D_H}{2L_F}$$

$$\tan \theta_R = \frac{D_M - D_T}{2L_R}$$

Practical design of such systems is largely based on prior experience and practical testing. However, an understanding of the likely consequences of any dimensional change is valuable as a pointer to a useful direction of development.

(1) Effective length L_E
Arguments rage over the true effective reflection point of the rear cone, but it is not of great practical consequence. The length L_E to the end of the rear cone is as good as any, and as previously stated:

$$L_E = \frac{\theta_E C_E}{12 N_M}$$

If L_E is defined to some other point, then a different effective pulse velocity C_E is found. However this varies anyway with the exhaust gas temperature and hence with the timing and exhaust pressure. The essential point is that the engine speed at which the correct exhaust effects occur is dependent on L_E, regardless of exactly how it is defined, and that the exhaust timing is also critical in the actual value needed. With a constant diameter header-pipe it is possible to have a sliding joint for adjusting L_E, the associated variation of L_H being a minor effect in comparison.

Increasing the exhaust duration makes L_E more critical because of the stronger exhaust pulse. It also raises the exhaust gas temperature, increasing the pulse velocity C_E, so L_E actually has to increase rather more than in direct proportion to θ_E. The overall average effective value is around 500 m/s (1,600 ft/s) and is consistent for similar designs.

(2) Header pipe length L_H
This length controls the timing of the start of the suction wave from the front cone. It may be varied whilst keeping the cone length L_F and L_R constant, then effectively also adjusting L_E. Alternatively, if L_M is kept constant then the front cone length decreases and angle increases, and the suction wave is not just later, but also shorter and more intense.

(3) Front cone length L_F
At a given cone angle, increasing L_F also increases D_E. In practical design the diameters may be chosen first, in which case increasing L_F reduces θ_E, giving a weaker return pulse, not necessarily longer. To maintain L_E, then L_H or L_R must be adjusted.

(4) Rear cone length L_R
For given diameters D_M and D_T, increasing L_R gives a smaller θ_R, which generally gives a longer positive return pulse with a slightly lower peak power but broader power band. To increase L_R at constant D_T requires changed D_M. To vary L_R whilst retaining L_E requires adjustment of L_R or L_F.

(5) Tailpipe length L_T
It is generally true that the tailpipe is proportionally longer for peaky maximum power engines and shorter for flexible wider-power band engines. However this may simply be

tradition or style. The writer has never seen any convincing explanation for the need for this. The length affects the flow resistance of course, although much less than does the diameter. It may be convenient in some cases to make small adjustments to the resistance by altering the length. The rear cone concentrates the pressure pulse, so a fairly strong pulse goes into the tailpipe and will be reflected from the final open end as a suction wave. It is probably desirable to have a tailpipe long enough to defer the appearance of this suction pulse back at the exhaust port until sufficiently after the main returning positive pulse from the rear cone. In some cases, regulations regarding the position of the exhaust outlet may also influence the choice of tailpipe length.

(6) Header pipe diameter D_H
This is governed by the need for efficient formation of the primary pressure pulse but without excessive resistance and losses before the front cone is reached. The value is usually around 0.7 of the bore.

(7) Maximum diameter D_M
At constant lengths, increase of the maximum diameter gives a larger front cone angle with a stronger suction pulse. Hence the positive pulse then enters the rear cone with less remaining energy. The maximum diameter D_M therefore affects the balance between the strength of the reflected pulses.

(8) Tailpipe diameter D_T
This diameter has a critical effect on the tailpipe flow resistance and therefore on the overall back-pressure, which again affects the balance between suction and plugging pulses. Hence a large D_M or greater θ_F may require a small D_T to balance the pressure profile optimally.

Practical values of some of the various dimensions could be categorised as follows:

Maximum diameter D_M/B
1.2 very small
1.4 small
1.6 medium
1.8 large
2.0 very large

Front cone half-angle θ_F
3° very small
4° small
5° medium
6° large
7° very large

Rear cone half-angle θ_R
8° very small
10° small
12° medium
14° large
16° very large

In all cases, the larger values are associated with maximum-power engines of high speed and narrow power band.

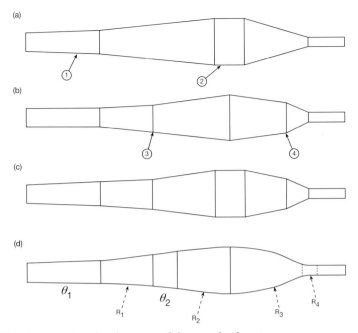

Figure 10.12.1. Progressive development of the tuned exhaust.
(a)   *1 Divergent header pipe.   2 Intermediate parallel section.*
(b)   *3 Twin-cone front.   4 Twin-cone rear.*
(c)   *Multi-section progressive profile (welded, piecewise linear).*
(d)   *Smooth profile, spun or pressed-sheet halves.*

10.12 The Di-Con Tuned Exhaust

The basic double-cone tuned exhaust evolved substantially in detail in the years following its introduction, so that its profile became more complex. More elaborate construction allowed multi-cone systems welded from steel sheet for racing motorcycles by 1970. Hence the term divergent-convergent exhaust system, or 'di-con', will be used for these more general systems, distinct from the more limited double-cone design. Progressive development of the di-con exhaust from the basic double-cone included the following features as seen in Figure 10.12.1:

1. Tapered header pipe at around 1.5 degrees half-angle
2. Parallel section between the cones
3. Twin-cone front diffusers
4. Twin-cone convergent section,
5. Many-cone profiled section from welded sheet, as in (c)
6. Spun-aluminium or pressed-steel smooth profile specified by profile radii (d)

Figure 10.12.1 (a) shows two of the improvements. The first was the introduction of a parallel section between the two cones, having various effects. It helps to separate the reflected pulses, preventing inefficient overlap. It reduces the sudden change of angle at the wall, which reduces inefficient flow turbulence and cooling, reducing the pulse strength. Finally, it provides a way to vary the position of the rear cone without changing the design or set-up of the front portion. The length of this intermediate section is typically 0.5 to 1.0 times the maximum diameter. As this part is of constant diameter, it is practical to introduce a sliding joint here for easy variation of the effective tuned length. This is especially advantageous when the second modification is introduced.

The second change in Figure 10.12.1(a) is that the header pipe is no longer of constant diameter, but now tapers outwards at a half-angle of typically 1.5 deg. This reduces the frictional losses, so the optimal initial diameter is possibly now a little smaller than for a parallel header, whilst the diameter at the junction with the front cone is certainly substantially larger. The angular change of direction at this junction is reduced, which can improve the efficiency of the front cone, or allow this to have a larger angle. In some case, a short front section of the mainly tapered header is of constant diameter, which facilitates variation of length at this point. The tapered header seems to offer a power increase of around 5% without any detrimental effects. Indeed, the handling and power band also seem to be improved.

Alternative improvements to the basic conical system were directed at the cones themselves, as in Figure 10.12.1(b). The front cone was staged, with an initial portion at a smaller angle compensated by a larger angle in the rear section to retain the maximum diameter. This reduces the wall angular deflection at any one point with a probable reduction of losses. It also allows a greater final angle because the flow is re-established after the first deflection. The final result is a more spread-out suction pulse with better efficiency of pulse reflection.

The other modification in Figure 10.12.1(b) is the staging of the rear cone with a larger angle in the rear section. This is said to give a more concentrated positive return pulse with a higher and narrower peak to the power curve. Again, the profile is smoothed out for reduced frictional and thermal losses. In the absence of an intermediate maximum-diameter parallel section, with the larger angle at the rear of a staged front cone then the reduced angle change at the maximum diameter may be helpful.

When the above four developments are combined, the result is the system of Figure 10.12.1(c). The added complexity of manufacture for the number of sections is apparent, but seems well worthwhile. The smoothing of the profile is apparent. In some cases, even more sections were introduced. The logical development from all this is to change the basic approach, and to cease specifying the profile by a piecewise-linear method, of successive cones, which is used because of the manufacturing method by welded steel sheet. The profile can be specified instead by a series of profile radii giving a smooth profile as in Figure 10.12.1(d). For maximum power output, this form of exhaust appears to be the ultimate, because it uses the exhaust pulse in the most efficient way, with minimum dissipation.

10.13 Exhaust Inserts

Whilst there is little doubt that, for maximum power, the previously described systems are generally optimal, for some applications the tuned exhaust systems are fitted with internal obstructions, or 'baffles'. These are used where power requirements give way to high torque requirements at lower engine speed and where low noise levels or a less harsh sound are important.

A common form of baffle is a plain disc with one or more holes in (Figure 10.13.1). An alternative is a short internal cone, which is more rigid. Chapter 5 explained how a pressure pulse behaves at such an obstruction, but broadly the pressure energy may be reflected, transmitted or dissipated, and there may be some effective delay and spreading of the transmitted pulse. The design intent of the baffle therefore hinges around the pulse dissipation and spreading, evidently with the intention of broadening the power band, and

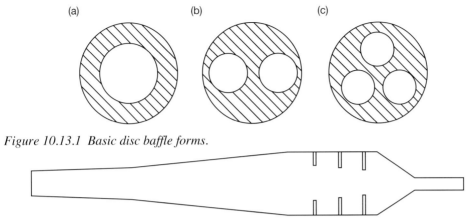

Figure 10.13.1 Basic disc baffle forms.

Figure 10.13.2. Longitudinal section of multi-baffle tuned exhaust system.

also, in some cases simply reducing the effect of the exhaust to limit the power which may otherwise be excessive. To disperse the pulse rather than reflect it, the area-ratio solidity of the baffle should be not much more than 0.5. To achieve adequate softening, two or even three baffles may be used, as in Figure 10.13.2, often with the baffles having progressively reducing flow areas. Obviously, with sufficient disruption it should be possible to largely eliminate the reflected positive pulse, leaving what is then effectively a silenced megaphone with a broad power band. The muffling effect can be extremely good. The baffles add mechanical integrity to the system, and stiffen the outer walls, which helps to reduce noise transmission.

10.14 Other Tuned Exhausts

Because of the intensity of the exhaust pulse, exhaust systems tend to be critical in dimensions, with great potential for unforeseen resonances, often adverse in effect. However, this also allows many options for other designs of tuned systems.

Figure 10.14.1 shows one possibility which can operate in a similar way to a double-cone system, although much less effectively. The step expansion reflects a suction wave and the end plate reflects a desired plugging pulse. This system can be converted into a compact form by, notionally, folding it in half. Assembled in concentric form, and with a rear tailpipe as shown in Figure 10.14.2, it has proved effective. In this way a fair degree of full-wave tuning can be achieved with an exhaust system that is much more compact than the full divergent-convergent system. Ultimate peak power is not achieved, but performance is

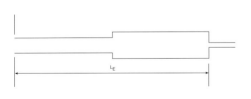

Figure 10.14.1. Simple full-wave tuned-length exhaust box.

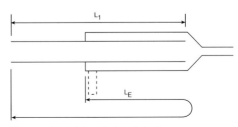

Figure 10.14.2. Folded full-wave system ('magic muffler') (alternative tailpipe shown dashed).

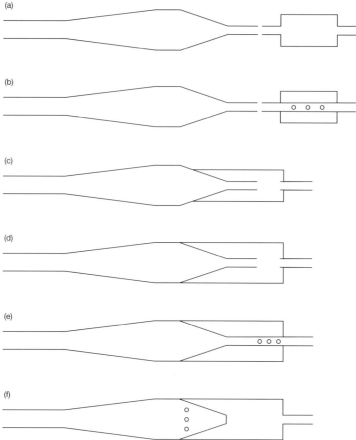

Figure 10.15.1 Supplementary mufflers:
(a) Independent add-on,   (b) Independent add-on,   (c) Integrated unit,
(d) Integrated unit of full diameter,   (e) Integrated tailpipe,   (f) Exit on rear cone.

markedly better than a simple expansion muffler, with a better power band width than the full system.

Length tuning must be observed carefully, and the dimensions are quite critical. For inner diameters, typically, $D_1 \approx 0.7B$ and $D_2 \approx 1.5B$. The axial internal clearance of the end of the inner pipe is critical so length adjustment should be by movement of the complete system. The tailpipe position is not critical, but its resistance is. This folded system retains the characteristic of the full di-con system of willingly accepting a supplementary muffler.

10.15 Supplementary Mufflers

Because the racing tuned exhaust requires significant back pressure for optimum power, normally provided by a suitably restrictive tailpipe, there is no great disadvantage in adding a supplementary expansion muffler to the system, since the overall flow resistance can be adjusted to the optimum value. Such supplementary mufflers certainly offer useful additional noise reduction, as the effect of the primary pulse from the tailpipe can be greatly reduced, and are widely used. Figure 10.15.1 shows in (a) and (b) simple add-on configurations, possibly linked by flexible pipe, whilst (c) shows a typical integrated unit. With increasing complexity and enlarging tailpipe diameter, it may be seen that these systems can ultimately blend into something similar to the multi-baffle systems of the previous section. In most cases, however, the basic power-improving portion remains distinct. If the additional chamber has a diameter equal to the maximum diameter of the di-con system, as in Figure 10.15.1(d), the appearance is rather different, disguising the true nature of the device, and looking like a muffled-megaphone type of system.

10.16 Tailpipes

Whatever the action of the pressure pulses within the exhaust system, the exhaust gas must be permitted to escape. The tailpipe permits this in a controlled way, giving a desired mean back-pressure, which depends critically on its inner diameter and weakly on its length. It is normal on a motorcycle for the tailpipe to be at the rear axle. In other applications this is not always needed, and the exit pipe, often still called a tailpipe, may be at other points of the system without detriment, as shown in Figure 10.16.1

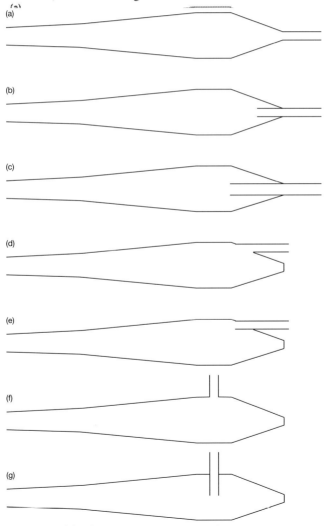

Figure 10.16.1. Some possible alternative exit pipe positions.

The exit pipe need not be flush with the inner surface of the system, and there is a case for positioning its entry around the inter-cone position or maximum diameter, as here the pulse is least intense and the noise output will be minimised. The tailpipe is often used as a mounting point, in which case it needs to be well attached to the main body of the exhaust system.

10.17. Exhaust Tuning

Tuning of the exhaust can be divided into the same categories as the physical parts, namely

    (i)   Exhaust port
    (ii) Exhaust passage
    (iii) Exhaust system.

Tuning of the exhaust port is primarily concerned with the timing, by raising the upper edge. The effect of this with a tuned exhaust is discussed elsewhere. For an open-exhaust engine, or with a simple expansion silencer/muffler, the effect has the trend as shown in Figure 10.17.1. Obviously the details depend upon other aspects of the engine, and will vary. Typically, however, absolute peak power can be obtained at an exhaust timing around 160°. Beyond this there is little, if any, gain, and probably a loss at 170° or more. Longer timings invariably raise the peaking speed. At lower rpm it will be better to have shorter exhaust timing, say 140°. For engines with restricted breathing (poor intakes, or non-Schnürle transfers) the optimum even for peak power may well be less than 160°.

Tuning of the exhaust passage is mainly concerned with smoothing it out and creating a progressive transition in shape and area from the port to the detachable system, the latter usually being circular in section.

The effect of the exhaust system on the power curve is illustrated in Figures 10.17.2 onwards for various system types. Again, this varies considerably with the particular engine and system, and varies with the exhaust timing for tuned exhausts. Longer timing makes a stronger exhaust pulse, so the power curve becomes more peaky. For a true tuned exhaust and an exhaust timing of around 180°, at 70% of the peaking rpm the power may be below 30% of the peak power. Of course this is why such set-ups require many gears, and why single-gear-ratio rules require moderation of the peakiness of the system to achieve usability and controllability, with less extreme exhaust systems or shorter exhaust timing to soften the pulse.

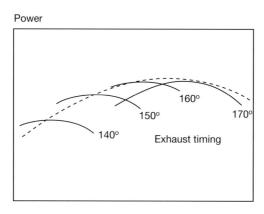

Figure 10.17.1. Example effect of exhaust timing on power input.

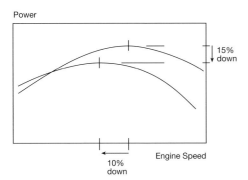

Figure 10.17.2. A simple box muffler typically reduces peak power by 15% and peaking speed by 10%. Power may be improved at low speed.

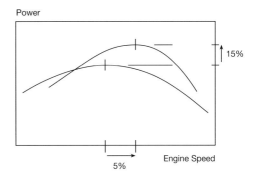

Figure 10.17.3. A simple tube minipipe typically raises peak power by 15% and peaking speeds by 5% to 10%.

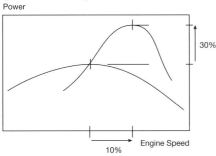

Figure 10.17.4. A folded full-wave system typically raises peak power by 30% and peaking speed by 10%. System length and exhaust timing must be matched for best results.

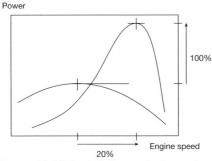

Figure 10.17.5. A full tuned-pipe exhaust with long exhaust timing can double the power output with peaking speed up by about 20%. Length is critical. One penalty is very poor low-speed performance. Peaking speed and peak power are typically greatest with the exhaust length set for a peaking speed 20% higher than without a tuned exhaust.

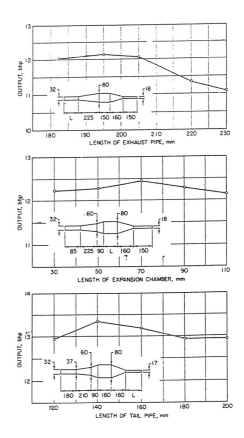

Figure 10.17.6. Some results of tests of tuned exhaust dimensions (from Shaeffer quoting Naito, 1966, SAE 660394).

221

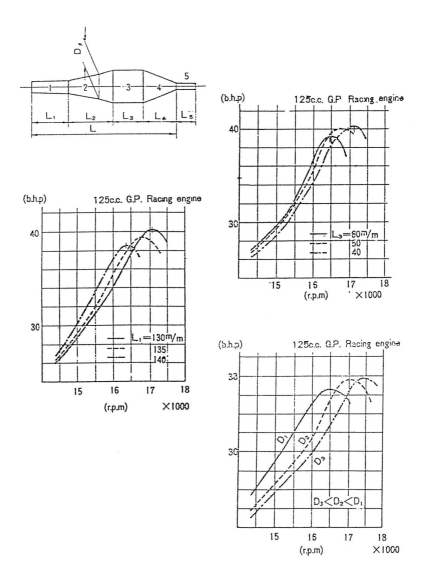

Figure 10.17.6 (cont.) Some results of tests of tuned exhaust dimensions (from Naito, 1966, SAE 660394).

CHAPTER 11:

Head Design and Combustion

11.1 Introduction

When the piston closes the cylinder at the end of the 'blow-up' period, it traps a complex combination of new air, fuel liquid and vapour, and old exhaust gas. The flow processes of the induction and transfer operations now give way to a non-flow process in which the working fluid is compressed, ignited, burned and expanded.

In the ideal Otto cycle of the thermodynamic texts, compression taken place with no heat transfer (called adiabatic). This raises the temperature because of the work done on the gas. The temperature is then further increased not by combustion but by an idealised heat transfer process at constant volume. This is followed by an adiabatic expansion. The ideal working fluid is chemically unchanged.

The real internal combustion engine differs drastically from this sequence of idealised processes. In fact the real processes are not even distinct because for a reciprocating engine the cylinder volume is only instantaneously at its minimum value. Combustion really begins before tdc, overlapping the end of compression, and continues well into the expansion. Combustion itself brings about a drastic change in the chemical state of the working fluid. Fuel (hydrocarbons) and air (O_2 and N_2) convert to CO_2, H_2O and N_2, although this process occurs only partially at first because of dissociation of the molecules at high temperature.

Because of these deviations from the ideal Otto cycle, the ideal cycle is of little value in predicting IC engine performance. For example, the ideal cycle predicts that increasing the compression ratio gives ever-greater power and efficiency, whereas any particular engine has an optimum value, beyond which there are major problems.

11.2 Compression

When the piston closes the cylinder, sealing it badly or well according to the condition of the piston, rings and bore, leaks can occur at the head-to-cylinder seat, at the ignition plug threads, or even, in some dire cases, through the plug insulator seal. Eliminating unnecessary leaks is a basic part of the engine preparation. Minimising leakage at the piston, consistent with avoiding excessive frictional forces at the piston and its rings, is much trickier, calling for accurate control of ring end-gap and piston clearances.

The ideal Otto cycle assumes an ideal gas with zero heat transfer during compression. The real situation is more complex. The trapped gas is a mixture of air, fuel vapour, fuel mist and hot old exhaust gas. The mixture is far from uniform with pockets of exhaust in some places, near-pure fresh mixture in others. At exhaust closure, the mean gas temperature is therefore not the low 'T_1' near ambient of the Otto cycle, especially if scavenging is incomplete because of poor design, high engine speed or throttled operation. Also the pressure at the moment of trapping may be lower or higher than atmospheric, as with a tuned exhaust.

In principle there is now an adiabatic compression from the actual T_1 and P_1, through the trapped compression ratio r_{TC}. The resulting (absolute) temperature and pressure would be

$$T_2 = T_1 r_{TC}^{\gamma-1}$$

$$P_2 = P_1 r_{TC}^{\gamma}$$

In these equations absolute temperatures and pressures must be used, so with T_C in Celsius and T in kelvin,

$$T = T_C + 273.15$$

The ratio of absolute temperatures is

$$\frac{T_2}{T_1} = r_{TC}^{\gamma-1}$$

and for pressures it is

$$\frac{P_2}{P_1} = r_{TC}^{\gamma}$$

For air in the ideal cycle, the ratio of specific heats γ has a value of 1.40. With a trapped compression ratio of 5 and initial conditions $T_{1C} = 15°C$ (288.15 K) and $P_1 = 100$ kPa (1 bar, 14.5 psi) the result is

$$\frac{T_2}{T_1} = 1.904$$

$$T_2 = 548.5 \text{ K } \left(275°C\right)$$

$$\frac{P_2}{P_1} = 9.52$$

$$P_2 = 952 \text{ kPa } \left(139 \text{ psi}\right)$$

These numbers illustrate the drastic increase in pressure and temperature that are expected during compression, even without combustion. The real engine deviates from the ideal because the gas is non-ideal, not least because it includes fuel mist. Heat transfer also takes place, with the gas heated by the hot metal of the piston, cylinder and head. However, later in the compression the gas may become hotter than the metal, and there may be some cooling of the hot gas. The liquid fuel (fuel mist) partially evaporates during the compression, taking energy from the gas. The result is that real compression is often better represented by a polytropic equation with an empirical n instead of γ:

$$\frac{T_2}{T_1} = r_{TC}^{n-1}$$

$$\frac{P_2}{P_1} = r_{TC}^{n}$$

where a value $n = 1.3$ is often used for analysis, especially for gasoline-fuelled engines. A lower value may be used for special fuels such as methanol or nitromethane, which are used

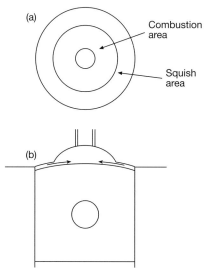

Figure 11.2.1. Squish action.

with a higher fuel/air ratio. Their evaporative cooling effect during the compression allows a higher compression ratio.

The resulting temperature and pressure evidently depend on the effective polytropic index n and on the trapped compression ratio. They prepare the mixture for the combustion process.

At the moment of trapping, the gas may be in strong motion, especially tumbling in the case of Schnürle porting. During compression this enhances mixing. It also increases heat transfer between metal and gas. Finally, it encourages fuel droplets to strike the metal surfaces. Most of the base fuel then evaporates from the surface, leaving the oil from the fuel/oil mixture to lubricate the piston motion. It also provides internal cooling of the metal.

As the piston approaches top-dead-centre, any squish area of the head comes into play, 'squishing' the mixture out of the squish area into the main combustion volume (Figure 11.2.1). Observation of piston tops shows that carbon deposits are softer and thinner on the piston area below a head squish zone, implying that the piston is cooler here as the main combustion heating of the piston occurs away from the squish area.

11.3 Ignition

Perhaps 20° before tdc, (according to the ignition system and auto-adjusting with speed) the electrical system creates a high voltage at the ignition plug. Because of the narrow plug gap, only about 0.75mm (0.030 inches) this voltage is sufficient to ionise the mixture in the plug gap, tearing electrons from the atoms of air. The resulting ionised gas is then electronically conducting, so the spark occurs. This brief burst of current produces a highly concentrated heating effect in the spark volume. The spark may last for 1 millisecond, but at 12,000 rpm this corresponds to some 72 degrees of crankshaft rotation. The ideal complete combustion period is about 40° which corresponds to well under 1 ms of time. For high-speed engines, combustion is complete long before the spark is finished. Much of the spark energy is therefore irrelevant. It is the initial part of the spark that is important. In the immediate vicinity of the spark the mixture rises to a temperature of about 6,000°C. This starts a chemical reaction between fuel and oxygen, which then propagates through the combustion volume.

A competition engine must have an ignition system in prime condition. One obvious problem is incorrect timing. Retarded timing causes low power and low fuel efficiency. Too advanced timing causes too much pressure rise before tdc, with high pressure and temperature over tdc. This can cause catastrophic mechanical stresses and heating of the engine.

A related problem is pre-ignition. This occurs when a hot spot in the cylinder, such as a carbon whisker on the tip of the plug, ignites the mixture before the spark would do so.

For good ignition the inner surface of the insulator must not become conductive through combustion deposits. This is prevented by running the plug within a suitable temperature range to vaporise or burn off any deposits. The running temperature of the insulator inner surface depends on the operating conditions in the engine cylinder, such as the temperature and pressure of the gas, and on the thermal resistance of the plug from central electrode tip to the mounting seat, where the heat is conducted away. A high specific power engine, with hot, high pressure, high density gas would make a plug run hotter than would the same engine throttled back, or a different engine in a lower state of tune. So critical is the plug temperature that different plug designs are needed for different engines. A 'hot' plug has a long conduction path, making it run hot in a given engine. A 'cold' plug has a short path, and runs cooler. Therefore, power-tuning or torque-tuning an engine may indicate that a cooler plug may be necessary. An incorrect heat rating can result in disastrous pre-ignition due to excess electrode temperature. Too cold a plug is safe, but will lead to carbon deposits on the plug with consequent poor ignition, especially in regularly throttled operation. Two-stroke engines, with combustion every cycle, generally require cooler plugs than four-strokes. A four-stroke plug in a two-stroke engine is likely to cause catastrophic pre-ignition.

In modern engines the plug is usually positioned centrally in the head. However, plugs have been used at all sorts of positions and angles. In some cases this is simply for accessibility. In other cases, drastic improvements have been obtained by moving the plug toward or away from the exhaust side. A probable cause is that the gas has not been mixed adequately, and that a pocket of exhaust gas or weakened mixture is presenting itself to the plug just when ignition is required. Moving the plug will then give it access to good mixture. With symmetrical banded porting and Schnürle porting a central plug normally works well. Baffled cross-flow engines are more problematic.

In summary the plug position is governed by

1. Scavenge action and good ignition
2. Body temperature
3. Accessibility

11.4 Combustion

Normal combustion begins in the extremely small volume of the spark, and progresses out three-dimensionally. Pressure then rises more-or-less exponentially up to about half of the peak. The rise over the first 10° or so of crank angle (Figure 11.4.1) is insignificant. This has given rise to the belief that there is an ignition delay before combustion gets properly under way.

Even at the ideal ratio, vaporised fuel and air has a very low velocity of flame front propagation, around 1 to 2 m/s in laboratory tests at room temperature, and not very dependent on the type of fuel. The flame front speed is mainly dependent on the temperature of the unburned gas ahead of the front. This is because flame propagation requires sufficient heat conduction forward from the hot burned gas into the cold unburned gas to start the latter reacting.

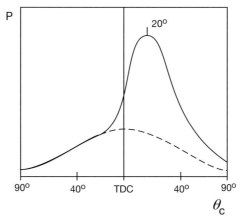

Figure 11.4.1. Cylinder pressure variation during combustion, versus crank angle (example). Dashed line shows pressure in absence of combustion.

An explosion is totally different from normal combustion. In an explosion a propagating high-pressure wave triggers local combustion because of the heating effect of the compression wave. The combustion front can then travel at the speed of the pressure wave, which is hundreds of times faster than the normal flame front speed limited by thermal conduction.

Correct engine combustion is not an explosion. It is a progressive combustion that must be made to occur rapidly but in a controlled way. Correct control of the combustion is an important part of engine design and tuning. Too slow a combustion gives low power, inefficient use of fuel, and a hot and noisy exhaust. Too fast combustion causes harsh running and mechanical damage. Technically, if the reaction proceeds by heat transfer, then it is a combustion. If it progresses as a pressure wave, at very much higher speed, then it is an explosion. The combustion fault called detonation is an explosion.

Complete combustion should take place over about 40° of crank angle. This raises several problems:

1. Normal flame front propagation is too slow
2. Explosion is too fast
3. The time available varies with engine speed.

Considering the example engine of bore 50 mm, the flame front needs to propagate about 25 mm from a central plug. At 12,000 rpm, 40° of crank angle is a time of 0.56 ms, requiring a mean speed of 45 m/s, or more than ten times the speed of the normal flame front.

The solution is the controlled use of turbulence. The swirling and rolling action of the gas causes a transfer of burning gas by convection forward into the unburned gas, thereby igniting it. The open secret of combustion control is turbulence.

In many cases the combination of scavenge action and compression automatically results in an appropriate level of turbulence. Also, happily, the turbulence velocities are proportional to the engine running speed, so combustion is faster at higher shaft speeds, tending to be constant in terms of crank angle taken. For high performance engines we often need to speed up the combustion. Squish areas where at tdc the piston crown and head are close together can achieve this. Close means about 2% of the bore or stroke, around 1 mm or so – less in many cases. For Schnürle-ported engines this usually takes the form of an annulus around the edge of the head, leaving a combustion bowl in the centre

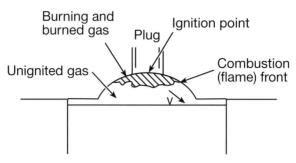

Figure 11.4.2. The combustion process. Burning occurs ideally between about 10° btdc and 40° atdc.

(Figure 11.4.2), the combustion space being axisymmetrical. This creates extra turbulence at tdc, and reduces the flame front propagation distance.

Obviously, as the piston arrives at tdc, shortly after ignition, the mixture in the outer reaches of the cylinder are 'squished' towards the centre, increasing the turbulence. The effect, however, may not be significant unless a large squish area is used, such as 50% of the bore area, with quite a small clearance.

For high compression high performance engines, squish heads provide a convenient way of reducing head volume. A flat head of the correct volume has little clearance from plug to piston. This may result in increased temperature at the centre of the piston, beneath the plug, because the combustion front will arrive at the piston before the cooling expansion has progressed significantly. In moderate output engines a flat head can perform as well, or even better, than a bowl-and-squish. If the piston tdc position is well below the cylinder top edge, the head needs to be inserted into the cylinder to provide the squish clearance, which may create problems with any crevice volume between the head and the cylinder. Fastest combustion will, of course, occur for the shortest path for the flame front. This requires a compact combustion chamber with a centrally located plug. Also, twin plugs can be used to reduce the path length.

Referring to Figures 11.4.1 and 11.4.2, the combustion runs approximately as follows. After ignition at 20° or more before tdc, combustion is established locally. Turbulence advances the flame front. Photographs of combustion through transparent heads show the burned gas region growing like an enlarging cloud around the ignition point. A useful concept of combustion is that the pressure is uniform. Obviously, the initially burned gas, which would have very high temperature and pressure if combusted at constant volume, actually expands considerably, compressing the unburned gas. As a result, there is a physical movement of the gas away from the plug.

The unburned gas, previously compressed mechanically, is therefore subject to considerable additional compression during combustion. Considering a constant-volume combustion, the final minute fraction of gas burned will be almost at the final pressure even before its combustion. In practice, peak pressure occurs at about 20° atdc, so the expansion stroke relieves the pressure in the last-burned gas. This last-burned gas, far from the plug, is called the end gas, and is nevertheless subject to considerable compressive heating. If the compression ratio is too high, in relation to the breathing and head design, then the combined mechanical and combustion compression can bring the end gas to a temperature at which it will react spontaneously. This is called detonation of the end gas. There is an associated sharp pressure rise and good chance of mechanical damage. Detonation will be worst around peak torque, at low speed, and with wide-open throttle.

The initial detonation creates a pressure wave which triggers the remainder of the gas to react. Detonation is technically an explosion and is often detectable by the engine sound.

Lowering the compression ratio helps, but this is generally an undesirable solution. Alternatively, a slow burning fuel can be used which, in the case of gasoline, means high octane. Also, the head design should be such that the end gas is well cooled by the metal surfaces to prevent an early reaction. This is why Sir Harry Ricardo introduced squish areas for four-stroke engines. The squish-band head discourages detonation whilst providing a compact chamber and extra turbulence.

As combustion proceeds, and the pressure rises, some of the end gas is forced into any crevice around the perimeter of the head, or around the piston above the rings, and into the ring groove itself. Although the volume of these is a small fraction of the total, their importance is disproportionate because of the combustion pressure rise in the end gas before its own combustion. The crevice volume around the plug threads, being behind the flame front from an early stage, is less significant than crevice volume at the cylinder periphery.

Ideally, the combustion process will be complete at about 30° atdc. By then the piston has descended down about 7% its stroke, perhaps 10% or more of the trapped stroke. Therefore there has already been significant expansion from the minimum volume tdc point, possibly 50% by volume, giving expansion cooling of the gas. This also helps to prevent detonation of the end gas.

The energy from combustion is considerable, and the theoretical temperature following constant volume combustion would be around 2,500 to 3,000°C. At these temperatures the H_2O and CO_2 molecules undergo substantial dissociation and are broken into fragments. This dissociation absorbs much of the early combustion energy, so the actual temperatures realised are only around 1,500°C or 1,800 K, some three to four times the compression temperature.

11.5 Expansion

The expansion power stroke begins at tdc, overlapping combustion, and proceeds to the opening of the exhaust port. In the ideal Otto cycle this is an adiabatic expansion, but reality deviates considerably from the ideal closed cycle. Early on, there continues to be significant heat transfer from the hot combusted gas into the head, cylinder and piston. The temperature drops, mainly due to the work done on the piston, and partly to heat transfer. The lower temperature allows dissociated molecules to recombine, releasing considerable extra energy compared with early in the process. Also, combustion itself will be imperfect early on, and will continue. Late reassociation of atoms into H_2O and CO_2 and retarded final stages of combustion tend to give lower power, lower efficiency and higher exhaust temperature than with an ideal early complete combustion. Heat transfer from combusted gas to metal tends to reduce power, efficiency and exhaust temperature. Retarded thermal energy yield is a disadvantage because it acts through a reduced useful expansion ratio for the production of power output.

Short timing of the exhaust port helps by allowing a longer power stroke, providing more useful work and releasing exhaust gases with lower temperature and pressure.

11.6 Practical Head Shapes

Design of a cylinder head internal shape is usually a matter of selection of a basic type followed by adjustment of particular dimensions and details. The intrusive piston baffle of cross-flow engines must be considered separately from Schnürle-ported engines and symmetrical porting, for which a flat or nearly-flat piston is used.

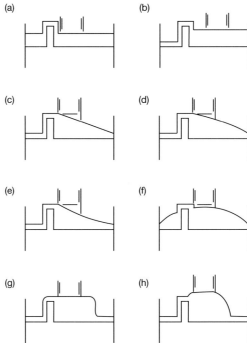

Figure 11.6.1. Basic head shapes for baffled pistons: (a) flat, (b) flat with squish, (c) wedge with squish, (d) low compression wedge, (e) high compression wedge, (f) hemi, (g) top hat, (h) bowler hat.

Figure 11.6.1 shows various head forms for cross-flow engines. The piston is basically flat, but with a baffle of height about 20% of the stroke. At a geometric compression ratio of 10, the mean head clearance, most visible in the case of the flat head, is about 11% of the stroke, so it is inevitable that the baffle will be intrusive. A clearance around the baffle is needed, typically 3% to 4% of the bore. Obviously the term 'flat' head is used loosely. One problem here is the volume on the transfer side of the baffle, because the flame propagation past the baffle may be poor. This volume may be reduced, as in the flat-head-with-squish of 11.6.1 (b). This leads on to the wedge-and-squish of 11.6.1 (c). The compression ratio can be altered by adjustments to the wedge profile, as in (d) or (e).

Another line of development is the basically axisymmetrical bowl with some sort of peripheral squish area. If the squish band is non-existent or very narrow, this is often called a hemi-head, as in Figure 11.6.1 (f), though falling far short of a true hemisphere if a realistic volume and compression ratio are to be achieved. This again has the problem of excessive volume on the transfer side. Introduction of a significant squish band gives the bowl-and-squish type of head. Where the bowl is relatively flat-topped and straight-sided this is often called a top hat head, as in Figure 11.6.1 (g). In this case there is usually a well-defined radius at the inner corner, which must be specified, as this has a substantial effect on the volume. The bowl diameter is often chosen to just reach the edge of the baffle slot, or its depth is set equal to that of the required baffle slot. Where the inner radius becomes very large then the result is a hemi-with-squish or bowler hat head, as in Figure 11.6.1 (h).

Considering the motion of hot gas during the combustion process, there must inevitably be significant forced-convection heat transfer from the hot gas to the baffle and the baffle clearance slot. This heating of the baffle and head cools the gas and inhibits rapid and complete combustion, so it is thermally inefficient. However, the hot baffle does help fuel vaporisation.

Schnürle-ported engines have flat or nearly flat piston crowns. The non-flat ones are usually domed or, occasionally, slightly concave. Sometimes a shallow cone or truncated cone shape is used. These are all axisymmetrical, and the head designs are all basically the same, but with minor adjustments to obtain the correct volumes and squish clearance distribution. The absence of the baffle clearance slot simplifies the head. Axial head symmetry is possible, though not actually required. Figure 11.6.2 shows basic shapes for such axisymmetrical heads. Obviously the particular choice depends upon achieving the correct volume, with the shape depending on personal views and preferences, individual experience, and specific testing. Results seem to depend on peculiarities of the particular engine, and heads seem to be inexplicably good or bad.

Squish bands vary considerably in clearance and profile (Figure 11.6.3). The first is simply flat with a sharp entry. The second is tapered (shown exaggerated) at up to 10

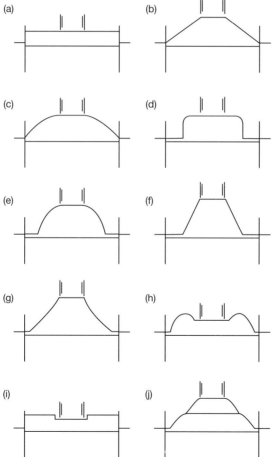

Figure 11.6.2. Axisymmetrical head shapes for flat-topped pistons in Schnürle-ported engines:
(a) flat, (b) conical, (c) hemispherical, (d) top hat, (e) bowler hat, (f) cone with squish,
(g) trumpet, (h) – , (i) – , (j) – .

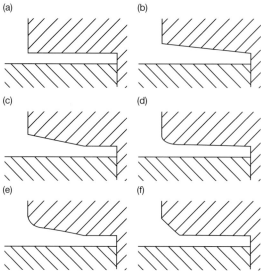

Figure 11.6.3. Squish band profiles: (a) flat, (b) tapered (angled), (c) partially tapered, (d) radiused entry, (e) radius and partial taper, (f) chamfered.

degrees, typically 4 degrees. The third is a compromise partially tapered one. Finally, the entry edge may be rounded at a radius between 3% to 8% of the bore. These features may be combined. For a non-flat piston, the whole squish band is slanted to the piston shape.

The head of an engine with a flat-topped piston need not be axisymmetrical. In fact, there are several reasons why to do otherwise:

1. to reposition the plug
2. to improve scavenging
3. to control piston heating and cooling

Figure 11.6.4 shows two typical non-axisymmetrical heads. The first is a simple adaptation of the symmetrical bowl-and-squish, with the bowl moved over, usually so that its

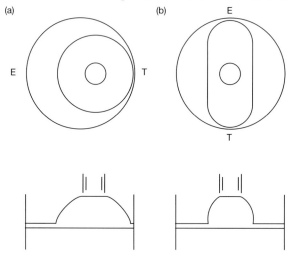

Figure 11.6.4. Asymmetrical heads: (a) offset bowl, (b) bathtub.

edge is almost at the extreme edge of the cylinder, as shown. The original design intended to position the broad squish area over the exhaust side of the piston, and the combustion bowl over the transfer side. This would make the piston crown temperature more uniform. However it was found that the engine ran better with the head on the wrong way round, apparently because this then placed the flat squish area over the rising scavenge stream which had previously been turned back by the bowl in too narrow a jet.

With a central bowl-and-squish the scavenge stream may not clear out a deep bowl very well. This will reduce overall scavenge efficiency, and possibly affect ignition. The bathtub head, as shown in Figure 11.6.4 (b), is an attempt to overcome this. The long axis of the 'bathtub' should be placed along the line of porting symmetry.

11.7 Fuels

The chemistry of special fuels is of great interest for two-stroke and four-stroke engines. Gasoline is most common, but alcohol (methanol) is a well-known racing fuel, and nitromethane is popular in drag racing. Such fuels are not necessary. Indeed, exotic fuels such as nitromethane can be hazardous for the engine, and for the operator. Actually, in its own way, gasoline can be as hazardous as anything else, because of its volatility and easy ignition. Alcohol fuels may actually be safer for the operator because of lower volatility and less intense flame, and they are often easier on the engine because they run cooler than gasoline. Apart from the obvious combustion hazard, some exotic fuels are biologically dangerous.

All fuels should be kept from the skin, and not breathed. High nitromethane content produces nitric acid in the exhaust fumes, which must not be breathed. With these cautionary notes, the following sections examine the characteristics of fuels and how they affect performance and fuel consumption.

Actually, because crankcase-scavenged two-strokes are relatively small, they consume little fuel, so non-gasoline fuels are of interest for competition purposes.

The fuel can be considered in three main elements:

1. Lubricant
2. Fuel base
3. Fuel additives

The distinction between these is sometimes rather blurred. The lubricant is normally assumed to remain unburned, but this is not entirely true. The quantity of an additive may become so large that it is better to consider the base fuel as a mixture. Nevertheless, the distinction of three components is a useful beginning.

The basic crankcase scavenged two-stroke engine cannot keep a large oil reservoir in the crankcase as a four-stroke does, and normally operates on lubricant added to the fuel. This system, sometimes called 'petroil' lubrication, has the merit of great simplicity, very appropriate to the two-stroke. The obvious disadvantage is that the oil admitted is entirely consumed. More elaborate engines have separate oil injection to the critical bearings. This may reduce the oil consumption, but is still a total-loss system. With gasoline, normal mineral oils are satisfactory, but with special fuels the choice of oil can become a serious problem.

The three main types of lubricant are:

1. Mineral oils
2. Vegetable oils
3. Synthetic oils

Vegetable oils, such as castor oil, blend well with alcohol fuels. Synthetics such as polyglycols may be needed for nitromethane-based fuels. Gasoline can use mineral oil or synthetics. The choice of lubricant depends on its compatibility with the fuel, not just on its lubricating properties. Combinations of oils are frequently used.

In an ideal plain-journal bearing, the metal surfaces remain separated by the oil film. The separation achieved under load depends on the load, the shape of the bearing surfaces, the speed of operation and the viscosity of the lubricant. In practice the lubricant in any particular bearing will be a hot oil-enriched fuel+oil mixture, because some of the fuel will normally have evaporated. To prevent rapid wear, the separation of the primary metal surfaces must exceed the size of metal protuberances due to manufacturing surface imperfections and operating distortions. In practice, high quality of manufacture permits lower oil percentages. Motorcycle engines for road use may go as low as 2%, with competition engines often around 5% to 6% with 8% for running in. The running-in process smoothes the surface imperfections, so an engine in optimum condition can operate on less oil than a new engine.

In practical operation, the ideal of complete separation of the metal surfaces of a bearing is rarely met. Some metal contact occurs, causing friction and progressive bearing wear. Under these boundary lubrication conditions, oil properties other than viscosity come into play. Vegetable oils, especially castor oil, can form a monomolecular layer on a metal surface. Castor oil can generally withstand adverse operating conditions better than basic minerals or synthetics. Chemical extreme-pressure additives, usually sulphur-based, as used in axle oils, can help minerals and synthetics under difficult conditions. The high temperature resulting from metal-to-metal contact causes the metals to react with the added sulphur compounds, changing the metal properties in a helpful way.

The list of fuel properties that can affect engine or vehicle behaviour includes:

1. Energy yield per unit liquid mass 'calorific value'
2. Stoichiometric ratio
3. Energy yield per unit liquid volume
4. Energy yield per unit mass of air
5. Energy yield per unit mass of mixture
6. Density
7. Melting point
8. Boiling point or range
9. Vapour pressure
10. Reactivity (burning speed)
11. Octane number, motor and research numbers
12. Cetane number
13. Propensity to detonate
14. Propensity to pre-ignite
15. Catalytic activity
16. Viscosity
17. Specific heat of liquid and vapour
18. Latent heat of vaporisation
19. Availability
20. Cost

Many items of the above list are mutually dependent. The calorific value is obviously important, but, as will be shown, this controls fuel consumption rather than power output.

The melting point may be rather high in some cases (e.g. nitrobenzene 5°C) but this may cease to be a problem once mixed. The boiling temperature (boiling 'point'), or boiling range for a mixture, is tied in closely with the vapour pressure at any given temperature. The surface tension is important in helping the fuel and oil lubricant to wick into narrow spaces in bearings, and to help sealing of narrow gaps.

The cetane number ($C_{16}H_{34}$, n-hexadecane) of a fuel is the result of a direct test measure of the reactivity of the fuel, and is more or less the opposite of the octane number. The latter measures resistance to detonation. A high cetane number or low octane number indicates high reactivity.

Specific heat (specific thermal capacity) of the liquid and gas, and especially the latent heat of vaporisation, calls for significant energy input to convert the fuel from its input liquid state into a burnable vapour. Vaporisation therefore results in significant cooling of the mixture with greater density of the gaseous fuel/air mix than would otherwise occur. Further vaporisation of the drops of fuel in the cylinder give significant internal cooling, greater for richer mixtures, lowering the cylinder temperature and improving reliability, but reducing thermal efficiency.

The explosive limits are the proportions by mass of fuel vapour in air, usually expressed as a percentage, indicating the range over which the mixture will sustain combustion after being independently ignited.

Flash point is the temperature at which sufficient vapour is produced over the exposed liquid to create a mixture with the air above the liquid which is ignitable by an independent spark or flame. Obviously this is related to boiling point, vapour pressure and explosive limits.

The flash point should be distinguished from the spontaneous ignition temperature (S.I.T.) (auto-ignition temperature). The S.I.T. is the temperature, much higher than the flash point, at which combustion of the stoichiometric fuel and air mixture will proceed of its own volition in the absence of any independent ignition. Obviously this is closely related to fuel reactivity, and octane and cetane numbers.

Of the many above factors, in addition to the obvious practical ones of availability and cost, the main factors in specifying a fuel are:

1. Energy yield calorific value
2. Reactivity
3. Volatility
4. Miscibility
5. Competition regulations

The first two factors are treated later. Some brief comments follow on the last three.

Obviously competition regulations are critical, and may explicitly require certain fuels and prohibit certain constituents. Typically permitted are pump gasoline or pure methyl alcohol with approved amounts of lubricant incorporated. However, less obvious regulations may have a decisive influence. In the absence of contrary rules, as in drag racing, maximum power will be obtained from alcohol and nitromethane fuels in preference to gasoline, but at the cost of much greater fuel consumption. In some cases a rule limit on the fuel tank capacity will be decisive here, in that such fuels will require too many refuelling pit stops. Under such rules, it may well be helpful to use range extenders such as benzene. This may be worthwhile even in the absence of tankage limitations, if pit stops would of necessity be slow, or if the fuel load is problematic.

Miscibility of fuel constituents is an important practical issue. Imperfect mixing often results in erratic running, because the small amount of fuel present in any particular cycle is irregular in constitution. The primary constituents must be compatible, or miscibility additives must be included, such as acetone or di-ethyl ether, at an appropriate percentage. Low ambient temperature generally worsens miscibility, which can cause unexpected problems due to separation of a previously satisfactory fuel.

Volatility is important. Apart from contributing to thermal efficiency, it aids starting cold engines. A starter additive might be di-ethyl ether, (boiling point 35°C) or propylene oxide (34°C), or light petroleum ether at typically around 10% by volume, or acetone (56°C) at a higher fraction. Gasoline is sometimes added to a methanol base for this purpose.

For a single fuel with a well-defined boiling point, Table 11.7.1 indicates roughly how cold-starting quality varies with the boiling-to-ambient differential. Methanol, boiling at 65°C, can easily run into problems at 5°C ambient, ethanol (meths) (boiling 78°C) at 18°C and nitromethane (boiling at 101°C) at any practical ambient. Volatile starter fractions are often useful.

TABLE 11.7.1. Relative volatility and starting properties – single fuel

$T_{boiling} - T_{ambient}$ °C	Relative Volatility	Starting Quality
30	Very high	Very good
40	High	Good
50	Medium	Medium
60	Low	Poor
70	Very low	Very poor

With fuel stored in large quantities over long periods, perhaps in underground tanks, there may be a problem with water contamination. As water and gasoline hardly mix at all, this can easily result in erratic running. Alcohols have a great affinity for water, mixing with it readily. A small amount of water can disrupt the miscibility of methanol and gasoline. Water may even be added deliberately at quite significant percentages, as an antidetonant. To ensure that a significant proportion of water will mix fully and not cause erratic running, a water tolerance additive may be needed. This is any substance that is readily miscible with both the base fuel itself and also with water. Acetone is sometimes used for this.

In considering additives to achieve general miscibility, volatility, anti-detonation, water tolerance, or other effects such as cooling or anti-pre-ignition, the substance chosen should be the one most compatible with the overall aims of the fuel mix.

The base fuel is normally one of:

1. Gasoline (petrol)
2. Kerosene (paraffin)
3. Aromatics (benzene family)
4. Alcohols
5. Nitroparaffins

Kerosene (and light diesel fuel) is a high cetane fuel (high reactivity, low octane) and therefore ill-suited to spark ignition.

The other base fuels listed are generally suitable for spark ignition engines if used correctly. Their power, range and other characteristics are fairly predictable. For best results the engine must be set up for the particular fuel. The compression ratio is critical; for methanol it may go half as high again as for gasoline. At about 50% nitromethane/50%

methanol the ratio is back down to that for gasoline, whilst pure nitromethane can be 40% to 50% lower than that. Spark-ignition timing variations are generally needed, perhaps 10° extra advance for methanol, and even more (30° or so) for nitromethane. Optimum port timing depends on the fuel, with nitromethane generally requiring extra exhaust lead (blowdown). Resonant exhaust design also depends on the fuel, largely because of the increased amount of exhaust gas generated by nitromethane. Methanol is high octane (low reactivity) and so tolerates higher compression ratios than pump gasoline, whereas nitromethane requires lower ratios, and is prone to pre-ignition. Compared with gasoline, fuel consumption is approximately doubled by methanol, and much worse than that for nitromethane, so fuel jets require attention, and often fuel pumps too.

In practical comparison with gasoline, methanol may deliver a power increase of 10% or so in an unchanged engine cylinder with lower running temperature and better reliability. Nitromethane can double the power, but usually with no reliability at all unless extreme care is exercised in engine preparation and operation.

Additives, of which there are several options, are typically as follows. Quantities vary considerably with application and operating conditions, the figures given being examples only.

1. Gasoline base:

    (a) Power/accelerator: methanol 10% (CR + 1), methanol 5% + nitromethane 5%, nitromethane 10% (CR – 1)
    (b) Starting: acetone 5%, propylene oxide 5%
    (c) Anti-detonant: methanol 10%, acetone 10%, benzol 10%
    (d) Anti-pre-ignition: –
    (e) Miscibility: acetone 5%
    (f) Water tolerance: acetone 5%
    (g) Coolant: methanol 10%, benzol 5%
    (h) Extender: benzol 10%+

2. Methanol base:

    (a) Power/accelerator: nitromethane 10%, propylene oxide 5%, acetone 5%
    (b) Starting: acetone 10%, gasoline 10%, di-ethyl ether 3%, propylene oxide 5%
    (c) Anti-detonant: water 5%, water 5% + acetone 5%
    (d) Anti-pre-ignition: acetone 10%, water 5% + acetone 5%
    (e) Miscibility: acetone 5%
    (f) Water tolerance: –
    (g) Coolant: –
    (h) Extender: gasoline 10%, benzol 10%, ethanol 10%

3. Nitromethane base:

    (a) Power/accelerator: propylene oxide 20%
    (b) Starting: acetone 5%, propylene oxide 5%
    (c) Anti-detonant: methanol 5%, benzene 5%, water 2.5% + methanol 7.5%, nitrobenzene 5%
    (d) Anti-pre-ignition: water 2.5% + methanol 7.5%, acetone 5%
    (e) Miscibility: propylene oxide 10%
    (f) Water tolerance: methanol 5%
    (g) Coolant: methanol 10%
    (h) Extender: methanol 10%

4. Benzol base:

- (a) Power/accelerator: –
- (b) Starting: acetone 10%, gasoline 10%
- (c) Anti-detonant: methanol 5% + acetone 5%
- (d) Anti-pre-ignition: acetone 10%
- (e) Miscibility: acetone 10%
- (f) Water tolerance: acetone 10%
- (g) Coolant: methanol 5% + acetone 5%
- (h) Extender: nitrobenzene 5%

The use of water may seem mysterious, as obviously this is not a fuel in the ordinary sense. Military aircraft with gasoline-fuelled spark-ignition four-stroke engines have used methanol-water injection to boost maximum power for take-off and combat. The methanol enriches the mixture for more power. The water, present as a fine mist, acts as a coolant as it evaporates, discouraging detonation. The water has a similar effect to reducing the compression ratio, so a higher mechanical ratio can be used, improving performance in normal operation. This suggests that for two-strokes, water could be added as a temporary fix for detonation, pending mechanical adjustment to the head. Oddly, high atmospheric humidity seems to act as an accelerator with nitromethane fuel, so abnormally high humidity may require reduced nitromethane content in favour of alcohol, or reduced compression ratio.

11.8 Fuel Energy

The so-called calorific value of a fuel, more correctly nowadays the energy or enthalpy of combustion, is measured by completely burning a sample in oxygen in a pressure-tight

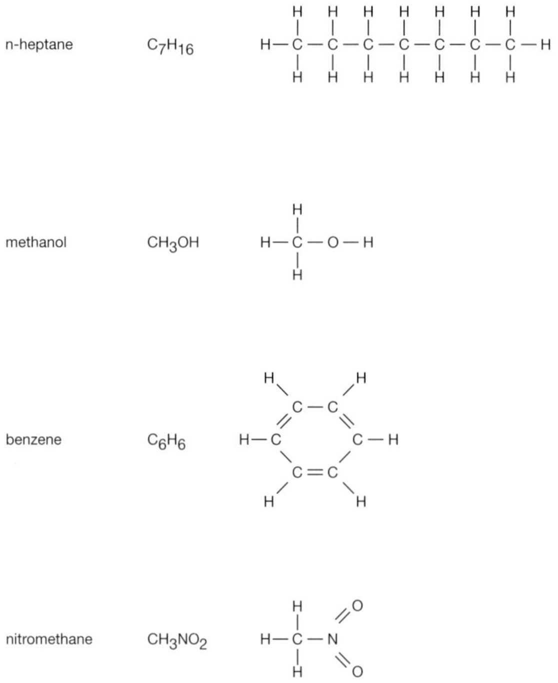

Figure 11.8.1. Molecular structure of some combustion constituents.

oxygen	O_2	O=O
nitrogen	N_2	N≡N
carbon dioxide	CO_2	O=C=O
water	H_2O	H—O—H

Figure 11.8.2 Air and exhaust molecules.

container. There are higher and lower values (HCV and LCV) according to whether the water produced is condensed as liquid or kept as vapour, respectively. Because engine exhaust is hot, it is usual to deal only with the lower value in engine calculations, although reference books tend to give the higher value. A typical value for gasoline is around 45MJ/kg or 45kJ/g (15.1 x 10^6 ft.lb/lb) so when one gram of gasoline is perfectly burned (about 1.36 cm³, 0.08 cubic inches or 0.035 oz) the thermal energy produced is 45 kilojoules (33.160 ft.lb). According to the overall efficiency of the engine in the prevailing operating conditions, from zero to about 15 kilojoules will be produced as useful work at the crankshaft.

Chemical analysis of perfect combustion throws light on the relative properties of various fuels. Gasoline is the fundamental fuel, but this is actually a complex mixture of many different sizes and shapes of molecules. For the purposes of this section (but not of the next, as explained there) we will consider simple heptane as an equivalent gasoline. Figure 11.8.1 shows the molecular structure of some prospective fuel constituents, from atoms of carbon, hydrogen and oxygen. Simple n-heptane is C_7H_{16} with seven carbon atoms in-line and sixteen hydrogens. Methanol (methyl alcohol) is a CH_3 group attached to an OH (alcohol) tail. Benzene is a ring structure of six carbons with six hydrogens. Nitromethane is a methyl group CH_3 with a nitro (NO_2) tail. In a complete molecule each atom wants to have its preferred number of links to other atoms, the valency. Hydrogen requires one, oxygen two and carbon four. Nitrogen is unusually versatile and can generally be satisfied by three or by five.

The fuel reacts by burning with air. This comprises oxygen molecules (O_2) and nitrogen molecules (N_2), in a ratio 1 to 3.76. Real combustion is, of course, messy and incomplete with many molecules failing to burn completely, giving pollutants. However in the basic ideal combustion all carbon goes to CO_2 and all hydrogen to water (or steam) H_2O whilst nitrogen is inert and unchanging.

Considering heptane in particular, one molecule of heptane, with 7 carbons and 16 hydrogens must produce 7 CO_2 molecules and 8 H_2O molecules. Therefore it requires 14 + 8 = 22 oxygen atoms, or 11 O_2 molecules. In air there will also be 3.76 x 11 N_2 molecules passing through unchanged. The complete combustion of heptane in air can be written as a chemical equation:

$$C_7 H_{16} + 11(O_2 + 3.76N_2) \Rightarrow 7CO_2 + 8H_2O + (11 \times 3.76) N_2$$

The number of each type of atom is preserved in any reaction, so the combustion equation for any fuel can be written. The CO_2 and H_2O molecules of the combusted material have atomic bonds of lower energy than the original fuel and air, so the surplus energy appears as thermal energy, associated with the calorific values.

TABLE 11.8.1 Atomic and Molecular Weights

Atomic:

Carbon	C	12.0110
Hydrogen	H	1.0080
Oxygen	O	15.9994
Nitrogen	N	14.0067
Sulphur	S	32.0640

Molecular:

Oxygen gas	O_2	31.9988
Nitrogen gas	N_2	28.08*
Carbon dioxide	CO_2	44.0098
Water	H_2O	18.0154

Heptane	C_7H_{16}	100.20
Methanol	CH_4O	32.04
Benzene	C_6H_6	78.11
Nitromethane	CH_3NO_2	61.04

*Effective value for real atmospheric nitrogen allowing for the presence of some argon etc.

The combustion equation indicates what happens in terms of numbers of atoms and molecules. To convert this into masses (kilograms or pounds) it is necessary to know the mass of individual atoms. These are the atomic weights, or molecular weights as in Table 11.8.1. Molecular weights are simply the sum of the values of the atomic weights of the constituent atoms. For heptane combustion, the masses are

Heptane	100.20	
Oxygen	11 x 31.9988	= 351.99
Nitrogen	(11 x 3.76) x 28.08	= 1,161.39
Air		1,513.38

The mass ratio of air to heptane for the ideal combustion is the stoichiometric ratio:

$$R = \frac{1,515.38}{100.20} = 15.1$$

Therefore one gram of heptane requires 15.1 grams of air for ideal combustion. The lower calorific value of heptane is $e_C = 44.73$ kJ/g, produced by burning proportions of one gram of heptane with 15.1 grams of air. A fuel with a high stoichiometric ratio will burn a larger amount of air. However, the amount of air being used by the engine is largely predetermined by the mechanical design and operating speed, so for different fuels it is better to think in terms of the amount of fuel used and the energy yield per unit mass of air. This is simply the calorific value divided by the stoichiometric ratio.

$$e_A = \frac{e_c}{R} \; \left[\text{kJ/kg of air}\right]$$

For heptane :

$$e_C = 44.6 \;\; \text{kJ/g of fuel}$$

$$R = 15.1 \;\; g_{air}/g_{fuel}$$

$$e_A = 2.96 \;\; \text{kJ/g of air}$$

This is a good indicator of the ability of the fuel to produce power in the engine. In a more detailed calculation, the energy release of a given volume of fuel vapour and air may be analysed. However, for other such fuels such as methanol or nitromethane this is unrealistic, as all the fuel cannot evaporate before trapping occurs.

Considering fuel consumption, the volume of fuel required to burn a given mass of air in the engine is important. The figure of merit for the fuel is then the calorific value e_C multiplied by the fuel density. For heptane the density at 15°C is 683 kg/m³, 0.683 g/cm³ (specific gravity or relative density 0.683), so

$$e_C = 44.6 \quad \text{kJ/g of fuel}$$

$$d = 0.683 \text{ g/cm}^3$$

$$e_V = 30.46 \text{ kJ/cm}^3 \text{ of fuel}$$

Considering the power output, the actual fuel volumetric consumption rate factor is

$$C = \frac{e_A}{e_V} \left[\text{m}^3 / \text{kg} \right]$$

For heptane this is:

$$C = \frac{2.96}{30.55} = 0.097 \text{ cm}^3/\text{g}$$

in cm³ of fuel per gram of air.

The above analysis any fuel will give a good indication of the prospects of any fuel as a power producer or for long-range economy as the base fuel (not as a minor additive).

TABLE 11.8.2. Basic fuel combustion properties

Fuel	e_C kJ/g	R –	e_A kJ/g	d g/cm³	e_V kJ/cm³	C cc/g
Heptane	44.6	15.08	2.96	0.683	30.46	0.0971
Methanol	19.7	6.43	3.07	0.791	15.60	0.1966
Benzene	40.3	13.19	3.06	0.876	35.33	0.0866
Nitromethane	10.6	1.69	6.27	1.124	11.90	0.527

e_C	lower calorific value
R	stoichiometric ratio
e_A	energy per gram of air
d	relative density (specific gravity)
e_V	energy per cm³ of fuel
C	fuel consumption cm³ of fuel per gram of air

The difference between the base fuels considered is summarised in Table 11.8.2, resulting from the following further combustion equations:

Methanol

$$CH_3OH + 1.5(O_2 + 3.76N_2) \implies CO_2 + 2H_2O + (1.5 \times 3.76) N_2$$

In this case note that account must be taken of the oxygen already present in the fuel itself to achieve complete balance of the equation.

Benzene:

$$C_6H_6 + 7.5(O_2 + 3.76N_2) \implies 6CO_2 + 3H_2O + (0.75 \times 3.76 + 0.5)N_2$$

Nitromethane:

$$CH_3NO_2 + 0.75(O_2 + 3.76N_2) \implies CO_2 + 1.5H_2O + (0.75 \times 3.76 + 0.5)N_2$$

In this case the single nitrogen atom in the fuel must be accounted for on the right-hand side, as half of an N_2 molecule.

Although some might claim that the analysis is over-simplistic, the results of Table 11.8.2 are undeniably realistic, and capture rather dramatically the actual character of these fuels.

First, column two shows the low calorific value of methanol, and especially that of nitromethane. In light of these figures it is often stated that methanol and nitromethane are powerful because they are fast burning. This is quite incorrect. Actually they are slow burning. Column three shows the low stoichiometric ratio for methanol and the extremely low value for nitromethane, indicating the amount of air needed to burn a given amount of fuel. Column four shows the power parameter e_A, kilojoules per gram of air, where methanol and benzene are seen to give a little more power than heptane (representing gasoline) and there is a gigantic power figure for nitromethane because the low calorific value is overwhelmed by the low stoichiometric ratio, all in good agreement with reality. Column five gives the relative density (specific gravity). Column six shows the volumetric energy e_V (kJ/cm^3) value, low for methanol, poor compared with heptane, the benzene value 16% higher than heptane, and the very low value for nitromethane. Column seven gives the fuel consumption parameter C, where methanol is twice the rate of heptane, benzene is 13% better than heptane, and nitromethane is over five times the figure for gasoline, and 2.7 times that for methanol. Therefore, benzene is the best range fuel of the group.

All these results are highly realistic, in agreement with practical results for most engines.

Even the power-doubling with nitromethane is realised in many cases, although this is not always achievable. Methanol may even give a little more power than that indicated. This simple calculation confirms that the power outputs achieved with methanol and nitromethane are certainly not due to the common fallacious explanation of fast combustion.

The energy yield can be applied to the products of combustion to predict a temperature for the burned gas. This indicates that methanol runs cool, not just because of evaporative cooling. It also correctly predicts that benzene runs a little hotter than heptane (for gasoline) and that nitromethane, despite considerable potential evaporative cooling, runs very hot at stoichiometric ratio. In practical operation, actual running temperatures generally need to be moderated by running rich to enhance evaporate cooling. Thermal difficulties are likely to arise when best fuel economy is essential.

In practice using methanol instead of gasoline will improve the power of an unmodified engine by more than 4%, perhaps by 10% in total, so there is another 6% to 7% to account for. In fact, three more factors need to be considered: molar expansion, dissociation and fuel evaporation. For a given temperature of the products of combustion methanol will have an advantage over heptane or gasoline. The power advantage of methanol is normally attributed to its high latent heat of evaporation (1,173 kJ/kg), which is much higher than that of gasoline (about 350 kJ/kg). In fact, evaporation of the fuel before trapping must be severely limited by the cooling effect, which will lower the vapour pressure and stop further evaporation. This suggests that the cooling effect is sensitive to the boiling point, which is low for methanol (65°C). Also, the evaporated fuel, as a gas, occupies volume, displacing air. For 20% of the methanol evaporated, the temperature lowers by about 30°C, about one tenth of the absolute temperature, increasing the mixture density by 10%. The fuel vapour adds 3% to the volume. The result would be a power increase of 7%. It would take the evaporation of all the gasoline fuel to achieve a temperature reduction of about 20°C, but this is not possible because of the higher boiling temperature (actually boiling range for gasoline). Therefore most of the evaporation probably occurs after trapping, when combustion begins. Another factor that acts in favour of methanol over gasoline is that because of the lower combustion temperature of methanol the combustion products are less liable to dissociate, so there is less power loss from this cause.

11.9 Fuel Reactivity

The analysis of the previous section assumes that the fuel is fully combusted, ignoring the process by which this is achieved. Apart from the physical processes in which early combustion energy progressively vaporises the fuel drops, an important chemical process occurs in the mixed gases.

Considering initially a stoichiometric ratio of fuel vapour and air, the fuel molecules are initially relatively stable, the heat of early combustion does not provide enough energy to disassemble all the fuel molecules and oxygen molecules to enable them to then recombine as CO_2 and H_2O. Instead, there is a progressive reaction based on the action of partial molecules called 'chain carriers'. This name arises because the partial molecule, with an unattached valency 'arm' or bond, normally on an oxygen molecule, is very reactive, and can cause the successful oxidisation of another complete or partial fuel molecule, but the reaction still leaves a free oxygen arm, or even creates two chain carriers in the process. So, the combustion process is perceived as a chain and the particular reactive molecules are the combustion chain carriers. The number of chain carriers can grow and the reaction proceed with increasing rapidity. The overall speed of combustion is therefore very sensitive to the number of chain carriers present at an early stage of combustion. If chain carriers are easily created, as when there are suitable molecules in the fuel to provide these, then the fuel is reactive. If the fuel is reluctant to create them, or tends to disarm the chain carriers and eliminate them, then it is unreactive, or high octane.

The basic reactivity of the fuel depends on how easily the molecules break up to create chain carriers. However, because the number of chain carriers needed is small relative to the total number of molecules, as each carrier can act on many molecules in due course, a small quantity of additive can have a large effect on the effective reactivity and octane number.

Long straight paraffin chains, similar to heptane but with perhaps 20 carbon atoms, are vulnerable and easily fractured thermally. Once a chain fractures, a carbon link is exposed, and this will soon acquire an oxygen atom and proceed as a chain carrier. Thus, kerosene is reactive, with a high cetane number and low octane number, and suitable for diesel engines, but not for spark ignition because it detonates too easily. Short chains are less vulnerable. Also, for a given number of carbon atoms, a branched chain is less vulnerable, and is therefore less reactive, with a lower cetane number and a higher octane number. Shorter highly-branched chains are good for gasoline, but bad for diesel fuel.

Benzene rings are robust and stable, so benzene and its derivatives are less reactive, high octane combustion retarders. Methanol is a small strong molecule, is of low reactivity, high octane, and a combustion retarder. Therefore, benzene and methanol can be used to improve the octane number of gasoline, allowing higher compression ratios.

The classic combustion retarder additive to reduce reactivity and consequent detonation of gasoline, allowing higher compression ratio, is tetraethyl lead. This operates by mopping up the chain carriers.

There are many possible combustion accelerators, generally organic nitrates, nitrites, aldehydes, peroxides or hydroperoxides. Considering, for example, n-propyl nitrite (C_3H_7ONO), contrasted with nitropropane ($C_3H_7NO_2$) in Figure 11.9.1, the nitrite molecule fractures easily between the O and N, the N=O separating off, leaving an incomplete C_3H_7O- which acts as a chain carrier. Nitropropane completely lacks this combustion accelerator property, although it can be a power improver because of its ideal combustion characteristics, analysed as in the previous section. Iso-propyl nitrate has the nitrate ($-NO_2$) attached to the centre carbon of the propyl group, instead of at the end as for n-propyl. Also nitrate is $-NO_2$ compared with nitrite $-NO$. These two molecules are both effective as combustion accelerators, despite their differences. Combustion accelerators are highly undesirable in gasoline fuels, but are useful for diesel fuels.

(a)   nitropropane (non-accelerator)

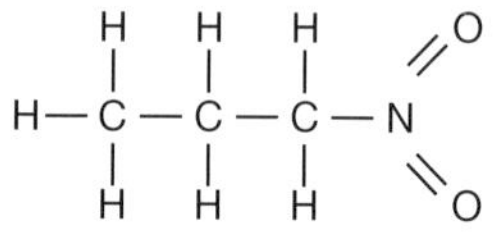

(b)   n-propyl nitrite (acclerator)

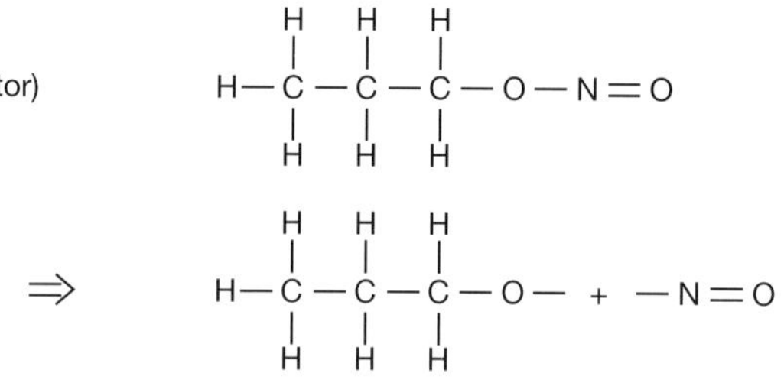

(c)   iso-propyl nitrate (accelerator)

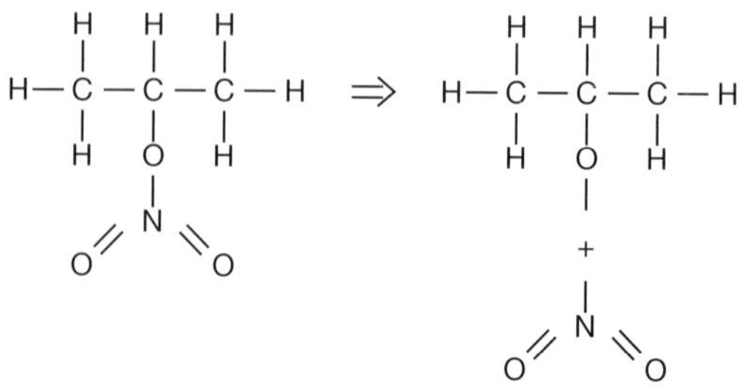

Figure 11.9.1. Fuel molecules and reactivity:
(a) Nitropropane (non-accelerator)
(b) n-propyl nitrite (highly reactive accelerator)
(c) iso-propyl nitrate (highly reactive accelerator)

244

As an illustration of the constituents of racing fuels, from 1945 to date, including four-stroke Grand Prix car fuels, racing motorcycle fuels, and kart fuels, some examples (by volume) to be found in the literature are:

1. Gasoline 100%
2. Methyl alcohol 100%
3. Gasoline 50%, benzol 50%
4. Gasoline 40%, ethyl alcohol 30%, benzol 30%
5. Ethyl alcohol 75%, benzol 14%, acetone 5%, water 6%
6. Methyl alcohol 60%, benzol 30%, gasoline 10%
7. Methyl alcohol 95%, acetone 5%
8. Methyl alcohol 80%, gasoline 10%, benzol 10%
9. Ethyl alcohol 56%, benzol 40%, gasoline 4%
10. Methyl alcohol 85%, benzol 10%, acetone 5%
11. Methyl alcohol 60%, gasoline 20%, benzol 20%
12. Methyl alcohol 80%, gasoline 10%, benzol 10%
13. Methyl alcohol 75%, benzol 14%, water 6%, acetone 5%
14. Methyl alcohol 80%, benzol 6%, gasoline 5%, water 4%, acetone 3%, nitrobenzene 2%
15. Methyl alcohol 56%, ethyl alcohol 28%, gasoline 7%, water 4%, acetone 5%
16. Methyl alcohol 82%, acetone 10%, nitrobenzene 5%, water 2%, di-ethyl ether 1%
17. Gasoline 40%, benzol 40%, ethyl alcohol 20%
18. Methyl alcohol 80%, ethyl alcohol 10%, acetone 5%, benzol 5%
19. Gasoline 50%, methyl alcohol 30%, methylated spirit 20%
20. Methyl alcohol 50%, gasoline 35%, benzol 10%, acetone 5%
21. Methyl alcohol 75%, benzol 10%, gasoline 10%, acetone 5%
22. Methyl alcohol 75%, water 15%, di-ethyl ether 10%
23. Gasoline 35%, acetone 35%, methyl alcohol 25%, ethyl acetate 5%
24. Methyl alcohol 75%, nitromethane 25%
25. Methyl alcohol 60%, nitromethane 20%, benzol 10%, gasoline 5%, acetone 5%
26. Methyl alcohol 50%, nitromethane 50%
27. Nitromethane 70%, methyl alcohol 25%, propylene oxide 5%
28. Nitromethane 80%, propylene oxide 20%
29. Toluene 94%, heptane 6% (turbocharged F1 Grand Prix)

(Benzol(e) is approximately 70% benzene, 20% toluene, 10% xylene.)
(Methylated spirit is 90% ethanol, 10% methanol, plus minor additives.)

Apart from some oddities, the main pattern in the above is the displacement of gasoline by alcohols, usually methanol (methyl alcohol), aromatics (benzene derivatives, benzol(e)) or nitroparaffins (especially nitromethane), and the inclusion of additives such as acetone, amyl acetate, diethyl ether, water, isopropyl nitrate and nitrobenzene. The possible combinations are virtually endless, so to understand the process of fuel design it is necessary to understand the reasons for choice of base fuels and additives.

CHAPTER 12

Engine Performance

12.1   Introduction

Considered as a black box, an engine has certain inputs and outputs (Figure 12.1.1). The purpose of the engine is, of course, to produce mechanical power from fuel and air. There are also undesirable by-products such as exhaust fumes, noise and vibration. The basic measures of performance are the power output and the fuel consumed to produce it. Power can be produced at lower or higher rpm, and there is the power band to consider. Power is not measured directly, but is derived from torque and shaft speed.

There are numerous performance parameters. These can be grouped in various ways. The first division is into measured or derived values. These can be subdivided into static and dynamic values. Some examples are:

Static measured:	swept volume, mass, frontal area
Dynamic measured:	shaft speed, torque, fuel consumption, air consumption, noise, and vibration, exhaust chemistry
Derived values:	power, specific power, brake specific fuel consumption, thermal efficiency, brake mean engine pressure.

12.2   Performance Parameters

It is often useful to measure pressures and temperatures, though these are not really performance parameters.

Measurement of swept volume is merely a matter of measuring the bore, stroke, and number of cylinders. Simple as this may seem, some issues may arise for competition engines operating close to the stipulated maximum. When measuring the stroke from the

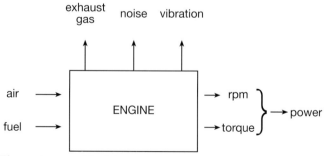

Figure 12.1.1. The engine as a black box.

piston depth in the cylinder, unless the piston is perfectly flat then exactly the same point on the piston crown must be used. For a ringed piston, the piston diameter is less than that of the liner, so the liner inner diameter should be used, but this may be tapered. Thermal expansion is small and the cold dimensions are generally accepted.

In measuring the engine mass, obviously for comparative purposes there must be uniformity in the inclusion of ancillary equipment, including the exhaust system.

The frontal area is of interest, particularly for multi-cylinder engines where the width may affect the vehicle drag, as with a straight four installed across a motorcycle. When defining the front profile, as of an air-cooled engine, one usually considers a profile line of the whole cooling barrel without subtracting the area between the fins.

12.3 Shaft Speed

Shaft speed measuring systems include:

1. Vibrating reeds
2. Mechanical rev control
3. Mechanical tachometers
4. Electronic tachometers using
   (i)   ignition sensor
   (ii) optical sensor
   (iii) magnetic sensor
   (iv) accelerometer sensor
5. Audio tachometers
6. Oscilloscopes

In the days of low-speed engines, shaft speed was usually measured by mechanical rev counters with a stopwatch. Later automatic ones counted the revs until an internal clockwork system disconnected the counter after a given time, often six seconds (0.1 minutes). Later, mechanical tachometers came into use. These could continuously indicate rpm with a slipping magnetic drive deflecting a needle against a torsion spring. These are often switchable for speed range, going up to typically 20,000 rpm or 50,000 rpm maximum, and are still useful. Good ones are quite expensive.

Vibrating reed tachometers come in two main types. A wire or thin metal strip indicates resonant response. The wire length may be varied to achieve resonance, with a corresponding scale to indicate rpm or hertz (cycles per second) directly. The other kind has a series of metal strips of different lengths covering a limited speed range in suitable steps. Vibrating reed tachometers can be fairly accurate if calibrated and used with skill, but generally lack the fine discrimination needed for accurate testing.

Mechanical tachometers have now been largely superseded by electronic ones, with digital display. Their discrimination is sometimes rather limited, e.g. to 100 rpm. Complete units are readily available and quite cheap. Alternatively, a frequency-indicating multimeter can be used with a suitable input. Cheaper electronic tachometers simply count the number of pulses in a given period, normally 0.01 minutes (0.6 seconds) to indicate to a discrimination of 100 pulses per minute. Better discrimination costs more. Extreme accuracy is not helpful because there is some inherent uncertainty in engine speed, due to variations in carburettion.

The signal pickup can be taken from the ignition system, giving only one pulse per revolution for a single cylinder engine. An optical pickup is common, operating by ambient light from black and white stripes on a rotating component such as a flywheel. This permits

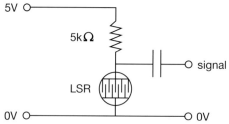

Figure 12.3.1. Optical pickup for tachometer, using a light-sensitive resistor (LSR). Most light-sensitive resistors are suitable, including miniature types, with dark resistance around 5,000 ohms. The decoupling capacitor may not be needed.

almost any number of pulses per revolution. Figure 12.3.1 shows a simple pickup circuit using a small light sensitive resistor, which can be used with a frequency-indicating multimeter. The series resistor is ideally equal to the average resistance of the LSR, but this is not critical. A 5kΩ resistance is often good. There may be difficulties with optical pickups. The signal amplitude is small at high frequency because of the slow response of the LSR, but usually adequate. An optical transistor or diode can be used instead. Indoors, the mains frequency causes variation of the intensity of artificial light, modest for incandescent light but severe for fluorescents. A strong direct current light often overcomes this. Alternatively, a non-optical pickup can be used, such as a Hall effect transistor.

A possible alternative is an accelerometer sensor on the crankcase or test bed, especially for single cylinder engines, which have plenty of vibration at the engine frequency. However the output is then limited to one cycle of signal per engine revolution.

Microphone audio pickups rarely work well in practice, as the audio signal is generally not well defined due to background noise and echo interference. An audio tachometer is a different device, which generates an engine-like sound of calibrated adjustable frequency. The sound of the tachometer is manually adjusted to agree with the engine noise frequency by detecting, and then eliminating, the interference beats. For workshop use this is less convenient than a passive tachometer, but has the advantage that it can be used remotely. In the latter case, however, Doppler effect must be considered as this causes a false frequency to arrive at the observer. Instead of calibrating the audio tachometer, which may in any case be subject to temperature variation or drift, a light-emitting diode can be added to the circuit, which will drive a digital optical tachometer to obtain the reading.

An oscilloscope can be used on almost any rotating member, with the advantage that multiple stripes can be painted or affixed to a flywheel or rotor to give several signals per revolution. Accurate oscilloscopes are quite expensive and the frequency must be set manually. AC artificial lighting, especially fluorescents, can be a problem.

12.4 Torque

Measurement of the engine torque is of prime importance. In principle it is independent from, but actually closely tied up with, the method of power dissipation. For a 100 cm^3 engine there may be 15 kW (20 bhp) or more to dissipate. Various forms of engine brake can provide suitable resistance, but the best method is generally a special adjustable resistance water pump. However these are expensive. In fact, setting up a test cell is difficult, time consuming and expensive, and beyond most private tuners, though essential for professionals.

Another approach is based on the reaction to torque from the load acting on the engine, which is equal to the output torque. On this basis, the engine can be mounted in a torque cradle and the torque measured on the engine rather than on the load. This eases the design of the load, so that an electrical generator can be used with an adjustable characteristic, with the power dissipated through electric fire elements or bulbs. The torque could then be measured on either the engine or the generator. It is not difficult to build a torque-reaction dynamometer, but to make one of scientific accuracy is another matter, especially for a severely vibrating single-cylinder engine. Early attempts to measure full size aero engine output in this way using propeller load suffered 50% errors.

Torque testing, though of profound importance, is something of a problem for the private engine tuner. In-vehicle performance testing may be more practical, simply using a straight-line acceleration test of a standard vehicle, especially if an acceleration data logger is available.

Whatever means is used, it is necessary to obtain torque output values for a series of shaft speeds over the relevant range.

12.5 Fuel Consumption

In principle, the pressure drop due to flow through a small orifice can be used to evaluate fuel consumption instantaneously. However, this will require calibration for varying fuel temperatures, and different fuels. This is a useful method if many such measurements are to be made on a standard fuel.

A more direct method is to measure the duration on a given volume of fuel, long enough for accurate stopwatch measurement, which is easier for a small number of readings, and has the confidence-building merit of being direct. However it is time consuming when many readings are required. Obviously the volume must be accurately established, usually by having a narrow neck at the critical fuel levels.

Because air and fuel temperatures greatly affect fuel vaporisation, it is important to measure this feature under standard temperature conditions, especially where adjustable fuel jets (needle valves) are used, as on many two-strokes.

The above methods measure volumetric fuel consumption. A possible alternative is gravimetric (mass) measurement using a tank on scales.

12.6 Air Consumption

Unlike fuel, air is free, but the air consumed in relation to the power is an important indicator of the scavenging quality of the engine. Air consumption is usually measured on a continuous basis by the pressure differential of a venturi meter, (Figure 12.6.1). Because the air flow into the engine itself is so cyclical, a generous size settling chamber is required, preferably fifty times the swept volume, so that flow in the measuring venturi is as steady as possible, which can be achieved if the settling chamber includes a rubber sheet on at least one side, so damping the oscillations.

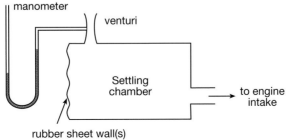

Figure 12.6.1. Measurement of air consumption.

The air consumption rate is derived from the venturi throat area and throat static pressure relative to ambient. Accurate calibration charts are available for standard venturi designs. The venturi must be sized to give a suitable throat pressure, using a manometer for accurate measurement, whilst avoiding excessive pressure losses. A venturi is generally preferred to a simple orifice.

A 100 mm water manometer indication requires about 1 kPa suction, with a throat speed of 40 m/s. For a 100 cm^3 engine, depending on its state of tune, this would correspond to a venturi bore of around 15 mm. This is smaller than the inlet system for a very highly tuned engine, so the need for good pressure recovery from the measuring venturi is apparent. Electronic equipment is available, at some expense, for the accurate measurement of smaller pressures. This will allow a larger venturi and ease the pressure loss problem, but such equipment lacks the confidence-building satisfaction of a visual reading, and raises concerns about change of calibration.

For a wide range of air consumption rates, different size venturis are commonly used. There is another method, where a single constant venturi at the small end of the range is used for pressure measurement, and replicas of that venturi can be opened or closed to multiply the corresponding flow rate by integer values.

If too small a settling chamber makes the flow through the sensing venturi unsteady, then the indicated air-flow rate will be too high because the venturi indicates the root-mean-square pressure. For very accurate testing this can be overcome by using a viscous pressure drop element in lieu of the venturi.

12.7 Exhaust Chemistry
Methods exist to analyse the engine exhaust gas, such as the Orsat apparatus or nowadays more elaborate, automatic equipment. Such equipment can help in evaluating how much unburned fuel is passing through the engine, but is beyond most amateur tuners.

12.8 Vibration
Engine vibration depends on unbalanced masses such as the piston(s), the number of cylinders and their configuration, and the way that the engine is mounted. With the engine fixed rigidly to an inert mass, an accelerometer can be used to evaluate the vibration, and to relate this to changes such as balance factor. When the engine is mounted in a vehicle, such as a motorcycle frame, then the net effect depends on the particular chassis. In that case, vibration is usually assessed subjectively.

12.9 Temperatures
Temperatures of interest include:

1. Ambient air
2. Fuel input
3. Engine head
4. Exhaust gas

Portable digital thermocouples are suitable and quite cheap. These indicate the temperature at the tip of a pair of flexible wires. The sensing tip of the wires needs to be attached firmly to the engine at the required point, most conveniently by trapping it under a screw head. For measurement of head temperature, the wires can be attached to the sparking plug washer or to a special bimetallic washer. Alternatively, a small screw can be tapped into the rear of the head.

Fluid temperatures are also easily measured by thermocouple. The usual target is the exhaust gas fairly near to the exhaust port, but others, including more remote exhaust gas, air input and fuel input, are of interest.

There may be some doubt about the closeness of the sensor tip temperature to that of the metal or fluid whose temperature is sought, though, for metal, a simple firm clamp is usually adequate. For fluids, the wires must be adequately exposed to the fluid to ensure that the tip temperature is not reduced significantly by conduction along the wires. This can be determined by testing.

Table 12.9.1 gives representative temperatures for an air-cooled 100 cm³ racing engine on gasoline fuel. The exhaust gas temperatures vary considerably with cylinder swept volume, increasing with cylinder size. These temperatures, after calibration of individual engines, are a useful indication of the carburation richness/leanness, and so are useful for set up and monitoring. The best values vary significantly from one engine to another, and according to the fuel, but with some experience are a guide to optimisation and reliable operation.

Table 12.9.1   Typical average temperature classifications for an air-cooled 100 cm³ racing engine (not sustained maximum power)

Head Temperature T_H:

220°C	very high
200°C	high
180°C	medium
160°C	low
140°C	very low

Exhaust gas temperature (near exhaust port) T_{EG}:

650°C	very high
625°C	high
600°C	medium
575°C	low
550°C	very low

12.10 Derived Values

The primary static engine parameters measured are:

1. V_S, swept volume (m³)
2. m_E, engine mass (kg)

plus other details such as fuel density.

The basic performance values obtained are:

1. N_M, shaft speed (revolutions per minute)
2. Q, shaft output torque (Nm)
3. V_F, fuel volumetric consumption rate (m³/s)
4. V_A, air volumetric consumption rate (m³/s)

normally for a range of values of shaft speed.

The basic SI units are shown, although other practical and consistent sets of units may also be used.

Derived values are then as follows:

1. Power
The shaft speed in rad/s is then

$$\Omega_S = \frac{2\pi}{60} N_M = 0.10472 N_M$$

The shaft power output is

$$P_S = \Omega_S Q = \frac{2\pi}{60} N_M Q$$

This is a power in the SI unit of watts, so in the common form of brake horse power (1 bhp = 745.7 W),

$$P_{bhp} = \frac{\Omega_S Q}{745.7} = 1.404 \times 10^{-4} N_M Q$$

The situation is further complicated by alternative units often used for the torque. Frequently engine torque is actually measured as kilogram (force) decimetres or as pound. feet (lb ft). Using

$$1 \text{ lb ft} = 1.357 \text{ Nm}$$

then for rpm, and torque in lb ft.

$$P_{bhp} = 1.905 \times 10^{-3} N_M Q_{lb.ft}$$

2. Specific Power
The term 'specific power' is used in two ways, for either

$$P_{SV} = \frac{P_S}{V_{SE}}$$

related to the engine swept volume, fundamentally W/m^3, but is often expressed in kW/litre or bhp/litre. Alternatively,

$$P_{SM} = \frac{P_S}{m_E}$$

related to the engine mass, fundamentally W/kg, but usually bhp/kg or bhp/lb.

3. Specific Fuel Consumption
The fuel mass flow rate is simply the density times the volumetric flow rate:

$$\dot{m}_F = \rho_F \dot{V}_F$$

The (brake) specific fuel consumption relates the fuel consumed to the power output

$$C_{SF} = \frac{\dot{m}_F}{P}$$

with fundamental units kg/(W.s) which is kg/J. In practical units this is normally expressed as kg/bhp.hr or lb/bhp.hr. The volumetric equivalent also known as the (brake) specific fuel consumption is often used, expressed as $cm^3/s/bhp$, which is a convenient unit, or as pints/bhp.hr. Sometimes the duration is preferred:

$$D = \frac{1}{\dot{V}_F}$$

possibly in s/cm^3 or minutes/gallon.

The specific duration is

$$D_{SF} = \frac{P_S}{\dot{V}_F}$$

in the fundamental units J/m^3, or practical units kJ/cm^3 or $bhp.s/cm^3$. The mass flow equivalent is

$$D_{SFM} = \frac{P_S}{\dot{m}_F}$$

in basic units J/kg, or practical units of kJ/g, or bhp.hr/lb.

4. Specific Torque

The specific torque, or torque per unit swept volume, is

$$q = \frac{Q}{V_S}$$

In SI units, the torque is in Nm, the specific torque in Nm/m^3 ($=N/m^2$), with practical units Nm/litre. Torque is sometimes found in kgf.m, kgf.dm (kilogram force decimeter = 0.9806 Nm), ounce.inches or pound.feet, and swept volume in litres, cubic centimetres and cubic inches, giving rise, *inter alia*, to kgf.dm/litre and lbf.ft/ci. Specific torque is also sometimes quoted as torque per unit mass.

5. Brake Mean Effective Pressure

The bmep is the notional pressure which when multiplied by the swept volume gives the energy output per revolution.

The shaft output per revolution (2π radians) is

$$E_S = 2\pi Q \qquad [\text{J}]$$

where Q is the torque, so

$$P_{BME} = \frac{E_S}{V_S} = \frac{2\pi Q}{V_S}$$

Hence, in SI or other consistent units, the brake mean engine pressure is simply 2π times the specific torque, i.e. 6.283 times the torque per unit volume.

The SI unit of bmep is the pascal Pa ($= N/m^2$), in practice in kPa, with psi (lbf/in^2) as the imperial unit value.

6. Delivery ratio

The air volumetric flow rate $\dot{V}_A$ can be reduced to the volume of air delivered per revolution

$$V_A = \frac{\dot{V}_A}{N_S}$$

The delivery ratio is then this volume divided by the swept volume

$$\eta_D = \frac{V_A}{V_S} = \frac{\dot{V}_A}{N_S V_S}$$

As in Chapter 8, this should be distinguished from the volumetric efficiency, which is lower because of the trapping efficiency.

7. Brake Thermal Efficiency
The fuel consumed per revolution is

$$m_F = \frac{\dot{m}_F}{N_S}$$

The notional combustion energy available from this amount of fuel is

$$E_C = e_C m_F$$

where e_C is the lower calorific value of the fuel. The (brake) thermal efficiency is then

$$\eta_{Th} = \frac{E_S}{E_C}$$

where E_S is the shaft energy output per revolution. This can also be expressed as

$$\eta_{Th} = \frac{P_S}{e_C \dot{m}_F}$$

12.11 Examples

The first example is a 98.2 cm³ engine delivering 18 bhp at 12,000 rpm:

Engine performance analysis from known speed and torque.
DATA:

Engine type	=	Demo 98 -3
Engine swept volume	=	98.20 cm³
Engine mass	=	7.000 kg
Fuel density	=	730.00 kg/m³
Fuel energy of comb.	=	45.000 MJ/kg
Air density	=	1.20 kg/m³
Speed	=	12.00 krpm
Torque	=	10.70 Nm
Fuel consumption	=	2.30 cm³/s
Air consumption	=	17.00 litre/s

RESULTS:

SPEED ANALYSIS:

Speed	=	12.00 krev/min 1.257 krad/s

TORQUE & MEP ANALYSIS:

Torque	=	10.70 Nm (7.889 lb ft)
Specific torque	=	108.96 Nm/litre (1.316 lb ft/ci)
Brake MEP	=	0.685 MPa (99.324 psi)

POWER ANALYSIS:

Shaft power	=	13.446 kW (18.00 bhp)
Specific power	=	136.925 kW/litre (1.166 bhp/lb)

FUEL ANALYSIS:

Fuel density	=	0.73 g/cm^3
Fuel vol. flow rate	=	2.30 cm^3/s
Fuel volume/rev	=	11.50 mm^3
Fuel mass flow rate	=	1.679 g/s
Fuel mass/rev	=	8.395 mg
Specific fuel cons	=	0.125 g/s/kW (0.740 lb/bhp.hr)
Specific fuel cons	=	0.128 cm^3/s/bhp

AIR ANALYSIS:

Air density	=	1.20 kg/m^3
Air vol. flow rate	=	17.00 litre/s
Air volume/rev	=	85.00 cm^3
Air mass flow rate	=	20.40 g/s
Air mass/rev	=	0.102 g
Delivery ratio	=	0.866

FUEL/AIR ANALYSIS:

Air/fuel mass ratio	=	12.15
Fuel/air mass ratio	=	82.304 E-3
Fuel/air vol. ratio	=	135.294 E-6

ENERGY ANALYSIS:

Shaft energy/rev	=	67.23 J
Fuel comb energy/rev	=	377.775 J
Thermal efficiency	=	17.796 %

The second example is a 125 cm^3 racing engine delivering 42 bhp at 12,500 rpm:

Engine performance analysis from known speed and torque.
DATA:

Engine type	=	Racing 125
Engine swept volume	=	125.00 cm^3
Engine mass	=	11.00 kg
Fuel density	=	730.00 kg/m^3
Fuel energy of comb.	=	45.00 MJ/kg
Air density	=	1.20 kg/m^3
Speed	=	12.50 krpm
Torque	=	24.00 Nm
Fuel consumption	=	4.80 cm^3/s
Air consumption	=	36.00 litre/s

RESULTS:

SPEED ANALYSIS:
Speed   =   12.50 krev/min(1.309 krad/s)

TORQUE & MEP ANALYSIS:
Torque   =   24.00 Nm (17.694 lb ft)
Specific torque   =   192.00 Nm/litre (2.320 lb ft/ci)
Brake MEP   =   175.02 psi

POWER ANALYSIS:
Shaft power   =   31.416 kW (42.056 bhp)
Specific power   =   251.327 kW/litre (1.734 bhp/lb)

FUEL ANALYSIS:
Fuel density   =   0.73 g/cm^3
Fuel vol. flow rate   =   4.80 cm^3/s
Fuel volume/rev   =   23.04 mm^3
Fuel mass flow rate   =   3.50 g/s
Fuel mass/rev   =   16.82 mg
Specific fuel cons   =   ¨0.11 g/s/kW (0.66 lb/bhp.hr)

AIR ANALYSIS:
Air density   =   1.20 kg/m^3
Air vol. flow rate   =   36.00 litre/s
Air volume/rev   =   172.80 cm^3
Air mass flow rate   =   43.20 g/s
Air mass/rev   =   0.207 g
Delivery ratio   =   1.382

FUEL/AIR ANALYSIS:
Air/fuel mass ratio   =   12.329
Fuel/air mass ratio   =   81.111 E-3
Fuel/air vol. ratio   =   133.333 E-6

ENERGY ANALYSIS:
Shaft energy/rev   =   150.796 J
Fuel comb energy/rev =   756.864 J
Thermal efficiency   =   19.924 %

The 'impossible' figure of 1.382 for the delivery ratio, that is 173 cm^3 of air burned each revolution of the 125 cm^3 cylinder, shows just how difficult it is to achieve the claimed power output. Nevertheless, this is based on published claims for racing motorcycle engines. The only conclusion is that the exhaust system must be capable of precompressing the large amount of air into the trapped volume of about 62 cm^3. Engines not set up to use the exhaust in this extreme way, with a very narrow power band, must have much lower power. Measuring the air consumption gives the delivery ratio. There is no easy way to deduce the volumetric efficiency or the trapping efficiency, so it is assumed to be 1.0.

12.12 Analysis

There are two main reasons for calculating the foregoing values:

1. To compare different engines
2. To assess the modifications

Tuning most often aims to improve the torque or power. However, if fuel consumption and air consumption can also be tested much more can be learned about the effect of the modifications.

For example, a modification that is found to increase the air and fuel consumption proportionally more than the torque at a given speed is evidently causing more mixture to exit unused from the exhaust port (lower trapping efficiency). In the absence of air consumption measurement, it is frequently assumed that the mixture is uniform and that the fuel consumption is proportional to the air consumption.

In either case, evidently a poor specific fuel consumption relative to a similar engine, or a deterioration arising from a modification, indicates that excessive mixture is being lost untrapped. At higher rpm the efficiency due to the shorter scavenge time may be restored, with improved torque and power at that higher speed – hence the need to test over the relevant speed range.

Observing how modifications affect fuel consumption is particularly important for events where fuel quantity is restricted, or where fuel weight is a problem.

Temperature of air and fuel, as well as humidity, can affect results, especially where the effect of small modifications is being investigated. Corrections can be made, but these are not really satisfactory because engines respond differently. The only good solution is to have uniform conditions for the comparative tests. Often this can be achieved by selection of stable conditions coupled with a rapid turnaround in engineering a specific series of changes and performing the tests.

Corrections of engine power output for ambient conditions are made according to the methods in Appendix E.

CHAPTER 13:

Tuning

13.1 Introduction

Tuning an engine is about fitness for purpose. Tuning must be for improving the engine with a particular application in mind, because the application dictates the characteristics needed. The existing engine may be less than ideal for many reasons, one of which is the manufacturer's limitations due to production costs, lack of knowledge, or the engine may simply have been designed for some other use.

Improved power is often the goal, but not always. Some aims of tuning are:

1. Improved appearance
2. Weight reduction
3. Frontal area
4. Reliability
5. Life (wear rate)
6. Ease of use (control)
7. Cooling
8. Lubrication
9. Ease of starting
10. Noise reduction
11. Oil tightness
12. Balance and vibration
13. Running characteristics
14. Tractability
15. Powerband width
16. Fuel economy
17. Carburettor suction
18. Torque
19. Power

These items can be collected into various groups of associated concepts, not entirely mutually exclusive, for example:

1. Appearance, weight, frontal area
2. Reliability, lubrication, life, cooling, starting, balance, ease of use
3. Economy, tractability, power
4. Noise, oil tightness

The first group comprises external static factors. The second group contains reliability and use qualities. The third group has the basic performance parameters. The final group comprises the side effects.

Items such as these will have different degrees of importance, so it helps to have a clear picture of their relative significance, not least because in many cases one must be traded off against another.

In practical tuning, operations generally fall into six categories:

1. External factors
2. Fits and alignments
3. Porting, gas flow and timing
4. Heads and compression ratios
5. Intake system
6. Exhaust system

13.2 The Build

The mystique of port angle-areas and directions and of the complexities of exhaust systems can easily obscure the fundamentals of engine preparation. At least as important as porting changes are the less glamorous but essential assembly skills; namely 'building' the engine correctly and 'blueprinting' it. Strictly, the first essential skill is disassembly. The second essential skill, 'assembly' or building, is a matter of getting from a bench of parts back to a well-built, preferably optimally built, engine. This poses genuine difficulties. The author has actually worked on engines that cannot be dismantled without distorting components, and which can only have been built by brute force, occasionally evidenced by hammer marks. Other engines are easily disassembled but require very careful thought to reassemble, for one reason or another. Finally, accurate assembly may require special tools or jigs. It is easy to lose critical set-up values when dismantling an engine, sometimes with no practical means of retrieving the data other than extensive testing.

Some parts, such as ball bearings in crankcase castings, or cylinders in cooling barrels, are likely to be a precise interference fit requiring controlled heating for assembly or disassembly.

There are many critical dimensions in an engine which must be observed on assembly, often involving adjustment or shimming. However, even if manufacturer's data or a handbook is available, this may apply to an untuned engine of lower output. Engine modifications will generally increase the running temperature, change the distribution of temperatures, and will usually invalidate the baseline set-up data.

The classic example of this is the ring end-gap value, which allows for the greater thermal expansion of the ring than of the cylinder. Ideally the ring gap verges on closing under maximum operating conditions. Torque-increasing modifications will generally increase the expansion differential, and demand a greater cold gap than the standard one. Equally, the correct cold gap will depend on the service conditions, intensity of load, cooling, and fuel used.

All parts need to be independently checked for accuracy and soundness. Then the engine is built progressively, checking each stage for problems such as inappropriate friction. Any such problems simply must be dealt with before continuing. There are many good books available on the practicalities of building of four-stroke racing engines, and there are sufficient similarities in the principles of assembly for these to be worth careful study for the two-stroke tuner, providing a useful supplement to books on two-strokes.

Depending on the work that has been performed, running-in may be necessary. This is so if any of the bearing surfaces have been replaced or modified, perhaps even if only cleaned. This also provides an opportunity for checking the correct operation of ancillaries such as ignition and carburettor, and oil-tightness. If all is well, then the engine can then be acceptance tested for performance and released for use, or subject to further performance testing if it is experimental.

13.3 Mechanical Set-up

Experienced tuners have long known that minor details of engine set-up can have a large effect on engine performance, reliability and ease of use. These aspects of tuning, contrasting with the more obvious port grinding, were bought to prominence in the public eye by certain developments in competitions in the 1960s. To provide close and economical competition, some classes were created calling for standard engines, or for only very limited modifications. The engines were required to conform to some or all of the manufacturer's dimensional tolerances. Predictably to the experienced, some engines were still noticeably better than others, and some tuners were still able to consistently produce superior engines. This is achieved by optimising each dimension within its permissible range – the process now well-known as blueprinting, conforming to the 'blueprint' (drawings) in an optimal way. In some cases this can be achieved by modifying the part, in others by part selection. The classic example is to maximise the compression ratio by obtaining the crankcase block with the lowest allowable deck height (by selection or machining), the connecting rods with greatest allowable length (by selection) and, the pistons with greatest crown height above the wrist pin (by selection), and the head of smallest volume. It will be apparent that the advantage here is likely to accrue to those operators with the best chance of selecting optimal components, so, despite the original intentions of the rule-makers, the private tuner is not necessarily helped by such regulations, which are in any case rather laborious to enforce.

Many dimensions other than the example given above are open to optimisation, perhaps most obviously the clearances between piston and cylinder, and the plain journal bearings. Castings must be selected for accurate and optimum ports, and so on. Even in those classes where modification is more freely permitted, grinding the ports does not substitute for accurate preparation of the details, but complements them.

The term blueprinting can also be used in a somewhat wider sense than optimal conformity to the drawings or tolerances, but to mean all those details of set-up and optimisation that are distinct from the usual gas flowing, porting, head and compression type of work. More broadly this can be called mechanical set-up.

This embraces the previous points and many others. For example, cylinders are best with a slight diametral taper when cold to compensate for greater thermal expansion at the top (Chapter 1). Around the ports, the cylinder has detailed relief by local taper and radiusing to help the ring. The piston is often slightly elliptical rather than round. The optimal piston is not simply parallel, but has tapers, is reduced in diameter in the ring lands, and has extra taper and slight radiusing of the upper and lower edges. This is called piston profiling. Piston rings are also profiled on the outer edge in various ways.

Hence the older tuning idea of making 'circles round and right angles 90 degrees' has given way to a more refined approach with optimisation of minute details slightly different from the simplistic ideal. The details of such deliberate discrepancies are idiosyncratic to particular tuners and are often closely guarded secrets. Another type of modification hard to recognise even on inspection of parts can be substitution of an improved material, or heat treatment of parts, or of other processes such as nitriding of shafts or of iron cylinder liners.

Some engines are prone to distortion on assembly. This can be due to poor design and may be hard to rectify. However it may also be due to inaccurate mating of parts, which can be rectified by reshaping, or lapping mating parts together, such as the head onto the cylinders. Six or eight head bolts are generally much better in this respect than four. One, possibly apocryphal, story is that an engine builder using a particularly large number of head bolts was asked 'Does it make any difference?' replied 'It probably doesn't make much difference to the engine, but it certainly frightens the opposition'.

13.4 External Factors
The external factors listed were appearance, weight and frontal area.

Appearance may seem a trivial aspect of tuning, but this is not always the case. An engine may as well look good, and a suitable engine appearance is beneficial to the professional image of the tuner. This leads on to weight saving by removal of surplus metal from the exterior. It may be possible to reduce the engine mass by around 10%, possibly as much as 20% with great effort. The value of such changes depends very much on the application. This generally involves some machining and hand work for metal removal, with substitution of lighter materials where possible, e.g. magnesium for aluminium, titanium for steel, or even plastics for aluminium in the case of low-stress parts.

In many applications the cooling is only marginally adequate, and greater reliability and consistency are achieved by attention to improving the cooling, possibly by using a larger diameter cooling barrel where the construction permits this change. Alternatively, the effectiveness of cooling may be improved by shrouding the fins so that the air flow is forced through the rear fin area. If the engine is out of the direct cooling air flow then forced convection cooling by a fan may be added, or, where weight permits, the engine may be converted to water cooling.

Titanium or even aluminium alloy bolts and screws can save a little weight where this is critical. For long cylinder-retaining screws the material choice from steel, brass, titanium or light alloy may also be influenced by the thermal expansion coefficient which may have a noticeable effect on the running characteristics in terms of the effect of running temperature and operational stability.

13.5 Reliability and Use
These listed qualities were reliability, lubrication, life, cooling, starting, balance and ease of use. These relate to some extent with the mechanical set-up issues of Section 13.3. Obviously, an engine of immense flash test-bed power output is of no use if in practical operation it will not start, has bad power loss by overheating, is impossibly sensitive to carburettor, ignition or weather changes, or breaks before the finish.

The prevention of breakage failures demands use of good quality materials, correctly heat-treated. Many tuners are not in a position to make fundamental changes of components. However, it is still possible to minimise problems by refinishing components such as the connecting rod to eliminate surface cracks, with normal visual crack examination techniques. All parts can be inspected. Finally, if necessary the problem can be tackled from the other end, reducing stresses by limiting the maximum rpm, to reduce reciprocating inertia stresses. Though perhaps a painful compromise, this may be the practical approach, and better than the alternative prospect of catastrophic failure, which, once experienced, is a strong motivator to caution.

Apart from outright breakage, the big reliability problem hinges around cooling and lubrication, especially of the top end where the two-stroke is especially vulnerable. Here, materials are critical, along with careful choice of cold clearances. Broadly speaking, reduction of head temperature improves reliability. This is best achieved by improved cooling, using ducting or forced convection or water-cooling. Problems can be alleviated by fuel mixes, lubricant type and quantity, mixture settings, ignition, compression ratio and head design. In particular, over-high compression can produce high short-term power on the test bed, but it increases the heat transfer and the running temperature with lower reliability and lower sustainable power.

Starting is largely a matter of technique. A two-stroke engine will start if the fuel quantities in the crankcase and head are to its liking, and if the ignition is correct. This obviously involves sparking plug type, gap, timing and general health of the system. In cold conditions, or with non-standard fuels, a volatile starter fraction is helpful. The art of starting is to introduce the correct quantity of fuel. For reliable results, this needs to be quantified, with measured fuel quantities, or at least with systematic priming and choking according to ambient conditions. Porting and head design can influence starting, but these must for the most part be dictated by other considerations.

Ease-of-use covers a host of details, largely to do with whether the engine can easily be persuaded to deliver its potential. A classic example hinges around carburettor size. An excessively large one can deliver excellent power at high rpm on the test bed, but be poor at lower rpm, and will be difficult to set up for good mixture feed and pickup during acceleration, and the poor suction will make for more difficult operation.

Ease-of-use includes smoothness of the torque and power curves. If these are erratic, the rider or driver will have great difficulty in obtaining maximum acceleration at low speed where wheelspin is possible.

Even at higher speeds, a power spike can upset the vehicle during acceleration in a corner, which may be exciting but doesn't win races. For equal powers, prefer an engine with a smooth power curve in the operating region.

13.6 Power, Economy and Tractability

These are the basic performance measures of the engine, and to a significant degree are traded off one against another, according to Figure 13.6.1. Any particular engine could be positioned on the diagram according to the designer's weighting of the relative importance of the three merits. Obviously the three characteristics, efficient use of fuel, tractability (smooth wide power band) and high peak power, are all separately desirable, but seeking to increase any one is likely to reduce the other two.

For a road-going motorcycle, in principle at least, the swept volume is not important, so a large swept volume low specific power engine could deliver the required power with a good balance of economy and tractability. In practice, this sound engineering approach is often compromised by legislation limiting engine volume by taxation classes or other factors, with the result that high specific powers are used with more rpm, worse noise and poorer fuel economy.

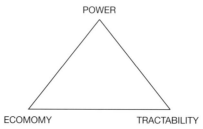

Figure 13.6.1. One gain in engine performance is usually traded off against another.

Outright racing engines optimise power with relatively little consideration for the other factors. In the most common case of the short-duration racing engine for motorcycles or karts, power may indeed seem to be paramount. However, this may be compromised by regulations regarding the number of gears. The engine is not a single speed device. Some power band is necessary to allow acceleration up through the gears. The engine must operate over an rpm range around its peak power, with the width of the band dependent upon the number of gears permitted, with some allowance for inaccurate changes. The power should be optimised over the necessary power band. The power band expressed as a fraction of the peak-power rpm is strongly influenced by the exhaust timing, with shorter timings being less peaky because the exhaust pulse is softer.

The heart of the trade-off in Figure 13.6.1 lies in the cylinder porting arrangements and the exhaust tuning. Maximum torque or power requires complete scavenge displacement of the old gas, only achieved if significant losses are tolerated, as perfect displacement scavenging is not achievable. This means poorer fuel efficiency for a carburetted engine.

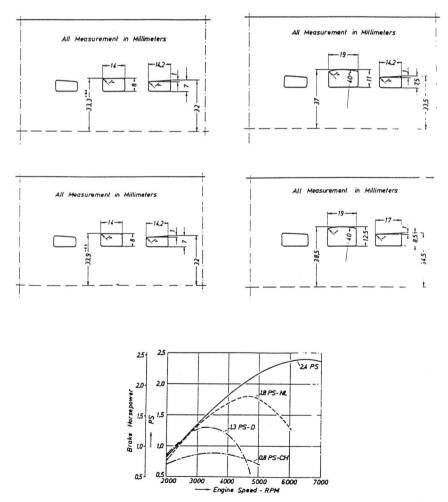

Figure 13.6.2. Example of exhaust and transfer port modifications – Sachs 50 cm³ (Waker, 1966, SAE 660009).

Maximum tractability with economy at low speed requires optimum scavenging at that speed, so at higher speeds scavenging will be incomplete, and torque low. If the scavenging is optimum at high speed, then at low speed there will be poor trapping efficiency and large losses. It just is not possible to optimise everything at once.

Therefore begin with a careful appraisal of what is required of the engine in terms of the three parameters. Identify the purpose, and then achieve fitness for that purpose.

The classic tuning situation is where it is desired to modify a conservatively designed road-going engine for racing. In this case, drastic modification to port sizes and timings, and exhaust and inlet systems, may be called for. In this case the engine is almost being redesigned. A simpler case is when a racing engine is to be improved. Manufacturers of commercial racing engines tend to use slightly conservative design to make engines easier to use, so there is often scope for detailed development, particularly in exhaust timing.

When an engine is required to deliver maximum power then, because of the nature of torque and power curves, it operates at a speed where the torque is in decline, possibly 15% to 20% below the peak value. At maximum power, therefore, the breathing is invariably incomplete due to lack of time. Hence, generally speaking, larger ports and lower flow resistances help the peak power. Hence practical power tuning usually includes a good deal of port grinding for timing, sizes and smooth shapes, and general opening up of the engine air flow.

Where optimum fuel efficiency is required then a single cylinder engine is normally preferred because this gives the largest individual cylinder size, and so gives lower thermal losses from the combusted gas. The swept volume will be a compromise, large enough for the gas to be transferred without large trapping losses, but, of course, not so large that the mechanical losses become excessive.

Equally, where a good torque spread with fuel efficiency is the aim, rather than outright specific power, as on road-going vehicles, then the advantage lies in few or single cylinders. The advantage of multi-cylinders in such applications is in balance and smooth running rather than performance, but of course multi-cylinders have a racy image arising from peak power racetrack performance.

A high crankcase compression ratio can be a significant help in improving vaporisation and fuel efficiency.

13.7 Cylinder Heads

The ease with which the head of a two-stroke engine is removed makes it a tempting target for modification. The most obvious change is skimming to raise the compression ratio. Bearing in mind that detonation is most likely at high torque, restriction of operation to high rpm, where the breathing is worse than at lower speed, may permit the successful use of higher compression ratio. On the other hand, porting and exhaust modifications improving the volumetric efficiency will generally require lower compression ratio. The ratio is easily reduced by inserting head spacers. This also changes the squish clearance, which is not ideal, but it provides a quick test which, if results are favourable, can be followed by a fully machined head with the desired squish.

A two-stroke can be rather idiosyncratic, in that a head shape that works well on one may be poor on another. It seems that for optimum performance there is no substitute for systematic testing of ratios and shapes to find what works well in any particular case. If all engines responded in exactly the same way, tuning would be easier but less fun. Anyone embarking on tuning a two-stroke engine sets out on an adventure into unknown territory.

Properties of Air

Standard sea-level properties for dry air are given in Section 3.2. For most ambient conditions, sufficiently accurate properties of air for engineering purposes may be calculated as follows. All results are in SI units. Temperature T_C (celsius), absolute pressure P and relative humidity r are measured experimentally. With data in Imperial units (Fahrenheit and psi), the SI values would be

$$T_C = \frac{T_F - 32}{1.8}$$

$$P = P_{psi} \frac{101,325}{14.7}$$

The absolute (kelvin) temperature is

$$T_K = 273.15 + T_C \ [K]$$

A sufficiently accurate saturated vapour pressure, P_S, of water at this temperature is given by

$$\log_{10} P_S = 3.231 + 0.02807 \left(T_C - 15\right) - 1.067 \times 10^{-4} \left(T_C - 15\right)^2$$

The relative humidity is commonly expressed as a percentage value, r_{pc}, of the saturation humidity at the prevailing ambient temperature. Expressing this as a simple decimal value r, not as a percentage,

$$r = \frac{r_{pc}}{100}$$

The actual absolute water vapour pressure is then

$$P_W = rP_S$$

The universal gas constant is now taken as

$$R_G = 8,314.5 \ J/kmol \ K$$

The molar mass for water is

$$m_W = 18.0154 \text{ kg/kmol}$$

so the specific gas constant for water vapour is

$$R_W = \frac{R_G}{m_W} = 461.52 \text{ J/kg K}$$

Using the basic gas equation for the water vapour, the absolute humidity, i.e. the actual water vapour density in the air in kg/m³, is

$$\rho_W = \frac{P_W}{R_W T_K}$$

The absolute pressure of the dry fraction of air is

$$P_D = P - P_W$$

The molar mass of dry air is

$$m_D = 28.965 \text{ kg/kmol}$$

so the specific gas constant for dry air is

$$R_D = 287.05 \text{ J/kg K}$$

The density of the dry air fraction is

$$\rho_D = \frac{P_D}{R_D T_K}$$

The total density is then the dry air density plus the absolute water vapour density:

$$\rho = \rho_D + \rho_W$$

To a good approximation, the humid air density can be expressed as

$$\rho = \frac{P - C_1 \, r_{PC} \, P_S \left(T_C \right)}{R_D T_K}$$

where $C_1 = 3.78 \times 10^{-3}$ %⁻¹ and r_{PC} is the relative humidity in per cent (i.e. $r_{PC} = 100 \, r$). The effective mean molar mass is

$$m_A = \frac{\rho}{\rho_D / m_D + \rho_W / m_W}$$

and the specific gas constant is

$$R_A = \frac{R_G}{m_A} \quad [\text{J/kg K}]$$

The dynamic viscosity of dry air, within 0.5% accuracy for the range 250 K to 400 K (−23°C to 127°C), is

$$\mu = 17.75 \times 10^{-6} \left(\frac{T_K}{285} \right)^{0.76} \quad [\text{Ns/m}^2]$$

The kinematic viscosity is

$$v = \frac{\mu}{\rho} \quad [\text{m}^2/\text{s}]$$

The ratio of specific heats is

$$\gamma = 1.400$$

The speed of sound is

$$V_S = \sqrt{\gamma R_A T_K} \quad [\text{m/s}]$$

For air cooling calculations, the thermal conductivity, within 1% from 240 K to 500 K (−33 °C to 227 °C), is

$$k = 0.02624 \left(\frac{T_K}{300} \right)^{0.8646} \quad [\text{W/mK}]$$

The specific thermal capacity at constant volume is

$$c_V = 717.8 + 0.07075 \left(T_K - 300 \right) + 261.25 \times 10^{-6} \left(T_K - 300 \right) \ [\text{J/kg K}]$$

which is within 0.2% for 275 K to 700 K and 1% for 175 K to 800 K.
The specific thermal capacity at constant pressure is

$$c_P = c_V + R_A$$

Where more accurate expressions are desirable, the dynamic viscosity is

$$\mu = 1.458 \times 10^{-6} \frac{T_K^{1.5}}{T_K + 110.4} \quad [\text{Ns/m}^2]$$

This is an SI version of an equation used to produce reference tables for 100 K to 1,800 K, so it is evidently accurate for engineering purposes.
A more accurate expression for the thermal conductivity is

$$k = \frac{2.646 \times 10^{-3} T_K^{1.5}}{T_K + 245.4 \times 10^{(-12/T_K)}} \quad [\text{W/mK}]$$

Again, this has been used for reference tables, over the range 100 K to 1,000 K.

Properties of Water

The fluid dynamic and thermodynamic properties of water influence engine cooling. The density of water varies with temperature according to the equation

$$\rho_W = 1,001.3 - 0.155T_C - 2.658 \times 10^{-3}T_C^2 \ [\text{kg/m}^3]$$

within 0.2% for 0–200 °C (pressurised sufficiently to prevent boiling, of course). The dynamic viscosity μ is given by

$$\log_{10}\mu = -2.75 - 0.0141T_C + 91.9 \times 10^{-6}T_C^2 - 311 \times 10^{-9}T_C^3 \ \left[\text{Ns/m}^2\right]$$

This is within 0.5% from 3 to 100°C.
The specific thermal capacity is

$$c_P = 4209 - 1.31T_C + 0.014T_C^2 \ \left[\text{J/kg K}\right]$$

which is within 0.2% for 3°C to 200°C.
The thermal conductivity is

$$k = 0.5706 + 1.756 \times 10^{-3}T_C - 6.46 \times 10^{-6}T_C^2 \ \left[\text{W/mK}\right]$$

which is within 0.3% for 1°C to 200°C.
For practical cooling circuits it is often accurate enough to use the properties at an appropriate constant mean temperature. At 90°C:

$$\rho_W = 966 \ \text{kg/m}^3$$

$$\mu = 0.315 \ \text{mPa.s} \left(\text{mNs/m}^2\right)$$

$$C_P = 4205 \ \text{J/kg K}$$

$$k = 0.676 \ \text{W/m.K}$$

The Helmholtz Resonator

This appendix presents the Helmholtz resonance equation (H. von Helmholtz, 1821–94) modified for application to engines. First consider the case of zero friction. Then add quadratic friction, as found in engine gas flows.

Figure C.1 shows the basic Helmholtz resonator representing the engine. The flask volume V_C is the crankcase, with an inlet pipe of cross-sectional area A_I and length L_I. The air in the pipe is considered to move in and out as a solid slug of gas. The original analysis was for acoustical vibration of very small amplitude. The volume of air in the neck is $A_I L_I$, with mass

$$m = \rho A_I L_I$$

where ρ is the density of the air. Actually, at the pipe entry the air just outside also takes part in the motion and has kinetic energy and inertia. Hence L_I should be the effective length, including the addition of an end correction L_{EC}. For a circular pipe,

$$L_{EC} = \frac{\pi}{4} D_I = \sqrt{\frac{\pi A_I}{4}}$$

The analysis proceeds for flow as far as the exit. Flow outside the exit is neglected because its energy is lost. Hence there is no end correction for the outlet end for large amplitude oscillations. For acoustics work a correction must be applied at entry and exit. Helmholtz's original analysis was for acoustical oscillation for a hole in a thin walled vessel, so the basic pipe length was zero, but there were two end corrections, as we would now express it.

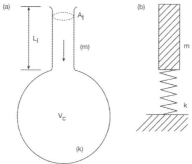

Figure C.1: Flask with neck forms a Helmholtz Resonator.
(a) physical configuration, (b) solid mechanical analogue of mass and spring, in vertical motion only.

Considering this slug of gas to be moved inwards a small distance x, the volume of gas inserted into the flask is xA_1. The existing gas in the flask is reduced in volume from V_C to $V_C - xA_1$.

This happens rapidly, so there is negligible heat transfer. The air in the flask is therefore changed in pressure according to the equation of state for a perfect gas undergoing an adiabatic process, i.e. with zero heat transfer, so:

$$\left(\frac{P}{P_0}\right) = \left(\frac{V_C - xA_1}{V_C}\right)^{-\gamma}$$

Because the volume change is considered to be small, the pressure equation may be approximated by

$$\left(\frac{P}{P_0}\right) = 1 + \frac{\gamma x A_1}{V_C}$$

The increase of pressure is therefore (approximately)

$$P - P_0 = \frac{\gamma P_0 A_1 x}{V_C}$$

As a result of the pressure change there is an outward force exerted on the slug of gas in the inlet tube, given by

$$F = (P - P_0)A_1$$
$$= \frac{\gamma P_0 A_1^2 x}{V_C}$$

This force opposes the displacement x. The equivalent restoring stiffness is therefore

$$k = \frac{F}{x} = \frac{\gamma P_0 A_1^2}{V_C}$$

Now a system with mass m, that of the air in the inlet pipe, and with restoring stiffness k, is a classical undamped vibrating system with the equation of motion

$$m\ddot{x} + kx = 0$$

and with a natural frequency

$$\omega_N = \sqrt{\frac{k}{m}} \qquad [\text{rad/s}]$$

$$f_N = \frac{1}{2\pi}\sqrt{\frac{k}{m}} \qquad [\text{Hz or cycles/s}]$$

where $\pi = 3.142$. Substituting for k and m gives the natural frequency in terms of the physical quantities of the flask, or engine:

$$f_N = \frac{1}{2\pi}\sqrt{\frac{\gamma P_0 A_1}{V_C \rho L_1}}$$

This equation can be simplified as the speed of sound C for a gas may be expressed as

$$C = \sqrt{\frac{\gamma P_0}{\rho}}$$

so the inlet natural frequency becomes

$$f_N = \frac{C}{2\pi}\sqrt{\frac{A_1}{V_C L_1}} \tag{C.1}$$

The velocity of sound C for air can be taken as 340 m/s. This equation then gives the natural frequency.

For a large pressure amplitude, as in a real engine, the effective friction force is not proportional to speed as a classical linear damping, but is proportional to the air speed squared. For a loss coefficient K (including exit energy) for the inlet pipe, the frictional pressure loss P_F is

$$P_F = K\tfrac{1}{2}\rho U^2$$

and the corresponding effective frictional force is

$$F_F = A_1 P_F = K\tfrac{1}{2}\rho U^2 A_1$$

This quadratic damping force can be expressed in terms of a quadratic friction coefficient C_Q, defined by

$$F_F = -\operatorname{sgn}(U)\,C_Q U^2$$

where sgn (U) is +1 or −1, giving the correct direction to F_F, opposing U, so

$$C_Q = \tfrac{1}{2}\rho K A_1$$

By dimensional analysis, the shape of the motion graph after release actually depends on the quadratic damping ratio

$$\zeta_Q = \frac{C_Q X_0}{m}$$

where X_0 is the initial displacement. Substituting for C_Q gives

$$\zeta_Q = \frac{\rho K A_1 X_0}{2m}$$

Parameter ζ_Q is non-dimensional, and analogous to the classic linear damping ratio ζ.

The initial displacement is

$$X_0 = \frac{F_0}{k} = \frac{P_1 A_1}{k}$$

where P_1 is the initial pressure difference, so

$$\zeta_Q = \frac{\rho K A_1^2}{2mk}\operatorname{abs}(P_1)$$

Substituting for the mass and stiffness terms in the denominator, i.e. for the mass

$$m = \rho A_1 L_1$$

and the stiffness

$$k = \frac{\gamma P_0 A_1^2}{V_C}$$

gives the non-dimensional quadratic damping ratio as

$$\zeta_Q = \frac{K}{2\gamma} \left(\frac{V_C}{A_1 L_1} \right) \text{abs} \left(\frac{P_1}{P_0} \right)$$

where P_1 is the initial pressure difference, i.e. the initial case gauge pressure, relative to the atmosphere, and K is the pressure-loss coefficient.

After release, the motion is governed entirely by the non-dimensional parameters P_1/P_0, ζ_Q and $\omega_N t$. The motion is as in Figure C.2. Because the damping is quadratic, a greater initial pressure ratio gives a more rapid damping, i.e.

$$\left(\frac{P}{P_0} \right) = f\left(\zeta_Q, \omega_N t, \frac{P_1}{P_0} \right)$$

Writing a quadratic damping parameter

$$\varepsilon_Q = \frac{K}{2\gamma} \frac{V_C}{V_I}$$

where V_I is the intake volume

$$V_I = A_1 L_1$$

then

$$\zeta_Q = \varepsilon_Q \, \text{abs} \left(\frac{P_1}{P_0} \right)$$

where ε_Q is a constant property of the system.

Figure C.2. Motion with linear stiffness and quadratic damping (curves obtained by numerical time stepping).

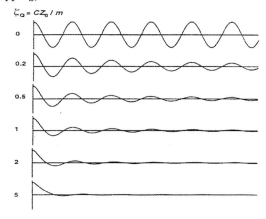

Amplitude ratio (half oscillation

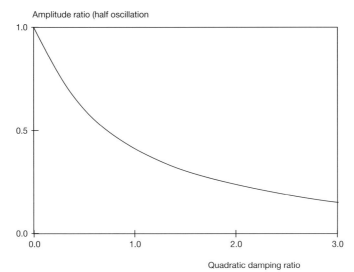

Quadratic damping ratio

Figure C.3. Amplitude ratios for half oscillation, with linear stiffness and quadratic damping.

Figure C.3 shows the amplitude ratios for half-wave and full-wave motions. Note that the full wave ratio is not the half-wave value squared because of non-linearity (the second half wave effectively begins with a smaller ζ_Q value because of the reduced amplitude). Figure C.4 shows the effect of damping on the frequency.

Frequency ratio (half oscillation)

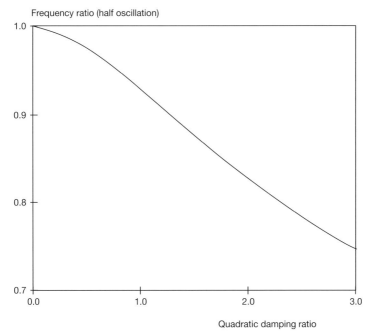

Quadratic damping ratio

Figure C.4. Frequency relative to undamped for the first half oscillation, as affected by the quadratic damping ratio.

273

TABLE C.1. Amplitude and time ratios with linear stiffness and quadratic damping

ζ_Q	half oscillation		full oscillation	
	$\dfrac{t_h}{T_u}$	$\dfrac{x_h}{x_1}$	$\dfrac{t_f}{T_u}$	$\dfrac{x_f}{x_1}$
0.0	0.500	−1.000	1.000	1.000
0.1	0.501	−0.882	1.001	0.789
0.2	0.503	−0.788	1.004	0.651
0.3	0.505	−0.712	1.009	0.553
0.4	0.509	−0.648	1.013	0.480
0.5	0.513	−0.593	1.018	0.424
0.7	0.522	−0.506	1.030	0.342
1.0	0.538	−0.410	1.048	0.263
1.5	0.569	−0.307	1.080	0.188
2.0	0.602	−0.241	1.114	0.145
2.5	0.636	−0.197	1.149	0.118
3.0	0.670	−0.165	1.183	0.098

Within the main range of practical interest of ζ_Q for engines, approximately, the time for a half oscillation is related to the undamped period T_u by

$$\frac{t_h}{T_U} = 0.50 + 0.038\zeta_Q^{1.42}$$

The displacement at half an oscillation is approximately related to the initial displacement by

$$\left|\frac{x_h}{x_1}\right| = 1 - 0.59\zeta_Q^{0.54}$$

Hence, for example, a possible value of $\zeta_Q = 1$ for a practical engine gives an amplitude ratio of 0.41 and a frequency reduction by about 8%.

APPENDIX D:

Engine Test Corrections

Engine power output varies with air pressure, temperature and humidity. Hence corrections to power measurements may be of interest for:

1. Adjusting tested power to reference conditions, for better comparison with other engines or other states of preparation.

2. Adjusting reference performance for prediction of performance in various expected field conditions.

Experimental and theoretical investigations of the sensitivity of performance to conditions have yielded somewhat varying results. This is because conditions can affect the engine in a variety of ways:

1. The mass of air charge inducted is affected by the air pressure and temperature.

2. Humidity affects the density, and the fractional oxygen content.

3. Mixture temperature after compression is altered by ambient temperature.

4. Cylinder cooling and operating temperature are affected by air temperature and pressure forced convection.

5. Exhaust cooling is affected, hence exhaust pulse speed varies.

6. Inlet temperature of the fuel affects its density and viscosity, and hence changes the fuel flow rate, for a fixed jet.

7. Fuel and air temperature both affect fuel vaporisation.

8. Water vapour is inert and acts as a combustion retarder and anti-detonant.

9. Carburettor suction is altered by air density.

10. Speed of sound in the inlet is affected, influencing choked flow rate.

The results were investigated in the early days of aviation because of the effect of altitude on engine performance. Different engines responded in different ways. Water vapour retards combustion, which is detrimental to an undercompressed engine, but may be advantageous to an overcompressed one.

Various correction standards were proposed for ground level testing of automobiles rather than to aircraft with large altitude variation. These are justified on the basis of the mass of air or oxygen actually induced by the engine. These test codes are formulated as a change from general conditions P, T_K, P_W to the reference conditions P_R, T_{KR}, P_{WR}, these being total air pressure, absolute temperature and water vapour pressure respectively (refer to Appendix A for calculations on humid air).

Some examples of formulae for the power correction factor C_p are:

SAE J816b:

$$C_p = \frac{P_R}{P}\left(\frac{T_K}{T_{KR}}\right)^n$$

$n = 0.70$ diesel engines
$n = 0.50$ spark ignition
Test P limited to 95 to 101 kPa, T to 15.5 to 43.3°C.

French standard 1:

$$C_P = \left(\frac{\rho_R}{\rho}\right)^{1.28}$$

French standard 2:

$$C_P = \frac{P_R}{P}\left(\frac{500 + T_C}{500 + T_{CR}}\right)$$

The SAE automobile engine correction is more elaborate and allows for test humidity, but corrects to dry air with

$$P_R = 29.92 \text{ in Hg} \quad (101,037 \text{ Pa})$$

$$P_{WR} = 0$$

$$T_R = 60\,°F \quad (15.56°C, 288.71 \text{ K})$$

The correction C_{PI} on indicated power is

$$C_{PI} = \left(\frac{P_R}{P - P_W}\right)\left(\frac{460 + T_F}{520}\right)^{1/2}$$

with air temperature T_F in Fahrenheit, or in Celsius:

$$C_{PI} = \left(\frac{P_R}{P - P_W}\right)\left(\frac{273.1 + T_C}{288.9}\right)^{1/2}$$

where it may be seen that the correction factor is proportional to absolute dry air pressure, and the square root of absolute temperature.

The SAE corrections are intended to be applied to the indicated power rather than the brake power, under the assumption that the mechanical losses are unchanged. This requires a value to be obtained or assumed for the mechanical efficiency η_M. The correction factor on brake power is

$$C_{PB} = 1 + \frac{C_{PI} - 1}{\eta_M}$$

so the mechanical inefficiency increases the changes made.

The SAE corrections are intended for four-stroke engines tested within the SAE code. Applicability of these codes to air-cooled two-stroke engines with tuned exhausts is dubious. The actual correction may even vary for different parts of the power curve. For example, an increase of tuned exhaust temperature will increase the pulse speed and increase the engine speed for peak power. At speeds below peak a consequent power reduction can be expected, and at speed above peak an increase would be expected.

When engines are tested by use of an aerodynamic load, such as the aerodynamic drag of a vehicle, the effect of air density on the resisting load at a given speed must also be considered. As increased density generally permits more power but also gives more drag, which is a compensating effect.

The writer does not know of any published tests of the variation of performance of racing two-strokes. However some tests on moderate performance two-strokes by Sher confirm in general unpredictability these effects.

The codes do not deal with the effect of ambient conditions on fuel consumption. In fuel-efficiency events, where this is critical, higher temperatures will improve efficiency due to better vaporisation, especially where fuel volatility is marginal due to the selection of high density fuels which tend to have low vapour pressure (high boiling point).

Mechanical Properties of Materials

Typical values. For design work refer to material specifications.

Material	Relative density (1) d (-)	Strength σ_F (MPa)	Stiffness E (GPa)	Specific strength σ_F/d (MPa)	Specific stiffness E/d (GPa)
Cast iron (grey)	7.80	200	170	26	22
Mild steel	7.80	250	205	32	26
High tensile (maraging) steel	7.80	1500	205	192	26
Brass	8.70	340	105	39	12
Aluminium bronze (10% Al)	7.80	850	118	109	15
Aluminium alloy (7075-T6)	2.81	500	71	178	25
Magnesium alloy (AZ31)	1.78	120	45	67	25
Titanium alloy (6Al, 4V)	4.46	1100	107	247	24

Thermal Expansion Coefficients – Selected Pure Elements

Parts per million per °C (averaged over 20 to 200°C)

Aluminium	Al	25.5
Beryllium	Be	13.5
Chromium	Cr	7.8
Copper	Cu	17.2
Carbon–graphite	C	2.4
Carbon–diamond	C	1.2
Gold	Au	14.5
Iron	Fe	13.2
Lead	Pb	30.5
Magnesium	Mg	27.0
Molybdenum	Mo	5.4
Nickel	Ni	14.2
Platinum	Pt	9.2
Silicon	Si	3.0
Silver	Ag	19.8
Tin	Sn	24.2
Titanium	Ti	9.2
Tungsten	W	4.5
Zinc	Zn	31.0

Approximate expansion coefficients – Engineering Materials

Parts per million per °C (averaged over 20 to 200 °C)

Aluminium alloy – wrought	22–24
Aluminium alloy – cast	18–22
Beryllium-copper (Be-Cu)	16.7
Bronze – phosphor 7%	18–19
Bronze – aluminium 7%–10%	17
Brasses (Cu-Zn):	18–21
Iron – wrought	12
Iron – cast	11
Magnesium alloy	27
Carbon steels	12–15
Steel – stainless – ferritic and martensitic	11
Steel – stainless – austenitic	16
Titanium alloys	8–9

Nomenclature

CHAPTER 1 – INTRODUCTON
No nomenclature for Chapter 1.

CHAPTER 2 – THE ENGINE AND ITS COMPONENTS

A_B	m^2	bore area
A_T	m^2	transfer passage cross-sectional area
B	m	bore
D_C	m	crankpin diameter
D_G	m	gudgeon pin (wrist pin) diameter
D_I	m	inlet diameter
D_S	m	main shaft diameter
e_C	J/kg	fuel energy of combustion (lower)
H_E	m	height of top of exhaust port above bdc
H_T	m	height of top of transport port above dbc
L_I	m	inlet length
L_R	m	connecting-rod length between centres
L_r	m	reference length
L_{RL}	m	connecting-rod CG position from little end
L_T	m	transfer passage length
m	kg	mass
N_M	rev/min	shaft rotational speed
N_S	rev/s	shaft rotational speed
P_S	W	shaft output power
Q	Nm	shaft output torque
R_C	–	geometric compression ratio
R_{TC}	–	trapped compression ratio
S	m	stroke
V_C	m^3	combustion volume
V_{CT}	m^3	crankcase volume
V_S	m^3	swept volume
V_{ST}	m^3	trapped swept volume

Greek:

η_M	–	mechanical efficiency
θ_B	deg	blowdown angular duration
θ_E	deg	exhaust port angular duration
θ_I	deg	inlet port angular duration
θ_T	deg	transfer port angular duration
Ω	rad/s	shaft rotational speed

Subscripts:

N	normalised (L/L_r, A/A_r, V/V_r)
S	specific (A/V_r)

CHAPTER 3 – ENGINE GEOMETRY

a	–	thermal efficiency scaling index
A_{AP}	deg.m^2	port angle-area
A_B	m^2	bore area
A_W	m^2	cylinder wall area
B	m	bore
B_P	deg.m^2	product of port maximum area and duration
f_P	–	power factor
f_R	–	ratio of rod length to crank throw
H_P	m	piston position above bdc
h_P	m	piston position above bdc as fraction of stroke
K_A	–	area scaling factor
K_{AV}	–	angular velocity scaling factor
K_{BMEP}	–	BMEP scaling factor
K_{GV}	–	gas velocity scaling factor
K_L	–	linear scaling factor
K_P	–	pressure scaling factor
K_{Power}	–	power scaling factor
K_Q	–	torque scaling factor
K_{RPM}	–	shaft speed (rpm) scaling factor
K_V	–	volume scaling factor
L_C	m	crank throw
L_P	m	length of piston
L_{PA}	m	length of piston above gudgeon pin centre
L_{PB}	m	length of piston below gudgeon pin centre
L_R	m	connecting-rod length between centres
N_C	–	number of cylinders
N_{DS}	deg/s	shaft angular speed in deg/s
N_M	rev/min	shaft angular speed in rev/min
$N_{M.P}$	–	shaft speed for peak power
N_{PN}	rev/min	normalised peaking speed
N_S	deg/s	shaft angular speed in rev/s
P	W	output power
P_M	W	maximum power output
P_{SN}	W	normalised specific power
Q	Nm	output torque
Q_N	Nm	normalised torque
r_{BS}	–	bore/stroke ratio
R_C	–	compression ratio
R_{CC}	–	crankcase compression ratio
R_E	–	expansion ratio
R_{TE}	–	trapped expansion ratio
S	m	stroke
T_{AP}	s.m^2	port time-area
V_C	m^3	combustion volume

Symbol	Unit	Description
V_{CB}	m³	crankcase volume with piston at bdc
V_{CR}	m³	crankcase reference volume
V_{CT}	m³	crankcase volume with piston at tdc
V_{II}	m³	volume of inlet interior passage
V_{NC}	–	normalised combustion volume
V_S	m³	swept volume
V_T	m³	volume of transfer passages
V_{TS}	m³	trapped swept volume
X	m	lateral co-ordinate
Y	M	vertical co-ordinate (along cylinder axis)

Greek:

Symbol	Unit	Description
η_M	–	mechanical efficiency
η_T	–	thermal efficiency
η_{TN}	–	normalised thermal efficiency
θ_B	deg	blowdown angular duration
θ_C	deg	crank position, clockwise after bdc
θ_{CE}	deg	crank position at exhaust closure
θ_E	deg	exhaust angular duration
θ_I	deg	inlet angular duration
θ_{IC}	deg	inlet closing angle after tdc
θ_{IO}	deg	inlet opening angle before tdc
θ_R	deg	con-rod angular position, clockwise from vertical rear view
θ_T	deg	transfer angular duration
θ_{TS}	deg	transfer angular duration spread

Subscripts:

C	crankpin
G	gudgeon pin (wrist pin)
P	piston
R	rod

CHAPTER 4 – KINEMATICS

Symbol	Unit	Description
A_C	m/s²	crankpin acceleration
A_P	m/s²	piston acceleration
D_{SJ}	m	shaft journal diameter
H_P	m	position of piston above bdc
K_{Acc}	–	acceleration scaling factor
K_L	–	linear sealing factor
L_C	m	length of crank throw
N_M	rev/min	shaft speed
N_S	rev/s	shaft speed
T_R	s	time for one revolution
V_{BJ}	m/s	big-end journal sliding speed
V_C	m/s	crankpin velocity
V_P	m/s	gudgeon pin velocity
V_{SJ}	m/s	plain journal sliding velocity
X	m	vibratory amplitude

Greek:

Symbol	Unit	Description
θ_C	deg	crank position abdc
θ_R	deg	rod position
λ	–	LC/LR
Ω_C	rad/s	crank shaft speed
Ω_R	rad/s	rod angular speed

CHAPTER 5 – DYNAMICS

Symbol	Unit	Description
A_{PY}	m/s²	acceleration of piston
A_V	m/s²	vibratory acceleration amplitude
d_P	m	crank pin diameter
F	N	force
F_{BC}	N	rod big-end centrifugal force
f_{CB}	–	counter-balance factor

Symbol	Unit	Description
F_{CB}	N	crank pin bearing force
F_E	N	effective vibratory force (amplitude)
F_F	N	Coulomb friction force
F_M	N	mounting force on engine (engine lugs)
F_{MBM}	N	algebraic sum of main bearing forces
F_{MR}	N	main bearing (reaction) force
f_N	Hz	natural (resonant) mounting frequency
F_N	N	normal force
F_{PGC}	N	force of cylinder gas on piston
F_{PGCC}	N	force of crankcase gas on piston
F_{PS}	N	side force of cylinder on piston
F_{RC}	N	force in connecting rod (compression positive)
F_V	N	vibratory force amplitude
F_{WP}	N	wrist pin force
I_P	kg m²	total system pitch inertia
K_M	N/m	mounting stiffness
m_{CBE}	kg	effective counter-balance mass
m_{eff}	kg	effective inertia at the engine
m_{ER}	kg	effective reciprocating mass
m_F	kg	flywheel mass
M_F	Nm	friction moment
M_{FM}	Nm	friction moment on shaft due to main bearings
M_I	Nm	input moment
m_M	kg	mass of mounting
M_O	Nm	output moment
m_P	kg	mass of piston
m_R	kg	mass of piston rings (total)
m_{RL}	kg	mass of connecting-rod little end (effective)
m_T	kg	total system mass (engine + vehicle)
m_{WP}	kg	mass of wrist pin
n	–	polytropic index for gas compression or expansion
P_{BMEP}	Pa	brake mean effective pressure
P_C	Pa	crankcase pressure
P_{Cm}	Pa	mean (average) crankcase pressure
P_{CS}	Pa	amplitude of crankcase pressure variation
P_I	W	indicated power
P_S	W	shaft power output
R_{CT}	–	trapped compression ratio
T	°C	temperature
T_K	K	absolute temperature (kelvin)
V_{ST}	m³	trapped swept volume
V_V	m/s	vibratory velocity amplitude
W_C	J	compression work
W_P	J	pumping work per revolution
W_X	J	work output
x_E	m	cylinder position relative to total centre of mass
X_V	n	vibratory displacement amplitude

Greek:

Symbol	Unit	Description
α_P	rad/s²	pitch angular acceleration
η_{CP}	–	crank pin efficiency
η_M	–	mechanical efficiency
η_{MB}	–	main bearing efficiency
θ_C	deg	crank pin angular position
θ_C	deg	crank position abdc
θ_R	deg	rod angular position

μ	–	coefficient of limiting friction
φ	deg	phase lead of crankcase pressure variation
Ω_C	rad/s	crankshaft angular speed

CHAPTER 6 – FLUID DYNAMICS

A	m^2	area
A	m^2	area
A_E	m^2	effective area
C	m	wetted circumference
C	m/s	velocity of pressure step on pulse
C_A	–	area coefficient
C_d	–	discharge coefficient
C_V	–	velocity coefficient
D	m	pipe (inner) diameter
D_H	m	hydraulic diameter
e	m	pipe internal roughness
f	–	area ratio
f	–	pipe friction factor
F	N	force
K	–	pressure loss coefficient
$k_{\mu T}$	–	viscosity – temperature factor
$\dot{m}$	kg/s	mass flow rate
N_{Re}	–	Reynolds number
P	N/m^2	pressure
P_{St}	Pa (N/m^2)	stagnation pressure
Q	m^3/s	volumetric flow rate
q	Pa	dynamic pressure
R_A	J/kg K	specific for constant for air
T_K	K	kelvin (absolute) temperature
U	m/s	fluid velocity
V_S	m/s	velocity of sound

Greek:

δ	–	dissipation coefficient
γ	–	ratio of specific heats
η_D	–	diffuser pressure recovery coefficient
η_R	–	static pressure recovery coefficient
μ	Pa.s	viscosity
ρ	kg/m^3	density
ρ	–	reflection coefficient
τ	–	transmission coefficient

CHAPTER 7 – THE INLET SYSTEM

A	m^2	area
A_A	m^2. deg	angle area of port
A_{AN}	–	normalised angle area
c	m/s	velocity of sound
C_Q	N/(m/s^2)^2	quadratic damping coefficient
D_G	m	gas passage diameter
D_I	m	inlet pipe diameter
D_S	m	shaft diameter
E	N/m^2 (Pa)	Young's modulus
F	N	force
f_N	Hz	natural frequency
h	m	valve lift
K	–	pressure loss coefficient
k	N/m	effective stiffness
L_G	m	interior gas passage length
L_I	m	inlet pipe length
L_P	m	gas port length
m	kg	mass
m_A	kg	air mass per revolution
m_f	kg	fuel mass per revolution
N_S	rev/s	shaft speed
P	Pa	pressure

P_0	Pa (N/m^2)	ambient pressure
q	Pa	dynamic pressure
R	m	bending radius
r_{FA}	–	fuel/air mass ratio
t	m	thickness
T_I	s	inlet duration
T_R	s	time for one revolution
U	m/s	velocity
V_{CT}	m^3	crankcase volume at tdc
V_F	m^3	fuel volume per revolution
w	m	valve width

Greek:

ε	–	strain
ζ_Q	–	quadratic damping ratio
θ_{PC}	deg	gas port angular width in case
θ_{PS}	deg	gas port angular width in shaft
ρ	kg/m^3	density
σ	N/m^2 (Pa)	stress
ϕ_I	deg	inlet pipe inclination

CHAPTER 8 – THE TRANSFER SYSTEM

A	m^2	area
B	m	bore
D	m	diameter
H	m	port height
K	–	pressure loss coefficient
N_S	rev/s	shaft speed
P	Pa	pressure
t	m	thickness
U	m/s	velocity
V_S	m^3	swept volume

Greek:

θ_H	deg	port horizontal angle
θ_V	deg	port vertical angle
ρ	kg/m^3	density

CHAPTER 9 – SCAVENGING

B	m	bore
m_{BE}	kg	mass of burned exhaust
m_{DA}	kg	mass of delivered air
m_{DF}	kg	mass of delivered fuel
m_{DM}	kg	mass of delivered mixture
m_E	kg	mass of exhaust
m_{RE}	kg	mass of trapped residual exhaust
m_{ref}	kg	reference mass
m_T	kg	trapped mass
m_{TA}	kg	mass of trapped air
m_{TF}	kg	mass of trapped fuel
m_{TM}	kg	mass of trapped mixture
m_{UA}	kg	mass of untrapped air
m_{UE}	kg	mass of unburned exhaust
m_{UF}	kg	mass of untrapped fuel
m_{UM}	kg	mass of untrapped mixture
N_S	rev/s	shaft speed
N_{Str}	–	Strouhal number
t	s	time
U	m/s	speed
X	m	distance of gas flow

Greek:

η_{ChA}	–	air charging efficiency
η_{ChM}	–	mixture charging efficiency
η_D	–	delivery ratio
η_{DM}	–	mixture delivery ratio

η_{PA} – purity of trapped air
η_{PM} – purity of trapped fuel/air mixture
η_{SCA} – air scavenging efficiency
η_{SCM} – mixture scavenging efficiency
η_{TA} – air trapping efficiency
η_{TM} – mixture trapping efficiency
η_V – volumetric efficiency
ρ_{AA} kg/m^3 density of ambient air

CHAPTER 10 – THE EXHAUST SYSTEM

A_T m^2 tailpipe cross-sectional area
C_E m/s exhaust pulse velocity
D m diameter
D_E m exhaust diameter
D_H m header diameter
D_M m maximum diameter
f_{NE} Hz exhaust system natural frequency
L_C m cone length
L_E m length of exhaust system
L_F m length of front cone
L_R m length of rear cone
L_T m tailpipe length
N_M rev/min shaft speed
N_S rev/s shaft speed
P Pa pressure
P_E Pa pressure at exhaust port
t s time
V_M m^3 muffler volume

Greek:

θ_B deg blowdown angle
θ_E deg exhaust angular duration
θ_F deg front cone diameter
θ_R deg rear cone diameter
θ_T deg transfer angular duration

CHAPTER 11 – HEAD DESIGN AND COMBUSTION

C – fuel consumption rate factor
d – fuel relative density (specific gravity)
e_A J/kg energy of combustion, per unit mass of air
e_C J/kg energy of combustion, per unit mass of fuel

e_V J/m^3 energy of combustion, per unit volume of fuel
n – polytropic index
P Pa pressure
R – air/fuel mass ratio
r_{TC} – trapped compression ratio
T K temperature (absolute, kelvin)

Greek:
γ – ratio of specific heats

CHAPTER 12 – ENGINE PERFORMANCE

C_{SF} kg/s/W specific fuel consumption
D s/m^3 fuel duration
E_C J fuel energy per revolution
e_C J/kg fuel energy of combustion
E_S J shaft output per revolution
m_E kg engine mass
m_F kg fuel mass per revolution
m_A kg/s air mass consumption
m_F kg/s fuel mass consumption
N_M rev/min shaft speed
N_S rev/s shaft speed
P_{BHE} Pa brake mean engine pressure
P_{bhp} bhp shaft power output
P_S W shaft power output
P_{SHF} W/m^2 power per unit frontal area
P_{SM} W/kg mass specific power
P_{SV} W/m^3 volumetric specific power
Q Nm output torque
q Nm/m^3 specific torque
T_{EG} °C exhaust gas temperature
T_H °C head temperature
V_A m^3 volume of air per resolution
V_S m^3 swept volume
v_A m^3/s air volumetric consumption
v_F m^3/s fuel volumetric consumption

Greek:

η_D – air delivery ratio
η_{Th} – brake thermal efficiency
Ω_S rad/s shaft speed

CHAPTER 13 – TUNING

No nomenclature for Chapter 13.

References and Bibliography

This bibliography is included to show the extensive literature that has accumulated over the years on two-stroke engines. Many of these books are now out of print. Second-hand ones are sometimes available through specialist bookshops or over the internet. Serious researchers will find the list useful.

GENERAL BOOKS:

There are many good books on engines in general. These provide material that is useful for the two-stroke designer and tuner, even if two-strokes are not explicitly dealt with.

Annand and Roe (1974) is an excellent book on gas flow, including pressure wave motion, in engines. This is primarily about four-strokes, but includes useful information on the characteristics of piston-controlled ports (9 pages), and about 6 pages on the principle of the two-stroke resonant exhaust.

Thomson (1978) covers basic principles of engine balance, although largely in a non-quantitative way.

Horlock and Winterbone (1982) (2 vols, 1,235 pages) mainly discusses general analytical methods, with a total of under 20 pages of direct relevance to two-strokes.

Irving (1987) is an excellent descriptive book on engine tuning, but is almost entirely devoted to four-strokes, containing only one chapter on two-strokes (20 pages).

SPECIFIC TWO-STROKE BOOKS

Irving (1967) is a specialised book on two-strokes (though now out of print), quite good in so far as it went, but purely qualitative, and lacking any in-depth discussion of, for example, resonant intakes or exhausts.

Burgess (1971) deals with practicalities of engine tuning and building.

Draper (1973) is a useful description of small two-stroke engines, without quantitative analysis.

Bossaglia (1972) is a high quality work describing practical principles of blueprinting and tuning.

Bell (1983) is a good description of tuning practice, including some case studies, with examples of modern exhaust system design.

Jennings (1973) again is a good explanation of tuning principles and design, with little theory.

Bacon (1981) gives only some general qualitative tuning guidance.

Robinson (1986) describes motorcycle two-stroke engine configurations and tuning principles, including some theory.

Blair (1990) is quite different in nature, being an extensive textbook on small two-stroke engine design. Of its 670 pages, 240 are devoted to computer programs. Inlet and exhaust design is dealt with entirely in terms of the method of characteristics, so that, for example, the Helmholtz model of inlet behaviour (gas column inertia) is not mentioned.

Blair (1996) is a very extensive revision and replacement of his previous book in 1990.

There are several useful books about two-stroke racing motorcycles, containing some information about the engines:

MacKellar (1995) covers Yamaha 1955 to 1993.

Walker (1996) covers MZ.

MacKellar (1998) covers Honda to 1997.

Walker and Carrick (1998) cover British specials.

GENERAL REFERENCES (BOOKS):

Annand, W.J.D. & Roe, G.E. (1974) *Gas Flow in the Internal Combustion Engine*, G.T. Foulis, ISBN 0-85429-160-1, 220 pp.

Benson, R.S. and Whitehouse, N.D. (1979) *Internal Combustion Engines*, 2 Volumes, ISBN 008-022718X, 008-022720-1, total 430 pp.

Fenton J. (Ed) (1986) *Gasoline Engine Analysis*, Mechanical Engineering Publications Ltd., ISBN 0-85298-634-3, 356 pp.

Ferguson, C.R. (1986) *Internal Combustion Engines – Applied Thermosciences*, J. Wiley & Sons, no ISBN, 550 pp.

Heywood, J.R. (1988) *Internal Combustion Engine Fundamentals*, McGraw Hill, ISBN 007-028637-X, 930 pp.

Irving P.E. (1973) *Motorcycle Engineering*, 5th Ed, Clymer Publications/Speedsport Motobooks, ISBN 0-85113-075-5, 325 pp.

Horlock, J.H. and Winterbone, D.E. (1982) 2 volumes, Oxford University Press, ISBN 0-19-856210- and 0-19-856212-8, total 1,235 pp.

Irving P.E. (1987) *Tuning for Speed*, 6th Ed, Turton and Armstrong, (1st edition 1948), ISBN 0-908031-297, 260 pp.

Smith, P.H. and Morrison, J.C. (1971) *Scientific Design of Exhaust and Intake Systems*, 3rd Ed, Robert Bentley Inc, ISBN 0-8376-0309-9, 274 pp.

Smith P.H. and Wenner D.N. (1977) 6th Ed, *The Design and Tuning of Competition Engines*, R. Bentley Inc., ISBN 0-8376-0140-1, 517 pp.

Stone, R. (1985) *Introduction to Internal Combustion Engines*, Macmillan, ISBN 0-333-37594-7, 319 pp.

Stone, R. (1989), *Motor Vehicle Fuel Economy*, Macmillan, ISBN 0-333-43820-5, 220 pp.

Thomson W. (1978) *Fundamentals of Automotive Engine Balance*, Mechanical Engineering Publications Ltd., ISBN 0-85298-409-X, 96 pp.

TWO-STROKE REFERENCES (BOOKS):

Titles published since 1970. Some of these may not be in print, but may be available from good reference libraries, or from second-hand bookstores.

Bacon R. (1981) *Two-Stroke Tuning*, Transport Bookman Publications, ISBN 0-8518-4039-6, 127 pp.

Bell A.G. (1983) *Performance Tuning in Theory and Practice – Two-Strokes*, Haynes, ISBN 0-85429-329-9, 228 pp.

Blair G.P. (1990) *The Basic Design of Two-Stroke Engines*, Society of Automotive Engineers Inc, SAE publication R-104, ISBN 1-56091-008-9, 672 pp.

Blair G.P. (1996) *Design and Simulation of Two-Stroke Engines*, Society of Automotive Engineers Inc., SAE publication R-161, ISBN 1-56091-685-0, G23.

Bossaglia C. (1972) *Two-Stroke High Performance Engine Design and Tuning*, Lodgemark Press, no ISBN, 230 pp.

Burgess A.T. (1971) *Rotary-Valve Two-Stroke Engines*, Lodgemark Press, ISBN 850770211, 104 pp.

Draper K.G. (1973) *The Two-Stroke Engine, Design and Tuning*, 5th Edition, Haynes, ISBN 0-85696-306-2, 127 pp.

Jennings G. (1973) *Two-Stroke Tuner's Handbook*, H.P. Books, Tucson, ISBN 0-912656-41-7, 156 pp.

Rauch S. (1988) DKW – *Die Geschichte Einer Weltmarke*, Motorbuch Verlag Stuttgart, ISBN 3-87943-759-9.

Boensch H.W. (1993) *Der Schnellaufende Zweitaktmotor*, Motorbuch Verlag Stuttgart, ISBN 3-87943-800-5.

Robinson J. (1986) *Motorcycle Tuning – Two Stroke*, Heinemann Newnes, ISBN 0-434-91741-9, 150 pp.

MacKellar (1995) *Yamaha – All Factory and Production Road-racing Two-Strokes from 1955 to 1993*, The Crowood Press, ISBN 1-85223-920-4.

Walker M. (1996) *MZ*, Transport Source Books, ISBN 1-85847-503-1.

MacKellar (1998) *Honda GP Racers*, The Crowood Press, ISBN 1-86126-073-3.

Walker M. and Carrick R. (1998) *British Performance Two-Strokes*, Transport Source Books, ISBN 1-85847-505-8.

TWO-STROKE REFERENCES (PAPERS):

Most of the useful papers of direct interest to two-stroke engine design have appeared either as SAE publications in the USA (www.sae.org), or have been published by the Institution of Mechanical Engineers in the UK (www.pepublishing.com). Only the ones of greater relevance are included.

Rizk W. (1958) *Experimental Studies of the Mixing Processes and Flow Configurations in Two-cycle Engine Scavenging*, Proc I. Mech.E., V172, pp. 417–437+plates.

Davies P.A.O.L. and Dwyer M.J. (1964), *A Simple Theory for Pressure Pulses in Exhaust Systems*, Proc.I.Mech.E. V 179, Pt 1, No 10, pp. 365–375.

Waker C. (1966) *The Present-Day Efficiency and the Factors Governing the Performance of Small Two-Stroke Engines*, SAE 660009.

Naito H. and Taguchi M. (1966) *Some Development Aspects of Two-Stroke Cycle Motorcycle Engines*, SAE 660394.

Nagao F. and Shimamoto Y. (1967) *The Effect of Crankcase Volume and the Inlet System on the Delivery Ratio of Two-Stroke Cycle Engines*, SAE 670030.

Jante A. (1968) *Scavenging Flow Ducts of 3-Cyl 2-Stroke Cycle Engines*, SAE 680468.

Huelsse W.A. (1968) *Investigation and Tuning of the Exhaust System of Small Two-Stroke Cycle Engines*, SAE 680469.

Leiker M. (1968) *The Exhaust System of the Two-Stroke Cycle Engine*, SAE 680470.

Thompson M.P. and Engelman H.W. (1969) *The Two Types of Resonance in Intake Tuning*, A.S.M.E. paper 69-DGP-11.

Krautter W. (1969) *Why Multicylinder Motorcycle Engines?* SAE 690748.

Hirake Y., Kobayashi T. and Tsai S. (1969) *A Study on the Exhaust System of a Small Two-Stroke Engine*, Bulletin J.S.M.E., V12, No.54, pp. 1,479–1,485.

Krieger R.B., Booy R.R., Myers P.S. and Uyehara O.A. (1969) *Simulation of a Crankcase Scavenged, Two-Stroke, SI Engine and Comparisons with Experimental Data*, SAE 690135.

Shaeffer B.L. (1970) *Better Breathing Improves Two-stroke Engine Power*, SAE Journal, July 1970, pp. 18–25.

Blair G.P. and Johnston M.B. (1970) *The Development of a High-Performance Motor-Cycle Engine*, Proc.I.Mech.E. V 185, 20/71, pp. 273–283.

Wright E.J. (1971), *Computer Simulation of Engine Gas Dynamic Processes*, SAE 710174.

Naitoh H. and Nomura K. (1971) *Some New Development Aspects of 2-Stroke cycle Motorcycle Engines*, SAE 710084.

Ohigashi S., Hamamoto Y. and Tanabe S. (1971) *Gas Flow Velocity in the Inlet Pipe, Exhaust Pipe and Cylinder of Two-Stroke Cycle Engine*, Bulletin J.S.M.E., V14, No71, pp. 470–482.

Jante A. (1971), *How to Obtain the Desired Shape of the Fuel-Air Ratio Curve in Two-Stroke cycle Gasoline Engines*, SAE 710577.

Blair G.P. and Cahoon W.L. (1971), *Design and Development of a High Specific Output 500 cc Single-Cylinder, Two-Stroke, Racing Motorcycle Engine*, SAE 710082.

Blair G.P. (1974) *Further Developments of a 500 cc Single-Cylinder 2-Cycle Engine for Motorcycle Racing and Moto-Cross Applications*, SAE 740745.

Ospring M., Karnopp D. and Margolis D. (1976) *Comparison of Computer Predictions and Experimental Tests for Two-Stroke Engine Exhaust Systems*, SAE 760172.

Way R.J.B. (1977), *Methods for Determination of Composition and Thermodynamic Properties of Combustion Engine Calculations*, Proc. I.Mech.E., V 190, 60/76, pp687-697.

Murphy M.J. and Margolis D.L. (1978) *Large Amplitude Wave Propagation in Exhaust Systems of Two-Stroke Engines*, SAE 780708.

Powell T. (1978) *High-Output Small-Displacement Two-Stroke Engines*, SAE 780737.

Baudequin F. and Rochelle P. (1980) *Some Scavenging Models for Two-Stroke Engines*, Proc. I.Mech.E. V194, pp. 203–210.

Sher E. (1984) *The Effect of Atmospheric Conditions on the Performance of an Air-Borne Two-Stroke Spark-Ignition Engine*, Proc. I.Mech.E., V 198D, No15, pp. 239–251.

Nuti M. and Martorano L. (1985) *Short-Circuit Ratio Evaluation in the Scavenging of Two-Stroke S.I. Engines*, SAE 850177.

Fleck R., Houston R.A.R. and Blair G.P. (1988) *Predicting the Performance Characteristics of Twin Cylinder Two-Stroke Cycle Engines for Outboard Motor Applications*, SAE 881266.

Index